A DICTIONARY OF EARLY MUSIC

A DICTIONARY
OF
EARLY MUSIC

from the Troubadours to Monteverdi

by
JEROME & ELIZABETH ROCHE

New York
Oxford University Press
1981

© Jerome and Elizabeth Roche 1981
Line drawings by Alec Roth

First published in the United States in 1981
by Oxford University Press,

Library of Congress Catalog Card Number: 81-82688
ISBN 0 19 520255 4

Printed in the United States of America

D.J.M.
in memoriam

Stabunt justi in magna constantia adversus eos, qui
se angustiaverunt, et qui abstulerunt labores eorum.
Videntes turbabuntur timore horribili, et mirabuntur
in subitatione insperatae salutis dicentes intra se,
poenitentiam agentes, et prae angustia spiritus
gementes: Hi sunt quos habuimus aliquando in de-
risum et in similitudinem improperii. Nos insensati
vitam illorum aestimabamus insaniam, et finem illorum sine honore: ecce quomodo computati sunt inter
filios Dei, et inter sanctos sors illorum est.

Wisdom 5[i-v]

INTRODUCTION

There are many one-volume reference books on music currently available in the English language. So why another such volume, devoted to early music? The short answer is that early music, here defined as that of the Middle Ages, Renaissance and early Baroque, has tended to receive short shrift from general dictionaries, whose primary concern is with the basic repertory from the middle Baroque period onwards. Nowadays music from before about 1650 can be heard in broadcasts, in concerts and on records, and listeners have been introduced to many unfamiliar composers and instruments. The aim of this volume, therefore, is to deal, as fully as possible within a compact format, with the instruments, musical forms, technical terms and composers of the centuries between, approximately, the rise of the troubadours and the death of Monteverdi.

It has been necessary for us to be selective. Though about seven hundred of the thousand or so entries are devoted to composers, this represents less than half of those known to have been active during the period. Our aim has been to include (1) composers who are, or have recently been, represented on commercial gramophone records and who can be identified with reasonable certainty, (2) composers a substantial amount of whose music has appeared in modern editions, (3) composers mentioned in the standard textbooks, and (4) composers known to be the subject of current scholarly study likely to lead to performance or publication. The amount of known biographical information varies greatly and it is this factor which accounts for the wide discrepancies in length between entries on composers of similar importance.

About a hundred entries deal with instruments. We hope we have included every medieval or Renaissance instrument likely to be heard in modern performances, but have largely restricted ourselves to descriptions of these rather than entering into (often controversial) matters concerning their history and ancestry. Line drawings of instruments are included where they can help to clarify written descriptions. The models for these drawings are modern copies, not surviving originals or contemporary pictures such as those in Praetorius' *Syntagma Musicum*. In some cases they inevitably include minor modifications to the original design made with modern performers in mind, and in others they represent only one version of an instrument which appeared in several forms or underwent significant changes over the years.

The remaining two hundred or so entries deal with technical terms, the various contemporary musical forms, major manuscript and printed sources, the principal Renaissance music publishers, and some of the more important theorists and writers on music active during the period. For reasons of space it has not, regrettably, been possible to include entries on (1) particular towns, courts or churches, (2) influential but not specifically musical figures such as patrons, poets, humanists and theologians, (3) performers who were not also composers. For information on these subjects readers are referred to 'Recommended Further Reading' below.

Names Composers and theorists from c1400 onwards are listed in the normal way, with surname followed by Christian name. The names of many medieval figures, however, are in the form 'X of Y' (as in Bernart de Ventadour), and for the sake of consistency all composers and theorists from before c1400–with the exception only of Machaut and Landini, who are normally referred to by their surnames–are listed with Christian name first; cross-references are provided where appropriate. We have not attempted to list or cross-reference all possible variants on composers' names (many occur in six or more forms, including translations).

Place-names Most Western European place-names are given in their modern form, with modern spelling where this has changed since the Renaissance (e.g. Strasbourg rather than Strassburg), or in an anglicized form where this is usual (e.g. Munich rather than München). But many Central European place-names have changed completely over the last few centuries, and many political boundaries have altered–the former Prussian city of Königsberg, for example, is now in the U.S.S.R. under the name of Kaliningrad, and the former Austrian province of Krain, or Carniola, is now in northern Yugoslavia. When referring to such places we have given the original name first, followed by the modern equivalent in square brackets. The same principle applies to places in northern Italy which was formerly part of the Austrian Tyrol.

Many composers of course lived and died not in large towns but in small villages; a few of these remain unidentified, but wherever possible we have indicated the name either of the region or of the nearest large town likely to be found in a standard atlas.

The term 'Franco-Flemish' is used to describe composers coming from an area covering modern Belgium and a part of northern France roughly comprising the regions of Artois and Picardy.

Cross-references   Cross-references to other entries are indicated by SMALL CAPITALS. This device has been used sparingly and is rarely used for composers' names, manuscript or printed sources, or musical forms, even though many of these have their own entries. The principal manuscript sources of the thirteenth century or earlier will be found listed under 'Manuscripts (before *c*1400)'.

Printed editions   Major scholarly editions are cited at the foot of composer entries where appropriate. These are confined to complete editions of a composer's work (whether self-contained or included in monumental series such as *Denkmäler Deutscher Tonkunst*), or to important selections of their music in series such as *Corpus of Early Keyboard Music* or *Early English Church Music*. A complete listing of individual editions is beyond the scope of a dictionary of this size and would, in any case, become out of date very quickly. (Discographies are also excluded since they would become out of date so quickly and could never apply to all relevant countries.)

Recommended Further Reading   While any sizeable bibliography of early music would be inappropriate here, the following suggestions may be helpful.

The compendious new sixth edition of *Grove's Dictionary of Music and Musicians* is recommended for general reference and for composers in particular. The one-volume *Harvard Dictionary of Music* (1969 edition) contains valuable entries on subjects such as forms, terms, genres, important collections and so on. For instruments and their historical background, we recommend David Munrow's *Instruments of the Middle Ages and Renaissance* and the relevant chapters of Mary Remnant's *Musical Instruments of the West*.

Useful introductions to medieval music are Richard Hoppin's *Medieval Music* and Albert Seay's *Music in the Medieval World*, while Howard Mayer Brown's *Music in the Renaissance* admirably fulfils this function for the later period. The last two both belong to the Prentice-Hall series, as does Claude Palisca's *Baroque Music*, with its helpful chapters on the new developments in music of the early 17th century. Gustave Reese's monumental studies *Music in the Middle Ages* and *Music in the Renaissance*, though written some decades ago, are still invaluable; the former is certainly out of date in some respects, and was in the process of being rewritten when Reese died. More accessible, perhaps, are the relevant volumes – II, III and IV – of the *New Oxford History of Music*.

The two most handy anthologies of music covering these periods are Apel and Davison's *Historical Anthology of Music* volume I (from the earliest times to *c*1600) and, for the Middle Ages, *Medieval Music*, edited by W. Thomas Marrocco and Nicholas Sandon. For excellent coverage of Renaissance vocal music of many genres and from many countries, we would single out the fifty-year-old *Das Chorwerk*, published by Möseler-Verlag and now past its 125th volume.

We would like to express our gratitude to all who have helped us in the preparation of this dictionary. Our thanks are due to those who have made instruments or photographs available to us, including Gill Munrow, Mary Remnant, John Turner and especially Richard Wood. We are also very grateful to those scholars who have personally added to or corrected our information on subjects of which they have specialized knowledge, especially David Fallows, Mary Remnant, Nick Sandon, Tim Carter and Graham Dixon.

Any new reference book is bound to contain mistakes, and we would ask that readers who find them will notify us, care of the publishers, so that they can be corrected.

Durham, November 1980
JEROME ROCHE
ELIZABETH ROCHE

KEY TO PRINTED EDITIONS CITED

AMMM	*Archivium Musices Metropolitanum Mediolanense*
CP	*Capolavori polifonici del secolo XVI*
CMI	*Classici Musicali Italiani*
CM	*Concentus Musicus*
CEKM	*Corpus of Early Keyboard Music*
CLF	*Corpus des Luthistes Français*
CMM*	*Corpus Mensurabilis Musicae*
DDT	*Denkmäler Deutscher Tonkunst*
DTB	*Denkmäler der Tonkunst in Bayern*
DTO	*Denkmäler der Tonkunst in Österreich*
EDM	*Das Erbe Deutscher Musik*
EECM	*Early English Church Music*
EL	*The English School of Lutenist Song Writers*
EM	*The English Madrigalists*
FVB	*The Fitzwilliam Virginal Book*
IM	*Instituta et Monumenta*
IMM	*Institute of Medieval Music*
MMRF	*Les Maîtres musiciens de la renaissance française*
MMI	*Monumenti di Musica Italiana*
MME	*Monumentos de la Musica Española*
MRM	*Monuments of Renaissance Music*
MB	*Musica Britannica*
MD	*Musikalische Denkmäler*
MRS	*Musiche Rinascimentali Siciliane*
PMFC	*Polyphonic Music of the Fourteenth Century*
RRMB	*Recent Researches in the Music of the Baroque Era*
RRMM	*Recent Researches in the Music of the Middle Ages and Early Renaissance*
RRMR	*Recent Researches in the Music of the Renaissance*
SCMA	*Smith College Music Archives*
TCM	*Tudor Church Music*

* Sets in the *CMM* series are mainly collected editions of a single composer.
However, the following 'anthology' sets of *CMM* have been cited:

CMM 8	Music of Fourteenth-Century Italy
CMM 11	Early Fifteenth-Century Music
CMM 32	Music of the Florentine Renaissance
CMM 53	French Secular Compositions of the Fourteenth Century

ABBREVIATIONS

b.	born
bd.	buried
bp.	baptized
B. Mus., Mus. B., Mus. Bac.	Bachelor of Music
c	*circa*
C13, C14, etc.	thirteenth century, fourteenth century, etc.
CE	collected edition(s)
fl.	flourished
Mm.	metronome
nr.	near
rev. edn.	revised edition
ser.	series
x (e.g. 1286x7)	between two dates indicates that the event specified took place between, or in either of, the dates mentioned

PITCH NOTATION

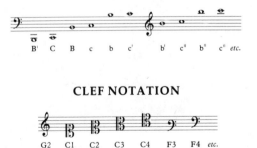

CLEF NOTATION

A

Abondante, Giulio (fl. 1546–87) Italian lutenist. Published several volumes of lute music, containing ricercars, fantasias in an ornamental rather than imitative style, dances in several sections which use variation techniques, and transcriptions of chansons, madrigals and motets.

Abyngdon, Henry (b. c1418; d. ?Wells, 1 Sep 1497) English composer. A member of the Duke of Gloucester's household chapel in 1447, and then Succentor at Wells cathedral; Master of the Children of the Chapel Royal from 1455 until 1478. In 1463 he became the first known recipient of a music degree (the Cambridge B.Mus.). He was highly esteemed as organist and composer (as Sir Thomas More's Latin epitaphs to him show), but none of his music survives.

A cappella see **Da cappella**

Accademia C16 and early C17 learned association devoted to the cultivation of science, literature and the arts, including music. An early example was the Accademia Filarmonica of Verona, founded in 1543. Many madrigals were intended for the exclusive circles of *accademie*: hence their high-flown style. The term was sometimes also applied to religious associations of lay people.

Acourt see **Haucourt**

Adam de la Halle (b. Arras, c1237; d. Naples, 1285x88) French composer, one of the later trouvères. The son of a burgher of Arras, Adam was educated at the Cistercian Abbey of Vaucelles and intended for the priesthood, but he fell in love and insisted on marrying (the marriage did not last). From 1262 he studied at the University of Paris, and in 1271 was in the service of Robert II of Artois, whom he accompanied to Naples, possibly in 1282; some of his most important works were performed at the Naples court. He was among the few C13 composers to apply polyphonic techniques to the various contemporary types of secular music–*ballade*, *rondeau* and *virelai*; 16 such pieces, in conductus style, survive. They are often very attractive and in some ways anticipate C14 developments. 7 motets and many monophonic songs also survive, but he is perhaps best known for his dramatic pastoral *Le Jeu de Robin et Marion*, performed at Naples in 1275 or 1285. This play with songs and dialogue pieces is sometimes called 'the first comic opera'. It is not known whether the melodies are folksongs or the composer's own (though he certainly wrote the texts) or whether instruments were used to accompany the voices.

CE: *Lyric works* (*CMM* 44), ed. N. Wilkins (Rome, 1967)

Adam of Fulda (b. Fulda, c1445; d. Wittenberg, 1505) German composer. From 1490 he was in the service of the Saxon court at Torgau, becoming court historiographer and later composer and *Kapellmeister*. He was professor of music at Wittenberg university in 1502 and a member of a humanist circle at Erfurt: his earlier treatise *De musica* was an important guide to German humanist musical learning. The humanistic spirit comes out in Adam's few German Lieder, one of which later became a Lutheran *contrafactum*. He wrote a 4-part Mass which looks back to the style of Dufay, and a number of hymn settings also redolent of an earlier Burgundian chanson style.

Adam of St Victor (b. Brittany, beginning C12; d. 1177 or 1192) French composer and Augustinian monk. A cantor at the Abbey of St Victor outside Paris, he was an important author of hymn and sequence texts and melodies, who brought to both forms a formal balance and regularity of metre and strophe-length.

Adriaensen, Emanuel (b. Antwerp; bd. Antwerp, 27 Feb 1604) Flemish lutenist. He published many volumes of lute music in collaboration with Phalèse, and arranged music for the lute ensemble, popular in France; his *Novum pratum* (1584) contains many pieces for 2 lutes and some for 3 or 4.

Adson, John (d. London, c1640) English composer and instrumentalist. In the service of the Duke of Lorraine in 1604–8, from 1625 he held various posts as recorder and cornett player and as music teacher at the English court. His *Courtly Masquing Ayres* for 'violins, consorts and cornetts' were published in 1621.

Afflighemensis, Johannes see **John of Afflighem**

Agazzari, Agostino (b. Siena, 2 Dec 1578; d. Siena, 10 Apr 1640) Italian composer. In 1602–6 directed music at the German College in Rome, and then returned to his native Siena as member of a cultural academy and from 1630 as choirmaster at the cathedral. He wrote 4 Masses, many motets, sacred concertos and madrigals, and the pastoral drama *Eumelio* (1606). His reputation, however, rests largely on his treatise *Del sonare sopra il basso* of 1607, one of the earliest and most important sources on continuo playing. *Eumelio* is noted for its early examples of melodic variation over a strophic repeated bass, while Agazzari's sacred concertos represent the first Roman publication of small-scale concertato church music with continuo in the manner of Viadana (though their style is relatively conventional).

Agostini, Lodovico (b. Ferrara, 1534; d. Ferrara, 20 Sep 1590) Italian composer. An Apostolic Protonotary (senior Curial secretary at the Vatican), and chaplain at the court of Alfonso II d'Este. He published 9 volumes of madrigals, containing many fine pieces, and a quantity of competently written church music.

Canzoni alla Napolitana in *MMI* 2nd ser., i, ed. A. Cavicchi and R. Nielsen

Agostini, Paolo (b. Vallerano, nr. Viterbo, c1583; d. Rome, 3 Oct 1629) Italian composer. A pupil and son-in-law of G. M. Nanino, he was in 1627 appointed *maestro di cappella* at St Peter's, having previously held similar posts in other Roman churches. His published church music includes 5 volumes of Masses; a Mass *à 48* for Pope Urban VIII and other works for up to 8 choirs survive in manuscript.

Agricola, Alexander (b. c1446; d. Valladolid, 1506) Franco-Flemish composer. Like many of his compatriots he went to Italy, serving at the Sforza court in Milan in 1471–4 and then dividing his time between Italy (Florence and the Aragonese court in Naples) and the north, where he was a choirman at Cambrai, a musician at the French court, and finally a singer at the Burgundian court of Philip the Handsome. He died while accompanying the Duke on a visit to Spain. 8 Masses,

25 motets and other sacred music of Agricola's survive, but he was notable as a composer of secular music–nearly 100 chansons and pieces with Italian and Dutch texts. His carnival songs are brilliant examples of chordal Italianate writing, and many of his secular pieces were published by Petrucci; he could also write elegantly complex melodic lines, and was especially adept at arranging chansons by his contemporaries.

CE: *Opera omnia* (*CMM* 22), ed. E. Lerner (Rome, 1961–70)

Agricola (real name **Sore**), **Martin** (b. Schwiebus, 6 Jan 1486; d. Magdeburg, 10 June 1556) German theorist and composer. The son of a farmer and self-taught in music, he was a schoolmaster in Magdeburg from 1524 and cantor there from 1527. A friend of Rhaw, who published much of his work, he composed hymns and motets but is more important for his theoretical writings, many intended for use in Protestant schools. Particularly useful is his *Musica instrumentalis deudsch* (1529, revised 1545) which contains valuable descriptions of the musical instruments in use in his time, with details of their tuning, fingering and technique.

Aguilera de Heredia, Sebastian (b. *c*1565; d. Saragossa, 16 Dec 1627) Spanish organist. He was organist at the cathedral of Huesca (Aragon) from 1585 until 1603, when he moved on to Saragossa. His fine and austere Magnificats *à 4–8*, published in 1618, remained long in use, and his *tientos* in various styles are among the best Spanish organ music of the period. He was one of the Spanish composers whose music was exported to Mexico.

Magnificats in *CMM* 71, ed. B. Hudson (Rome, 1975)

Aich, Arnt von (b. ?Aachen; d. Köln,

?before 28 June 1530) German printer. In about 1520 he issued a book of 75 anonymous 4-part Lieder, which may represent the repertory of the Bishop of Augsburg's court, and are comparable with the Lieder by such outstanding composers of the day as Isaac and Hofhaimer.

Aichinger, Gregor (b. Regensburg, 1564; d. Augsburg, 21 Feb 1628) German composer and priest. Between 1578 and 1584 and after 1588 he studied in Ingolstadt and served the Fugger family there and in Augsburg. The years 1584–7 he spent in Venice, studying with G. Gabrieli, and in Rome. At the time of his death he was singer and canon at St Gertrude in Augsburg. He published at least 18 volumes of church music, whose clear textures and flowing counterpoint show the influence of Lassus and of the contemporary Roman school. He cultivated the Venetian style, was one of the first Germans to imitate Viadana, and also wrote some purely instrumental music.

Cantiones in *RRMB* xiii, ed. W. Hettrick; Selected works in *DTB* x/1

Aimeric de Peguilhan (b. Toulouse, *c*1170; d. 1230) Troubadour. His first patron was Raimon V of Toulouse, and in the course of a wandering life he came to know all the greatest musical patrons of the time. Of his work there survive 54 poems and 6 melodies.

Air de cour French late C16 and early C17 strophic song for one voice (sometimes more) and lute accompaniment, in syllabic style and binary form. The texts were sometimes set in MUSIQUE MESURÉE. It displaced the polyphonic chanson in popularity in the 1570s.

Alanus see **Aleyn**

Alba (Alva), Alonso de Late C15/early C16 Spanish composer. A singer at the Court of Queen Isabella from 1491, he is represented in the *Cancionero de Palacio*, and also wrote a quantity of sacred music.

Albert de Rippe see **Rippe**

Alder, Cosmas (b. Baden, Aargau, c1497; d. Bern, 7 Nov 1550) Swiss composer. A chorister at Bern cathedral till 1511 and a singer there till 1524, he stayed in the city as town clerk after the Reformation. He was one of the few post-Reformation Swiss composers to write polyphony, a volume of hymns *à* 3–5 appearing posthumously in 1553.

Alexander (known as **'Der Meister'** or **'Der Wilde'**) Late C13 Minnesinger. 4 of his melodies survive, including a relatively mature example of the *Leich* (or *lai*).

Aleyn (Alanus), Johannes (d. ?Windsor, 1373) English composer. He enjoyed the favour of King Edward III, who sent him to collect money from the Kentish monasteries and rewarded him with a canonry at Windsor (1362) and also with other ecclesiastical posts including posts at Exeter and Wells cathedrals. In 1384 St George's, Windsor, possessed a roll of MS music bequeathed to it under Aleyn's will. His complex isorhythmic motet *Sub Arturo plebs* in the Chantilly MS may have been written for the celebrations on 23 April 1358 of the victory at Poitiers; its texts contain a list of English musicians and a list of famous theorists including Pythagoras, St Gregory, Boethius and, at the end, Aleyn himself.

Alfonso X (known as **'El Sabio'** = the Wise) (b. Toledo, 23 Nov 1221, d. Seville, 4 Apr 1284) King of Castile and León (from 1252) and brother-in-law of Edward I of England. A patron of Castilian literature and historiography, and of the arts, he initiated the study of music at Salamanca University. Many troubadours found favour at his court, and it was here that the MS known as the CANTIGAS DE SANTA MARÍA was compiled; Alfonso himself may have composed some of its melodies.

Alison (Allison), Richard (d. ?before 1609) English composer. His *Psalms of David in Meter* (1599) was a much-admired collection of settings *à* 4 or for one voice and lute; *An Hour's Recreation . . .* (1606) is a mixture of madrigals and anthems. He also contributed to East's psalter, and Morley's *Consort Lessons*.

An Hour's Recreation in *EM* xxxiii

Allegri, Gregorio (b. Rome, 1582; d. Rome, 7 Feb 1652) Italian composer. In his youth he sang in the choir of S. Luigi dei Francesi, Rome, and studied with G. M. Nanino. He was later a chorister and composer at Fermo cathedral and at Tivoli, and became a Papal chapel singer in 1629. It was for the Papal choir that Allegri wrote the famous *Miserere*, a psalm setting mainly in simple *falsobordone* for 2 antiphonal choirs transformed by exceptionally high ornamented passages. These were a closely guarded secret for many generations; Burney, the historian, caused the work to be made available to English cathedral choirs, Mozart copied it out by ear, and several Romantic composers enthused over it. Allegri also wrote fine polyphonic Masses in the idiom of Palestrina without continuo, and small-scale concertato motets in the modern manner for churches with limited resources.

Allison see **Alison**

Allwood (Alwood), Richard English early C16 composer and priest. He composed a 6-part Mass (in the Forrest-Heather partbooks) and contrib-

uted 5 pieces to the Mulliner Book
Mass in *EECM* i, ed. J. Bergsagel

Alman, almain C16 dance in moderate duple time. The English word is a
corruption of 'Allemande', and gave its
name to many keyboard and lute
pieces and movements in suites for
consort.

Alternatim In Catholic liturgical
music, a scheme of performance by 2
alternating groups, whereby plainsong alternates with polyphonic vocal
or organ elaborations of it. In the Office
it was found in PSALMS, MAGNIFI-
CATS and HYMNS; the ORGAN MASS
also used the scheme.

Alva see **Alba**

Alwood see **Allwood**

Ammerbach, Elias Nicolaus (b.
Naumburg, *c*1530; bd. Leipzig, 29 Jan
1597) German organist. Studied at
Leipzig University and was organist at
the Thomaskirche in 1561–95. His 2
published organ tablatures include
German dances and simple chorale settings as well as transcriptions of songs
and motets by composers such as
Isaac, Senfl and (especially) Lassus,
which he tended to overload with
stereotyped ornamentation.

Amner, John (b. Ely, 1579; d. Ely,
1641) English composer. He was
organist and choirmaster at Ely
cathedral in 1610–41, and was a competent composer of church music, producing Anglican service music and
anthems, and publishing *Sacred Hymns*
(*à 3–6*: 1615) which are in a largely syllabic style.

Amon, Blasius (b. Hall, Tyrol, *c*1558;
d. Vienna, June 1590) Austrian composer. He was a chorister at the
archducal court at Innsbruck until

1577, when he went to study in Venice
(possibly with A. Gabrieli). He later
joined the Franciscan Order, and in
1585 was cantor at the monastery of
Heiligenkreuz, moving to Vienna in
1587. His 5 volumes of published
church music (some posthumous)
show a strong Venetian influence, and
he may have been the first German-
speaking composer to use the polychoral style, in his motets of 1590.
Sacred works in *DTO* lxxiii

Ana, Francesco d' (d. Venice,
1502x03) Italian organist and composer. Initially at the church of S.
Leonardo in Venice, in 1490 he became
the first holder of the second organist's
post at St Mark's. An early writer of
frottolas, published in Petrucci's collections, he was the most important
Venetian composer of his time; one of
Petrucci's volumes of Lamentations
contains a notable *Passio Sacra* (not a
true Passion setting).

Anchieta, Juan de (b. Azpeitia, nr. San
Sebastián, 1462; d. Azpeitia, 30 July
1523) Spanish composer; relation of
St Ignatius Loyola. From 1489 to 1519
he served at the courts of Castile and
Aragon and may have visited the
Netherlands; in 1519 he retired to
become a parish priest at Azpeitia. He
was one of the leading Spanish church
composers of the time; the 2 Masses
and many motets which survive show
extensive use of plainsong and much
chordal writing.
Masses in *MME* i, ed. H. Anglés

Andrea da Firenze (d. 1415) Italian
composer. A member of the Servite
Order in Florence from 1375 (he was
also known as Andrea dei Servi).
Organist at the Servite church of SS.
Annunziata in 1378, several times Prior
in Florence and Pistoia, and rose to
become Provincial (regional head of
Order) of Tuscany (1407–10). In 1378

he and Landini supervised the building of a new organ at SS. Annunziata, and in 1387 he drew up plans for a new cathedral organ. He is portrayed in the Squarcialupi Codex. His surviving output consists of c30 *ballate* which show the influence of Landini; cadential melismas are contrasted with passages of more syllabic word setting, and use is made of imitation and sequence.

CE: in *CMM* 8/v, ed. N. Pirrotta; in *PMFC* x, ed. W. T. Marrocco

Andrieu (known as **d'Arras**) (b. c1180; d. Arras, 1248) Trouvère. A member of the PUY D'ARRAS, he was connected with Guillaume le Vinier, and may have been a knight. 16 poems with melodies survive.

Andrieu, Franciscus (?Magister Franciscus) Late C14 French composer. His lament for Machaut in *ballade* form in the Chantilly MS is the earliest known of many 'Déplorations' (elegies) for famous composers; it has sustained chords (possibly quoted from the Gloria and Credo of Machaut's Mass) at the words 'La mort Machaut'.

Anerio, Felice (b. Rome, c1560; d. Rome, 26x27 Sep 1614) Italian composer. The brother of G. F. Anerio, he sang as chorister and adult falsettist in various Roman churches, including the Cappella Giulia under Palestrina. He succeeded Palestrina as composer to the Papal chapel in 1594, and also worked at the English College. He collaborated with Soriano on the 1614 revision of the *Graduale*, and published 7 volumes of motets and spiritual and secular madrigals; much more church music exists in manuscript. Though his style closely resembles Palestrina's, he gradually assimilated new ideas, such as word painting, Venetian-style polychoral effects, and the use of the basso continuo.

Anerio, Giovanni Francesco (b. Rome, c1567; bd. Graz, 12 June 1630) Italian composer, brother of Felice Anerio. He was a choirboy under Palestrina at St Peter's, Rome, and from 1600 held many choirmaster posts in that city – at St John Lateran, S. Spirito in Sassia, the Collegio Romano, and S. Maria dei Monti. He also worked for a time at Verona cathedral and his last years were spent directing music at the Polish court; he died on his way back from there to Rome. He published a volume of Masses, several volumes of motets and a collection of psalms, antiphons and litanies; his *Teatro armonico* (1619) was an important contribution to the development of oratorio, being a collection of *laude* in dialogue for soloists, choir and instruments. His church music illustrates the transition from a Palestrinian idiom (as in the fine Requiem Mass) to the concertato manner pioneered by Viadana.

Angélique see **Lute**

Angicourt see **Perrin d'Angicourt**

Animuccia, Giovanni (b. Florence, c1514; d. Rome, 25 Mar 1571) Italian composer. He directed music at St Peter's, Rome, in 1555–71 (as Palestrina's predecessor) and published one book of Masses, one of Magnificats, 4 of madrigals and 2 of *laude*. The latter were written for St Philip Neri's oratory (where Animuccia also ran the music) and proved a formative influence on the nascent oratorio. That he was aware of other progressive movements in the church is shown by the heading 'according to the stipulations of the Council of Trent' in the 1567 Mass collection, though in fact the Masses are hardly chordal in style, being plainsong-based settings in a beautifully-wrought imitative manner.

Annibale Padovano (b. Padua, 1527; d. Graz, 15 Mar 1575) Italian organist and composer. The first organist at St Mark's, Venice, 1552–64, he became in 1566 organist, and in 1570 *Kapellmeister*, to the archducal court at Graz. A distinguished instrumental composer, he published toccatas and ricercars for organ and ensemble, a well-known battaglia for 8 wind instruments, and also church music and madrigals.

Keyboard works in *CEKM* 34, ed. K. Speer

Antegnati, Costanzo (b. Brescia, 1549; d. Brescia, 14 Nov 1624) Italian organist, composer and organ builder; member of a famous family of organ builders. He was organist of Brescia cathedral from 1584–1619, and published volumes of Masses and psalms for double choir, motets and madrigals; also a volume of organ ricercars (1608) containing an introduction entitled *L'arte organica*, which discusses registration and lists the organs his family had built.

Ricercars in *CEKM* 9, ed. W. Apel

Anthem Derived from ANTIPHON. A motet to an English sacred text designated for the Anglican service, where it fulfilled a function similar to that of the MOTET in Catholic rites. Its development therefore began at the Reformation; within decades two types could be distinguished—the verse anthem, accompanied and with parts for solo voices, and the full anthem for choir without soloists and with optional accompaniment.

Anthonello da Caserta (b. Caserta, nr. Naples) Late C14/early C15 Italian composer. He is represented in the Chantilly and Reina MSS. He set French texts in preference to his native Italian ones, but though some of his music makes use of the 'mannered' style, other pieces are simpler in idiom, with a greater emphasis on a treble melody.

CE: in *CMM* 53/i, ed. W. Apel; in *PMFC* x, ed. W. T. Marrocco

Antico, Andrea (b. Montona [Motovun, N. Yugoslavia] 1470x80; d. after 1539) Italian early C16 publisher active in Rome and Venice, and composer important in the transition from frottola to madrigal. He published frottola arrangements for keyboard and a *Liber XV missarum* (Rome, 1516) including Masses by Josquin, Mouton, de la Rue, Févin and Brumel.

Canzoni etc. in *SCMA* iv, ed. A. Einstein

Antiphon Short texts from the scriptures or elsewhere set to plainsong in mainly syllabic style, sung before and after a psalm or canticle. The term also applies to more elaborate chants, especially the 4 Marian antiphons of the Roman rite, one of which was sung at the end of the divine Office. These were often set polyphonically for voices or organ from 1400 onwards.

Antiphonale Latin name (usually 'antiphoner' in English) for a Catholic liturgical book containing the texts and music for all the hours of the Office apart from Matins.

Antonius de Civitate (b. Cividale, Friuli; d. after 1423) Italian composer and Dominican monk. Some of his surviving compositions (3 Mass movements, 5 motets and 5 secular pieces) are dated 1422 or 1423. He adopted the rhythmically simple, melodious style favoured by Franco-Flemish composers of the early C15, and was one of the few Italian composers of his generation known to have written an isorhythmic motet (for a wedding in 1423).

CE: in *CMM* 11/v, ed. G. Reaney

Antonius Romanus (fl. 1414–25) Italian composer. He may have lived in Venice, as 2 of his 3 surviving 4-part motets are for Doges (the 3rd is for the Dukes of Mantua). He also left 3 Mass movements. One of those composers who adopted the simpler, melodious style of the early C15.

CE: in *CMM* 11/vi, ed. G. Reaney

Appelby (Appleby), Thomas (fl. 1537–63) English composer. He spent several periods as organist and instructor of the choristers at Lincoln cathedral, and was *Informator Choristarum* (master of the choristers) at Magdalen College, Oxford, in 1538–41. He is known by a Magnificat in the Peterhouse partbooks, and a 'Mass for a Mene', somewhat resembling a similar piece by Taverner.

Appenzeller, Benedictus (b. Oudenarde, Flanders, fl. 1542–51) Flemish composer, probably of Swiss descent. From at least 1542 until 1551 he was master of the choristers at the Brussels court. He may have been a pupil of Josquin, on whose death he composed the fine motet *Musae Jovis*; he also published a collection of chansons in 1542, and his double canon *Sancta Maria* was worked into a tapestry presented to Mary of Hungary in 1548.

Appleby see **Appelby**

Aquila, Marco d' (fl. 1505–36) Italian lutenist and composer. He was granted a privilege (never used) to print lute music at Venice in 1505, and is represented alongside F. da Milano in a lute anthology of 1536. Here he makes unusually early use of the term 'fantasia' as applied to lute music, preferring this form to dances or transcriptions of vocal pieces. His technique shows the influence of Josquin, and his fantasias are balanced and symmetrical in form.

Arauxo see **Correa de Arauxo**

Arbeau, Thoinot (b. Dijon, 17 Mar 1520; d. Langres, 23 July 1595) An official at Langres in the later C16, whose real name was Jehan Tabourot. He published in 1588 his *Orchésographie*, an important dance tutor, in which he describes most of the French dances then in use, and prints many of their accustomed tunes with diagrams from which the steps can be reconstructed.

Arcadelt, Jacob (b. c1500; d. Paris, 14 Oct 1568) Franco-Flemish composer. Spent much of his life in Italy. After a brief trip to Florence, he sang tenor in the Cappella Giulia, Rome, and was master of the boys there in 1539. He was a singer in the Papal choir in the 1540s and early 1550s, after which he returned north to Paris with Charles of Lorraine, Duc de Guise; in 1555 he had the title 'regius musicus'.

Arcadelt was perhaps the most important of the northern composers who settled in Italy at the time when the madrigal was developing. As a distinguished polyphonist, he brought a contrapuntal element to the song-like chordal Italian style to produce madrigals of balance and polish. The several volumes of 4-part madrigals he published around 1540 were an instant success, and the first book (1539) was reprinted more than 30 times over a period of more than a century; it was this that contained the famous (and beautiful) *Il bianco e dolce cigno*. This illustrates the melodic poise of Arcadelt's madrigals; others show his sensitive use of harmonic colouring and the dissonances characteristic of Franco-Flemish polyphony. His output also included Masses, motets and chansons.

CE: *Opera omnia* (*CMM* 31), ed. A. Seay (Rome, 1965–   )

Archlute General term for any large

bass plucked string instrument, with 2 pegboxes, especially the THEORBO and CHITARRONE; in the C16 applied also to an extended LUTE.

Arezzo, Guido d' see **Guido**

Aria A strophic song in a light, tuneful vein. We can discern the following types:
1. alternative name for the late C16 CANZONETTA, becoming after 1600 a tuneful triple-time or common-time type of dance song.
2. strophic song for voice and continuo by Caccini and his followers, sometimes involving melodic variation over a fixed bass. Its tuneful style and moving bass line distinguish it from the freer solo madrigal.
3. within opera, an elaborate, self-contained solo song usually in an organized, flowing melodic style distinct from recitative; before 1650 it had not yet acquired any fixed musical form.

Arnaut Daniel (b. Ribérac, nr. Périgueux, fl. 1180–1200) Troubadour. No melodies survive for his 18 poems, but Dante esteemed him above all other troubadours, even Guiraut de Bornelh, and paid him the tribute of writing a few lines of verse in Provençal.

Arnold von Bruck see **Bruck**

Arnt von Aich see **Aich**

Arras see **Moniot d'Arras**

Ars antiqua A term applied by some early C14 theorists to late C13 motets, to distinguish them from those of their own day; recently it has been generally applied to all music of the C13.

Ars nova Generic term for C14 French music, in distinction to ARS ANTIQUA; properly it should apply only to early C14 French music (e.g. that of Philippe de Vitry, who coined the term in the title of a treatise). The difference between the two manners was seen at the time as mainly one of notation.

Ars subtilior A term applied to the rhythmically complex, manneristic music of late C14 France, as distinct from the music of the earlier ARS NOVA period.

Artusi, Giovanni Maria (b. Bologna, 1540; d. Bologna, 18 Aug 1613) Italian theorist and humanist. His conservative stance led him into conflict with Monteverdi, whom he attacked in a polemical work of 1600 for not observing the rules of counterpoint in the madrigal *Cruda Amarilli.*

Ashewell, Thomas (b. *c*1478; d after 1518) English composer. A chorister at St George's, Windsor, in 1491–3 and singer at Tattershall College, Lincs, in 1502–3, he was master of the choristers at Lincoln cathedral by 1508, and in 1513 became master of the Lady Chapel choir at Durham cathedral. His church music includes 2 fine festal Masses in the florid style in the Forrest-Heather partbooks, and he was represented in the songbook printed by Wynkyn de Worde in 1530.
    Masses in *EECM* i, xvi, ed. J. Bergsagel

Asola, Giovanni Matteo (b. Verona, 1528x29; d. Venice, 1 Oct 1609) Italian composer. A pupil of Ruffo, he held the post of *maestro di cappella* successively at Treviso and Vicenza cathedrals, and led the Italian musicians' tribute to Palestrina in 1592. His very large output, though largely conventional in style, does include some double-choir pieces and works requiring basso continuo. He also published

3 volumes of madrigals, one of which consists entirely of 2-part canons.

Motets in *RRMR* i, ed. D. Fouse

Aston, Hugh (d. 1558) English composer. He served at St Mary Newark College in Leicester (1525–48) and wrote church music, including 2 imaginatively written festal Masses in the Forrest-Heather partbooks and 5 votive antiphons, as well as the 'Hornpipe' for keyboard for which he is best known and which marks the beginning of the English keyboard variation style.

Sacred music in *TCM* x

Attaingnant, Pierre (b. ?Douai, *c*1494; d. Paris, 1552) The first Parisian music printer. His publications spanned the years 1528–50, beginning with the *Chansons nouvelles*, which inaugurated a very important series of 4-part chanson books. He used single-impression printing, with movable type manufactured by P. Haultin.

Attey, John (d. Ross-on-Wye, *c*1640) English composer and lutenist. His *First Book of Ayres* (1622) was the last of its kind and came some 10 years after the bulk of the English lute-song publications, though resembling them in style.

Lute songs in *EL* 2nd ser., ix

Ayre English strophic song of the period 1590–1650, in simple dance-like homophonic style. Dowland, an important exponent of the genre, provided for its performance either by 4 voices with or without instruments, or by voice and lute. Holborne, W. Lawes and others applied the term to movements of dance-like character in their suites for consort.

Azzaiolo, Filippo (b. Bologna, 1530×40; d. ?Bologna, after 1569) Italian composer. A singer in various Bolognese churches, he published 3 volumes of *Villote del fiore* – simple 4-part songs in a light, popular style using devices such as dance rhythms and nonsense syllables. *Chi passa* was especially widely known, and was used as the basis of a keyboard piece by Byrd.

B

Bagpipe Wind instrument, very widely used at all social levels during the Middle Ages, but later of primarily rustic associations. Though bagpipes vary enormously in size and appearance, all have the following common characteristics: (1) bag or reservoir of air filled by (2) mouthpipe with non-return valve; (3) chanter or melody-pipe with double or single reed, and usually 8 finger-holes giving a 9-note compass; a fixed-pitch drone-pipe (4), though common, was not universal. The bagpipe's continuous sound made it more suitable than other wind instruments for dance music.

complexities this entailed–and fantasias that were scarcely less intricate; he was particularly fond of pieces by Gombert, Clemens and their generation, and applied only restrained and delicate ornamentation. A colourful character to the last, he destroyed his manuscripts on his deathbed, since only he could play the music to his own satisfaction.

CE: *Opera omnia*, ed. I. Homolya and D. Benkö (Budapest, 1976–   )

Balbulus see **Notker Balbulus**

Ballade A medieval French poetic

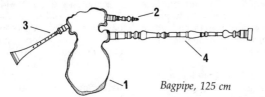

Bagpipe, 125 cm

Bakfark, Valentin (Greff) (b. Kronstadt [Brasov], Transylvania, 1507; d. Padua, 22 Aug 1576) Hungarian lutenist. He became court lutenist to the King of Hungary (1526–40) and was ennobled by him; later he served at the Polish court (1549–66), travelling widely as a renowned virtuoso. Having fled Poland after being denounced as a spy, he went to Vienna, then returned to the Hungarian court in Transylvania and ended his career as a lute teacher in Padua. Bakfark wrote lute arrangements of contemporary madrigals and motets that were astonishingly faithful to the counterpoint of the originals–despite the technical

and musical form, usually 3 stanzas of 7 or 8 lines, the last one or 2 of which are a refrain. Many trouvère and troubadour songs are in *ballade* form; Machaut revived it as a polyphonic composition of refinement. Its musical structure is *a a b*, sometimes with a textual refrain at the end of *b*. The form had fallen out of use by the mid-C15.

Ballard, Robert (b. Paris, *c*1575; d. Paris, *c*1645) French lutenist. The son of the publisher Robert Ballard, and partner and possibly pupil of A. Le Roy, he was a lutenist at the royal court from 1612 until his death. He took part in performances of *ballets de cour*, and published 2 volumes of airs and dances for the lute.

CE: *CLF* iv–v, ed. A. Souris and S. Spyket

Ballata A late C13 and C14 Italian poetic and musical form, similar to the VIRELAI (not to the *ballade*). Landini wrote many polyphonic examples.

Ballet de cour French court ballet, 1570–1660, with vocal and instrumental music and mythical or allegorical scenes; chorus, air, dance and poetic declamation were all connected with the plot. The earliest surviving example is the *Balet comique de la royne* (1581).

Ballett, balletto A type of light dance song or madrigal often with a 'fa-la' refrain. Introduced in Italy by Gastoldi in a publication of 1591, it was imitated in England by Morley and Weelkes, though in less plainly homophonic vein. In Germany Schein and others used the term for instrumental pieces in similar style.

Banchieri, Adriano (b. Bologna, 3 Sep 1568; d. Bologna, 1634) Italian composer and theorist. Became a Benedictine monk and, apart from a period as organist at Imola (1601–7), was organist and later abbot of S. Michele in Bosco, Bologna. He also belonged to cultural *accademie* (founding one himself) and wrote under various pseudonyms. His publications included 6 treatises on organ playing, continuo practice, composition and plainsong accompaniment, and about 20 books each of sacred and secular music. His name is famous on account of his frolicsome madrigal comedies, written to his own texts for the entertainment of Bologna's brilliant social circles; his *Festino* (1608) burlesques several current musical idioms and presents an imitation of animals improvising 'bestial counterpoint' over a cantus firmus.

Instrumental canzonas in *RRMR* xx, ed. L. Bartholomew; Madrigal comedies in *CP* i, vi, ix, xii

Bandora, pandora Plucked string instrument in bass register, with flat back, 6 or 7 double courses of metal strings tuned upwards from C, fixed frets, and a characteristic scalloped shape. Invented in London c1561, it was mainly used in England to accompany the voice or as part of the BROKEN CONSORT, as in Morley's *First Book of Consort Lessons.*

Bandurria see **Guitar**

Banester, Gilbert (b. ?London, c1445; d. London, 19 Aug x 1 Sep 1487) English composer. Master of the Children of the Chapel Royal from 1478, he contributed a carol in florid style to the Fayrfax MS, and wrote and produced pageants at Henry VII's court; his Latin motets include one probably for Henry's wedding. He is represented in the Eton Choirbook.

Barbarino, Bartolomeo ('Il Pesarino') (b. Fabriano, nr. Ancona; d. after 1617) Italian composer. *Maestro di cappella* at the cathedrals of Pesaro and (from 1605) Parma, he published some church music but is mainly important as one of the earliest and most prolific monodists. His style is often dramatic, with extravagant word painting, but in general his best music is in a more melancholy and expressive vein.

Barberiis, Melchiore de (b. ?Padua, c1500; d. after 1549) Italian lutenist. Nothing is known of his life, but between 1546 and 1549 he published 10 volumes of lute music including a pavane and saltarello on Janequin's *La guerre*, a fantasy for 2 lutes, and some *canzone francesi* which appear to be original instrumental conceptions with no vocal model.

Barbireau, Jacques (b. ?Mons, *c*1408; d. Antwerp, 8 Aug 1491) Franco-Flemish composer. From 1448 onwards Barbireau was master of the boys' choir at the church of Notre Dame, Antwerp, where he was succeeded by Obrecht. The choir there grew in his time from 38 to as many as 69 singers. By 1490, when the Emperor Maximilian sent him to Buda on a diplomatic mission, he had achieved a wide reputation. His small output includes 2 Masses and 3 chansons, one of which (*Een vroylic wesen*) became a 'hit' of the period round 1500, surviving in many versions, both vocal and instrumental, especially in Germany; Isaac wrote a Mass on it, while Obrecht wrote one on another of Barbireau's songs. Despite many assertions to the contrary, he is not identical with Barbingant, who composed some of the music ascribed to Barbireau and is mentioned by Tinctoris.

CE: *Opera omnia* (*CMM* 7), ed. B. Meier (Rome, 1954–7)

Bardi, Count Giovanni (b. Florence, 5 Feb 1534; d. Rome, 1612) Italian aristocrat, member of various *accademie* and particularly leader of the Florentine Camerata, a group of musicians, poets and scholars who met at his home between the late 1570s and early 1590s to discuss music in Greek culture. He wrote music for the *intermedi* of 1586 and 1589, and a theoretical work, *Discorso sopra la musica*, in 1590.

Barform Important German musical form *a a b* related to the BALLADE, and consisting of 2 *Stollen* (*a*) and the *Abgesang* (*b*). It was used in both monophonic and polyphonic German song and later adopted for chorale melodies.

Barré, Antonio (b. ?Langres; d. Rome, *c*1579) Italian publisher and composer of French descent. Sang in the Cappella Giulia, Rome, and published a book of madrigals. He subsequently started a music publishing business in Rome and later in Milan, which issued collections of madrigals and church music including some of his own works.

Bartolino da Padova (fl. 1375–1405) Italian composer. Portrayed in the Squarcialupi Codex as tonsured and wearing a habit, he may have been Prior of the Carmelites in Padua in 1380. In 1405 he was forced into exile in Florence as a result of unfavourable allusions in some of his works to the political and moral behaviour of the Visconti family who controlled Padua. Most of his 11 madrigals and 27 *ballate* are *à* 2, though some are *à* 3. His style lacks the sense of flow and clear-cut melodic lines characteristic of his Italian predecessors, and shows more strongly the influence of the music of the contemporary French *ars subtilior*, especially in its rhythmic complexity.

CE: in *PMFC* ix, ed. W. T. Marrocco

Bartolomeo da Bologna Late C14/early C15 Italian composer and Benedictine Abbot. His surviving compositions consist of 2 *ballate*, 1 *rondeau*, 2 secular Latin pieces, and 2 Mass movements; the Mass movements are based on his *ballate* and show a pioneering use of parody technique. His music shows the influence of the rhythmically straightforward, melodious Franco-Flemish style of the early C15.

CE: in *CMM* 11/v, ed. G. Reaney

Bartolomeo degli Organi (called **Baccio**) (b. Florence, 24 Dec 1474; d. Florence, 12 Dec 1539) Italian composer. He held a church post in Florence and published motets whose style is in some ways similar to that of contemporary Franco-Flemish polyphony, but is important as a leading composer of *canti carnascialeschi* and *ballate*.

CE: *CMM* 32/ii, ed. F. d'Accone

Basiron, Philippe (?=**Philippon**) Franco-Flemish composer *c*1500. Mentioned in Crétin's Déploration, an elegy on the death of Ockeghem, whose *D'ung aultre amer* he used as the basis for a chanson of his own. He also composed church music, including a *L'homme armé* Mass, some of which was published by Petrucci.

Bassadanza see **Basse dance**

Bassanello Wind instrument with double reed and conical bore, invented in the later C16, possibly by the father of the composer Giovanni Bassano. Praetorius lists 3 sizes, alto, tenor and bass, each with 7 finger-holes and the compass of a 10th or 11th. The tone is like that of a soft shawm, and Praetorius recommends the alto for tenor parts in ensembles.

Bassano, Giovanni (b. ?Venice; d. ?Aug x Sep 1617) Italian composer. A fine cornettist, he was employed from 1576 in various posts at St Mark's, Venice, including (from 1601) conductor of the orchestra. He published canzonets, motets with organ bass and keyboard music, and in 1591 issued a collection of ornamented versions of motets and madrigals by leading composers such as Palestrina, Lassus and Rore. He also made highly decorated arrangements of existing music for the viola bastarda, in which the polyphonic texture disappears. His father was probably the inventor of the bassanello.

Basse dance, bassadanza French, Netherlandish or Italian court dance of the C15–16 in moderate duple time, though some surviving notated settings are in slow triple time. Its music was often improvised over a cantus firmus, one of the most popular of which (*La Spagna*) appears in both French and Italian dance manuals. The basse dance was usually followed by one or two quicker dances, e.g. a recoupe (based on the same musical materials as the basse dance) and a tordion.

Basso continuo A method of indicating a harmonic accompaniment (for keyboard, lute, etc.) by the bass notes together with figures and/or accidentals showing the chords to be played above them. Universally used in the Baroque, it grew out of C16 improvised methods of accompaniment (e.g. the *bassus pro organo*–a separate organ bass, sometimes with the treble part added).

Basso ostinato see **Ground**

Baston, Josquin (fl. 1542–53) Franco-Flemish composer. He may have served at the Polish court 1552–3, and also at the Danish and Swedish courts a few years later. His chanson-motets combine expressiveness and charm with expert use of devices such as canon; in his 6-part lament on the death of an unidentified 'Lupus' the two middle voices repeat the Gregorian *Requiem* chant in canon 6 times with different counterpoints.

Bataille, Gabriel (b. *c*1575; d. Paris, 17 Dec 1630) French lutenist and composer. In 1617 he was chamber musician to the French queen; he contributed to various *ballets de cour* and between 1606 and 1615 published 6 volumes of other composers' psalms and songs arranged for solo voice with fully polyphonic lute accompaniments. Some songs of his own appeared in Ballard's collections 1617–20.

Bateson, Thomas (b. Cheshire, *c*1570; d. Dublin, 2 Mar x 30 Apr 1630)   English composer. After serving as organist of Chester cathedral (from 1599) he went to Holy Trinity (now Christ Church) cathedral, Dublin, as a singer in 1609, becoming master of the choristers in 1618; in 1615 he became the first Dublin B.Mus. He wrote church music, and published 2 volumes of madrigals, including some fine serious pieces which show an excellent taste in poetry.

Madrigals in *EM* xxi–ii, rev. edn.

Battaglia   Italian 'battle'; a term used of music imitating the sounds of battle. An early example is Isaac's instrumental *La Battaglia* (*c*1485), but a more famous one is Janequin's programmatic chanson *La guerre*, which was frequently arranged for instruments (e.g. by Susato, A. Gabrieli) under the heading 'bataille' or 'battaglia'.

Batten, Adrian (bp. Salisbury, 1 Mar 1591; d. London, 1637)   English composer. A singer at Westminster Abbey from 1614, and from 1627 at St Paul's cathedral, he was a most prolific composer of Anglican service music and anthems, some of which continued long in use; he was represented in much later collections such as Boyce's *Cathedral Music*. An organ book of his at St Michael's College, Tenbury, contains much C16 church music in organ score, for some of which it is the only extant source.

Baude Cordier see **Cordier**

Bauldewijn, Noel (b. *c*1480; d. Antwerp, 1529x30)   Franco-Flemish composer. Choirmaster at S. Rombault in Malines from 1509 and at Notre Dame in Antwerp from 1513. He composed Masses (probably including the *Da pacem* Mass ascribed to Josquin) and motets (including a *Quam pulchra es* on which Gombert based a Mass), some of the latter being published by Petrucci.

Beaulieu, Estorg (Hector) de (b. Beaulieu-sur-Menoire, Limousin, *c*1495; d. Basel, 8 Jan 1552)   French poet and musician; organist, music teacher and Catholic priest. Lived in Langres from 1534 to 1537, and was a friend of the poet Marot. In 1537 he became a Protestant, fleeing to Geneva and studying theology in Lucerne before becoming a Reformed pastor. In 1546 he published his *Chrestienne Resiouyssance* – 160 sacred *contrafacta* of secular song texts (the music does not survive).

Bedyngham, John (d. ?London, 1459x60)   English composer represented in the Trent Codices. His chansons, in the Burgundian style of Dufay and others, were popular throughout Europe; his Mass *Deuil angoisseus*, on a chanson by Binchois, shows the beginnings of parody technique, and is exceptional in treating all 3 voices of its model to very free variation, both melodic and rhythmic.

Beldemandis see **Prosdocimus de Beldemandis**

Bellavere (Bell'Haver), Vincenzo (b. ?Venice, *c*1530; d. Venice, Sep 1587)   Italian composer. He was a pupil of A. Gabrieli whom he succeeded as first organist of St Mark's, Venice, in 1856; composed keyboard toccatas, madrigals and church music.

Belli, Giulio (b. Longiano, Forlì, *c*1560; d. ?Imola, after 1621)   Italian composer and Franciscan monk. From 1582 to 1611 he held a succession of appointments as *maestro di cappella* at various north Italian churches, beginning and ending at Imola. Between 1580 and 1613 he published many volumes of church music, including motets with cornett *obbligati;* some of this music later appeared in German anthologies. He also published madrigals and *canzonette.*

Benet, John (fl. 1430–50) English composer. His music was known on the Continent, and is found in the Trent Codices. His motets illustrate the use of total isorhythm, and his Mass movements, which contrast a declamatory style in settings of the Gloria with a more melismatic one in Sanctus and Agnus settings, mark an important stage in the development of the cyclic Mass (the complete Ordinary). These are all *à 3;* his sonorous 4-part Kyrie trope *Deus Creator* has 2 strict canonic and 2 untexted parts and shows great technical skill.

Bennet, John (b. ?Cheshire, c1570; d. after 1614) English composer. His best-known work is the madrigal *All creatures now* from the *Triumphs of Oriana,* whose relatively simple but attractive style is also present in his 1598 madrigal book. He also wrote church music and contributed to Ravenscroft's psalter.

CE: Madrigals in *EM* xxiii

Berchem, Jachet (b. ?Berchem, nr. Antwerp; d. Ferrara, 1580) Flemish composer; became court organist at Ferrara in 1555. Most of his output is secular, including 3 volumes setting extracts from *Orlando furioso,* and madrigals and chansons in anthologies, but he also published 3 Masses.

Bergamasca A popular tune presumably from the Bergamo district. The melody or its harmonic scheme was used as a basis for instrumental music in the C16–17 by Frescobaldi, Scheidt and others.

Bergamasca

Bermudo, Juan (b. Ecija, Andalusia, c1510; d. c1565) Spanish theorist and organ composer. In 1550 he served the archbishop of Andalusia together with Morales, whom he esteemed highly. His *Declaración de instrumentos musicales* (1549) combined instruction in keyboard playing, musical rudiments and tuning.

Bernardi, Steffano (b. Verona, c1585; d. ?Salzburg, 1636) Italian composer. From 1611 to 1622 he was *maestro di cappella* at Verona cathedral and then entered the service of the Bishop of Breslau [Wrocław]. In 1627 he became *Kapellmeister* at Salzburg cathedral, for whose consecration he composed a Te Deum for 12 choirs. Between 1610 and 1634 he published much church music, in both old and new styles; he also composed *madrigaletti* and early examples of the trio sonata.

Sacred music in *DTO* lxix

Bernart de Ventadour (Ventadorn) (b. Ventadorn, c1125; d. Dalon, Périgueux, 1195) Troubadour. The son of a kitchen scullion, he served Eleanor of Aquitaine (for whom many of his best and most expressive songs were written) at the court of her husband, Henry II of England, and also Raimon of Toulouse, before entering the monastery where he ended his life. Few other troubadours left so many melodies which have survived; there are 18, and many of them became well known all over medieval Europe, some being given German texts by Minnesingers such as Friedrich von Hûsen and Dietmar von Aist. Some of his songs, including the especially famous *Quan vei l'aloete*, show the melodic influence of Gregorian chant.

Berneville see **Gillebert de Berneville**

Berti, Giovanni Pietro (d. Venice, 1638) Italian composer. Originally a singer at St Mark's, Venice, he became second organist there in 1624 and by 1637 was receiving an exceptionally high salary. His strophic ground-bass arias with instrumental *ritornelli* and ingeniously varied treatment of the bass follow the example of Grandi, and mark an important stage in the development of the solo cantata; in their long phrases and use of triple time they also foreshadow the *bel canto* style.

Bertran de Born (b. Born, Périgord, c1140; d. Dalon, Périgueux, before 1215) Troubadour, later Vicomte d'Hautefort. He made trouble between Henry II of England and his sons, and Dante therefore portrays him in the *Inferno* as carrying his head in his hands as punishment; he ended his life in a monastery. Only one of his melodies survives, but he is one of the finest troubadour poets.

Bertrand, Antoine de (b. Fontanges, Auvergne, c1540; d. Toulouse, c1581) French composer. Best known for his settings of the *Amours de Ronsard* (1576–8). These contain some fine music as well as showing his fondness for harmonic experiment and chromaticism more characteristic of madrigal than chanson. The *Amours* were reissued in 1580 with spiritual texts, and a volume of French and Latin sacred songs was published posthumously in 1582.

Chansons in *MMRF* iv–vii

Besard, Jean-Baptiste (b. Besançon, c1567; d. c1625) French lutenist.

Trained as a lawyer and lived in Germany, where he published his monumental lute collection, *Thesaurus harmonicus*, in 1603. This is a remarkable compendium of the lute music of the period: 26 French *airs de cour* (the first French solo songs of the C17), countless arrangements of madrigals and villanellas, and free idiomatic pieces such as fantasias and preludes, these admirably exemplifying variety of texture and expressive melancholy. The large number of dance sets look forward to the baroque suite. Music from Dowland's *Lachrymae* is included. Besard's instructions on lute playing appear in their turn in Robert Dowland's *Varietie of lute lessons*.

CE: in *CLF* ix, ed. A. Souris

Béthune see **Conon de Béthune**

Bevin, Elway (b. ?Wells, 1554; d. ?Bristol, ?1639) English or Welsh composer and theorist. A pupil of Tallis, he was organist at Bristol cathedral from 1589 and also a member of the Chapel Royal from 1605, but on account of his adherence to Catholicism lost both posts in 1637. He composed some Anglican church music and a setting of the folk song known as 'Browning' in the Cosyn Virginal Book, and wrote a treatise on methods of constructing canons in up to 60 parts.

Bicinium C16 term for contrapuntal composition in 2 parts, used mainly in Germany. Collections such as those by Rhaw of 1544 and Lassus of 1577 had an educational function: demonstrating counterpoint or teaching singing and playing. Scheidt used the term for the 2-part versets or variations in organ music.

Binchois, Gilles (b. ?Mons, c1400; d. Soignies, 20 Sep 1460) Franco-Flemish composer. From c1419–23 he was organist at S. Waudru, Mons; later he was in the service of the Duke of Suffolk in Paris (1424/5) and may have come with him to England. From before 1431 till 1453 he was a chaplain at the court of Burgundy. He was also a canon at a church in Mons along with Dufay, whom he must have come to know in middle life.

Binchois wrote some 28 Mass sections, 4 Magnificats, some 30 motets and hymn settings and about 55 chansons; it was in the latter genre that he shone, ranking with Dufay as a major exponent of the form. Most of these are settings of *rondeaux*, while a few are *ballades*; most adopt the usual 3-part texture, with a melodious top line accompanied by 2 instrumental parts of equal range. Many have a somewhat sad, nostalgic quality, the words treating of unrequited love in the rather stilted manner of the courtly tradition of chivalry. Often formal in his treatment of the poetic forms, Binchois could nevertheless achieve depth of feeling as in *Amoreux suy*. Other chansons are more routine, with successive short melodic phrases dominated by cadence formulas. Some of his church music (Magnificats, hymns) is simple in manner, elaborating the plainsong with chords in simple *fauxbourdon*, occasionally decorated.

CE: Chansons in *MD* ii, ed. W. Rehm

Bladder pipe Double-reed wind instrument with a bladder between the reed and the player's lips which acts as a reservoir of air. This preserves the most useful feature of the bagpipe, its ability to generate a continuous sound, yet at the same time makes possible a degree of articulation impossible on the bagpipe. It was in use from the C13 to C16, and could be curved, like the crumhorn, or straight. Virdung illustrates it in his treatise *Musica getuscht* (1511) under the name 'Platerspil'.

Blitheman, John (alias **William**) (b.

c1525; d. London, 1591) English composer. In 1564 he was master of the choristers at Christ Church, Oxford, and in 1585 organist of the Chapel Royal, where Bull was his pupil and eventual successor. An outstanding composer of keyboard music, he is represented by 15 pieces in various styles in the Mulliner Book. The organ hymn *Eterne rerum* uses bold dissonances fluently, and an In nomine contains what may be the earliest example in English keyboard music of triplet figuration.

Blondel de Nesle (b. Nesle, nr. S. Quentin, c1155) Trouvère. The picturesque tale in which Blondel rescues Richard I of England from prison by singing a particular song outside the castle walls is regrettably untrue; he was however one of the most important early trouvères. His melodies, which show the influence of Gregorian chant, were well known and popular all over Europe, and were often used for *contrafacta*.

Bodel see **Johan Bodel**

Boësset, Antoine (b. Blois, 1586x87; d. Paris, 9 Dec 1643) French composer, of good family. The son-in-law of Guédron, he was superintendent of music to Louis XIII and wrote ballets for court festivities. He continued the series of *air de cour* publications begun by Bataille, issuing 9 volumes between 1617 and 1642.

Boethius, Anicius (b. Rome, c480; d. Milan, 23 Oct 524) Roman philosopher and statesman. His *De institutione musica* (5 vols) was the most extensive of the Latin writings on music, and provided a link between the musical theory of ancient culture and the Middle Ages. It became the foundation of medieval theory, circulating in many MS copies and finally being printed in the late C15.

Bologna, da See under the first name of composers known thus.

Bombard Medieval name for a large shawm – one of the few sustaining tenor instruments available during the C14, and specified (as 'Pumhart') in a song by Hermann of Salzburg. In the C16 the name came to apply interchangeably with POMMER to all sizes of shawm.

Bonini, Severo (b. Florence, 1582; d. Florence, 5 Dec 1663) Italian composer; Benedictine monk. Resided in various Italian monasteries, notably S. Trinità at Florence, and was for 20 years organist at Forlì. A singing pupil of Caccini and one of his earliest imitators, he published monodies and small-scale madrigals and church music in the new style. His MS *Discorsi e regole sovra la musica* contains much useful information about Caccini and Monteverdi.

Bono, Pietro see **Pietrobono**

Borchgrevinck, Melchior (b. *c*1569; d. Copenhagen, 20 Dec 1632) Danish composer of Dutch descent. Entered Danish court service in 1587; studied in Venice with Giovanni Gabrieli in 1599–1600 and 1601–2, returning to Copenhagen as court organist and becoming *Kapellmeister* there in 1618. He published 2 volumes of madrigals shortly after returning from Italy, and also composed dances.

Borlet (?fl. 1409) Composer whose name is probably an anagram of Trébol –a French composer who was in the service of Martin V of Aragon in 1409. His *Hé tres doulz roussignol* belongs to the extremely popular genre of the bird imitation piece. Another unascribed

version of the same piece (*Ma tredol rosignol*) seems somewhat contrasted in mood and style; the nightingale in the first, 4-part, piece is gentle and pensive while that in the second, in 3 parts, is gay and extrovert.

Born see **Bertran de Born**

Bornelh see **Guiraut de Bornelh**

Bossinensis, Franciscus (fl. 1509–11) Lutenist, possibly from Bosnia (Yugoslavia). He published 2 volumes of transcriptions of frottolas (mainly by Cara and Tromboncino) for voice and lute, which also contain ricercars and preludes to the vocal pieces for lute solo.

CE: Transcriptions in *Le Frottole per canto e liuto,* ed. B. Disertori (Milan, 1964)

Bottegari, Cosimo (b. Florence, 27 Sep 1554; d. Florence, 31 Mar 1620) Italian singer and lutenist. Starting in 1574, he compiled an MS songbook which is an important source for the few surviving Italian solo songs of the period. (He should not be confused with the Italian theorist Ercole Bottrigari.)

CE: *The Bottegari Lutebook,* ed. C. MacClintock (Wellesley, Mass., 1965)

Bourgeois, Loys (b. Paris, *c*1510; d. *c*1561) French composer. One of the first composers to set psalm translations by the poet Marot, he assisted Calvin by publishing in 1547 a volume of simple psalm settings for congregational use. He established the final forms of a number of tunes and introduced the idea of displaying the numbers of the psalms to be sung on a board in the church. He also published more elaborate and chanson-like psalm-settings suitable for private devotions.

Bouzignac, Guillaume (b. end C16; d.

after 1643) French composer, from the Languedoc region. Master of the choristers at Grenoble cathedral in 1609; also worked in Angoulême and Tours. His sacred music (all in MS) is of a higher standard than that by his French contemporaries, being dramatic and intensely expressive in the new baroque manner. He had great influence on later baroque French composers such as Charpentier.

Bovicelli, Giovanni Battista (b. Assisi) Italian singer, in the choir of Milan cathedral. In 1594 he published *Regole, passaggi di musica*, a treatise on the vocal ornamentation of madrigals and motets. The ornaments are often of considerable complexity.

Bowed lyre see **Crowd**

Brade, William (b. 1560; d. Hamburg, 26 Feb 1630) English composer. Spent his entire working life after 1594 abroad, with periods at the Danish court in Copenhagen and in many German cities. He published 5 volumes of dances which mark an important stage in the development of the suite, and was one of the C17 English composers who had a strong influence on German instrumental music.

Brando see **Branle**

Brandt, Jobst von (b. Waldershof, Oberpfalz, 28 Oct 1517; d. Brand, Oberpfalz, 22 Jan 1570) German composer. From 1530 studied in Heidelberg and sang in the court chapel under Lemlin; became an administrator for the monastery of Waldsassen (Oberpfalz) in 1548. More than 60 of his songs were published in Forster's collections (1549–56) including quodlibets and songs in more than 4 parts. He also wrote Lutheran polyphony, and a volume of his psalm settings appeared posthumously.

Branle A popular C16 dance with many local variants. The *branle simple* was in duple time, the *gay* in triple. The word was synonymous with the English 'brawl' and Italian 'brando'.

Brassart, Johannes (b. Lowaige, nr. Tongeren, c1405) Franco-Flemish composer. A priest in Liège until 1431, in which year he spent a few months in Rome as a Papal singer, he was employed by the Emperor Sigismund from 1434–43. His sacred music—8 Introits, 9 3-part Mass movements and 12 3- and 4-part motets—is partly found in the Trent Codices and Aosta MS, and includes some attractive pieces, such as *O flos fragrans*, with ornamented upper parts which recall Dunstable.

CE: *Opera omnia* (*CMM* 35), ed. K. Mixter (Rome, 1965–70)

Brawl see **Branle**

Breitengraser, Wilhelm (b. Nürnberg, c1495; d. Nürnberg, 23 Dec 1542) German composer. Studied in Leipzig from 1514 and then became a schoolmaster in Nürnberg. His songs are included in Ott's 1534 songbook alongside those of Senfl and A. von Bruck; he also composed Masses and other church music.

Bretel see **Jehan Bretel**

Breviary A liturgical book containing all the texts for the Catholic Office.

Broken consort A relatively recent term for a consort of instruments from different families (as distinct from a 'whole consort' where the instruments are from a single family). A good example is that of Morley's 1599 *Consort Lessons*, consisting of flute, treble and bass viols, lute, bandora and cittern.

Brolo (de Bruollis), Bartolomeo (fl. ?1430–40) Italian composer. One of the few known native composers in early C15 Italy, he wrote festal Mass movements, imitative motets, and *rondeaux* which combine Italianate melody with characteristics of the new Franco-Flemish style.

CE: in *CMM* 11/v, ed. G. Reaney

Browne, John (b. *c*1452) English composer; the most prolific contributor to the sacred music of the Eton Choirbook, his music belongs to the middle, climactic stage of the repertory and marks him as one of the finest composers of that era in England. He wrote 15 works for the MS and contributed carols to the Fayrfax MS. His polyphony combines imaginative technique and use of vocal sonority (in up to 8 parts) with dramatic treatment of the text (especially in the *Stabat Mater*) and some imitative writing.

Bruck, Arnold von (b. Bruges, *c*1490; d. Linz, 6 Feb 1554) Austrian composer of Flemish origin; possibly a pupil of Heinrich Finck. Served the Emperor Ferdinand I as *Kapellmeister* from at least 1527 until 1546, when he became an ecclesiastic at Laibach [Ljubljana]. His relationship with the Catholic Church was however ambivalent, the bulk of his sacred music being for Protestant use. He produced many settings of Lutheran chorales, some very simple, some more complex and polyphonic, 17 of which were published in Rhaw's 1544 collection. His German secular songs approach the quality of Senfl's, and he was extremely highly regarded in his time, a medal in his honour being struck in 1536.

Motets in *DTO* xcix

Brudieu, Joan (b. Limoges area, *c*1520; d. Urgel, Catalonia, 1591) French composer and priest who worked in Spain. Except for a brief period in Barcelona, he served from 1539 until his death at the cathedral in Urgel, becoming choirmaster in 1578. His Requiem is one of the finest of the period and makes use of bold dissonances, as do his madrigals of 1585. These set Catalàn as well as Italian texts and are comparable with those of Brudieu's more talented Italian contemporaries.

Bruhier, Antoine (fl. 1504–17) French composer. A singer at the French court and (1514–17) in the Papal choir; composed a little church music and some chansons which foreshadow the new Parisian style. A motet by Moulu mentions him alongside composers such as Dufay and Obrecht.

Brule see **Gace Brule**

Brumel, Antoine (b. *c*1460; d. Ferrara, after 1520) Franco-Flemish composer. Held church posts in Chartres (1483–6), Laon, Paris (master of the boys at Notre Dame 1498–1500) and Lyons before becoming *maestro di cappella* to Alfonso I d'Este at Ferrara in 1506–9. His output includes 12 Masses, 29 motets, 3 Magnificats and several chansons. His considerable prominence in his own time is suggested by the fact that he was only the third composer to have a volume of Masses published by Petrucci (after Josquin and Obrecht), and by the many appearances of his music in MSS. His *Missa Et ecce terraemotus* is a remarkable piece for 12 voices. Many of his motets use borrowed cantus firmi, maybe with a different text, and are in a flowing, rhythmically intricate style, but his *Sicut lilium* has an attractive simplicity suggestive of Italian influence.

CE: *Collected works (CMM* 5), ed. B. Hudson (Rome, 1969–72)

Bruollis see **Brolo**

Buchner, Hans (b. Ravensburg, 26 Oct 1483; d. Konstanz, ?early March

1538) German composer; pupil of Hofhaimer and teacher of Sicher. Organist at Konstanz cathedral until the Reformation and thereafter at the minster in Überlingen. His *Fundamentbuch* is the earliest organ tutor, giving instruction in playing, intabulation and improvising as well as containing more than 140 pieces. These include preludes and song transcriptions as well as the enormously varied collection of plainsong-based pieces for which Buchner is most significant.

CE: *Sämtliche Orgelwerke* in *EDM* liv–v

Buisine or **claro** Medieval straight TRUMPET, 6 feet or more in length, with flared bell, used especially for ceremonial purposes. It acquired an S-shape in the later Middle Ages and developed into the slide trumpet.

Bull, John (b. *c*1562; d. Antwerp, 12 x 13 Mar 1628) English composer; received his musical training at the Chapel Royal under Blitheman. In 1582 became organist at Hereford cathedral and in 1585 a member of the Chapel Royal, where he succeeded Blitheman as organist in 1591. From 1596 to 1607 he was professor of music at the new Gresham College; in 1601 he travelled abroad, causing a sensation as an organist. Because of his Catholic beliefs, he emigrated in 1613, becoming organist to the Archduke Albert in Brussels and in 1617 organist at Antwerp cathedral.

Though it includes a few vocal and consort pieces, Bull's output is dominated by keyboard music–some 150 compositions, about a third of them in the Fitzwilliam Virginal Book. Along with Byrd and Gibbons, Bull was a major master of keyboard music, as well as a virtuoso player. His writing was experimental in its exploration of skilful finger techniques and often con-

cerned with the invention of patterns. His fantasias and cantus firmus pieces have a chilling intellectual quality, whereas the dances and character pieces show Bull's more accessible side. Through his musical activities in the Low Countries he had connections with Sweelinck, whom he admired and also influenced.

CE: Keyboard works in *MB* xiv, xix, ed. T. Dart, J. Steele and F. Cameron

Buonamente, Giovanni Battista (d. Assisi, 1643) Italian composer. After serving the Gonzagas in Mantua, worked at the courts of Vienna and Prague, and became *maestro di cappella* to the Franciscans at Assisi in 1636. His 7 volumes of instrumental music include pieces for various combinations of violin, lute, cornett and sackbuts. He was one of the first composers to treat the violin as a virtuoso instrument, and he also contributed to the development of the sonata as an instrumental form.

Burck, Joachim a (b. Burg bei Magdeburg, 1546; d. Mühlhausen, 24 May 1610) German composer. Lived in Mühlhausen from 1563 as cantor at the Latin school (where Eccard was his pupil), organist and local government official. He acknowledged Lassus and Rore as among the models for his many publications of songs, motets and through-composed Passions, and his approach to word-setting in Protestant music shows Lassus' influence. He is somewhat overshadowed by Eccard, on whose early publications he collaborated.

Burden 1. An English term for a self-contained textual and musical refrain in vocal pieces, especially the C15 CAROL.

2. English name for the apparently lowest (plainsong) part of FABURDEN, which was actually transposed a 5th

higher and sung by the middle voice (meane).

Burton, Avery (b. *c*1470; d. 1542x47) English composer. A Gentleman of the Chapel Royal from about 1509 to 1542; travelled abroad with the choir on several occasions and associated with Cardinal Wolsey's Oxford chapel choir for a time in 1527, which probably explains the inclusion of his fine hexachord Mass in the Forrest-Heather partbooks. The Mass is rather unusual in its abstract cantus firmus and its use of 2 bass parts in a 6-part scoring (one of these is missing from the partbooks).

Busnois, Antoine (d. Bruges, 6 Nov 1492) Franco-Flemish composer. Before 1467 he was a singer in the service of Charles the Bold of Burgundy, after whose death in 1477 he served his widow Margaret of Burgundy. Up to 1482 he was at the court of Archduke Maximilian after the latter's marriage to Maria of Burgundy. He may have visited Italy in the 1480s (his chansons are often found in Italian sources), and spent his last years as choirmaster at S. Sauveur, Bruges.

Busnois wrote some 3 Masses, 2 Magnificats, a Lamentation, 8 motets and about 63 chansons; like Binchois, he was primarily a chanson composer, and was widely esteemed in his day as a worthy contemporary of Ockeghem. His chansons use the standard forms, especially the *rondeau* and *bergerette*, and have a wide inventive range and feeling for musical structure. He moved towards writing for 4 voices rather than 3, and developed a melodic style of shapely elaboration with long-breathed phrases. He tended to widen the overall vocal compass and to use imitative writing to weld the texture, a feature particularly apparent in *Bel aceuil*. Busnois was poet as well as

musician, and may have written the texts of some of his chansons.

Buus, Jacques (b. ?Ghent; d. Vienna, Aug 1565) Franco-Flemish composer. In 1551, having abandoned the first organist's post at St Mark's, Venice, because of excessively low pay, he became court organist at Vienna. He published motets which show the influence of Gombert, and also some madrigals, but is primarily an instrumental composer, issuing 5 volumes of ricercars in motet-like style and canzonas, for organ or ensemble.

Buxheim Organ Book German manuscript collection of organ music (*c*1470) containing over 250 pieces, mostly arrangements of Burgundian chansons; one of the principal sources of C15 keyboard music.

CE: *EDM* xxxvii-ix

Byrd, William (b. ?Lincolnshire, 1543; d. Stondon Massey, Essex, 4 July 1623) English composer. In 1563 he succeeded Parsons as organist of Lincoln cathedral. Though appointed a Gentleman of the Chapel Royal in 1570, he only moved to London in 1572; he shared the post of organist with Tallis. In 1575 the two composers were granted a monopoly to publish music for Queen Elizabeth I, the immediate fruit of this being the joint *Cantiones Sacrae* of that year; on Tallis' death in 1585, Byrd enjoyed the patent alone. Between 1577 and 1593 Byrd lived at Harlington and later Stondon Massey; as a staunch Catholic he could not hold a post in the Established Church, but he ascribed his freedom from persecution to his position and work at court.

Byrd occupies a pre-eminent position in English music between the Tudor polyphonists and the 'golden age' around 1600, and his sheer versatility compares with that of Lassus on the Continent. His Latin music includes 3 Masses and the Mass Propers of the *Gradualia* (doubtless destined for recusant services) and 3 volumes of motets, all of this illustrating a blend of the traditionally rugged English polyphonic style with new, declamatory elements from the Netherlands and Italy. His Anglican services and anthems gave the new English rite some of its finest music and introduced into it the novelty of the verse anthem. This arose out of Byrd's contribution to secular song, a field in which he firmly resisted the fashion for the Italianate madrigal, preferring a sober type of accompanied solo song to high-flown if not religious texts; such 'consort songs' could be sung just by voices or accompanied by viols. Byrd also contributed to the viol consort literature a number of fine fantasias, In nomines and dance pieces. Lastly, his keyboard music stands out in a repertory that represents a high point in English music; here stylised dance pieces and brilliantly inventive sets of variations command attention.

CE: *The Collected Works of William Byrd*, ed. E. Fellowes (London, 1937–50); Keyboard music in *MB* xxvii–xxviii, ed. A. Brown; *The Byrd Edition*, ed. P. Brett and others (London, 1976–)

Byttering   Late C14/early C15 English composer; possibly a member of Henry V's Chapel Royal – his motet *En Katharina* may have been written for the wedding of Henry and Catherine de Valois. Most of his surviving music is in the oldest part of the Old Hall MS. The style of some of his pieces, with a highly ornamented treble melody and 2 accompanying parts, is reminiscent of the C14 Italian style, and anticipates that of English C15 music. Other works show his extremely skilful use of canon and the isorhythmic motet principle.

C

Cabezón, Antonio de (b. Castrojeriz, nr. Burgos, 3 May 1510; d. Madrid, 26 Mar 1566) Spanish composer and organist. Born blind, he served the Empress Isabella from 1526, and from 1539 was royal court and chapel musician to Charles V and later to Philip II. He came to London with Philip II in 1554–6, and his music and playing may have had a significant effect upon the English virginalists.

Cabezón's keyboard works were collected and published by his son Hernando 12 years after his death; they are a monument to his mastery of the various keyboard idioms of the day. Included are little *versillos* (contrapuntal settings of plainsong psalm tones), hymn elaborations, arrangements of motets by Josquin and other north European composers and, most noteworthy of all, *diferencias* (sets of variations on well-known melodies). Cabezón was indeed the first to develop the keyboard variation; each variation is linked without a break to the next, and he infuses the plainest secular material with a lofty seriousness of manner.

CE: *MME* xxvii–xxix, ed. H. Anglés; *IMM* Collected works ser., iv, ed. C. Jacobs (Brooklyn, 1967–   )

Cabezón, Hernando de (bp. Madrid, 7 July 1541; d. Valladolid, 1 May 1602) Spanish organist. The son of Antonio de Cabezón, he succeeded him as organist to Philip II in 1566. In 1578 he published an edition of his father's works which also includes 5 pieces of his own in a similar style.

Caccia Type of C14 Italian madrigal. Its texts deal with hunting, fishing or other vivid scenes from real life; the music, in lively descriptive style, consists of a strict canon for 2 voices usually accompanied by a free tenor in longer notes.

Caccini, Francesca (b. Florence, 18 Sep 1587; d. ?Lucca, c1640) Italian singer and composer, daughter of Giulio Caccini. She wrote music for court entertainments and a collection of monodies and duets. Her sister Settimia was also a well-known singer, who may have taken part in the first performance of Monterverdi's *Arianna*.

One *ballo* in *SCMA* vii, ed. D. Silbert

Caccini, Giulio (b. Tivoli, c1550; bd. Florence, 10 Dec 1618) Italian composer and singer. He was taught by Animuccia in Rome, and came to Florence in 1565 at the behest of Cosimo I de' Medici; he studied singing and became a singer at the Medici court, a post he retained for the rest of his life. He was involved in the *intermedi* for the Medici weddings of 1579 and 1589 as composer, singer and harpist. His only absence abroad from Florence was in 1604–5, when he visited the court of Henry IV and his queen, Maria de' Medici, in Paris. He was a renowned singing teacher; both his wives and two daughters were singers.

Caccini was a member of the Florentine CAMERATA, whose discussions led to a new style of song; it was in this field that he was most important as a composer. He also wrote music for some of the earliest operas – *Il rapimento di Cefalo*, performed by 100 musicians at Maria de' Medici's wedding in 1600, and *Euridice* (a rival setting to that of

Peri). His songbook *Le Nuove Musiche* (1602), one of the first collections of monodies, contains 12 madrigals and 10 arias; its preface expounds the 'new music' and especially matters of singing style and embellishment, which Caccini used with moderation and expressive intent. A further book of 29 monodies followed in 1614.

Monodies in *RRMB* ix, xxviii, ed. H. W. Hitchcock.

Cadéac, Pierre (fl. 1529–58) French composer. In 1556 he was master of the choristers at the cathedral of Auch. His chansons and motets were included in anthologies from 1529 onwards, and he also published 4-part Masses. His chansons are truly French in feeling and show considerable talent for setting both merry and melancholy texts. Gombert based a Mass on his *Je suis desheritée*.

Caimo, Gioseppe (b. Milan, 1540; d. Milan, 1584) Italian composer of noble birth. He worked as an organist in Milan (from 1580 at the cathedral) and between 1564 and 1585 published 7 volumes of madrigals and canzonets. Some of his madrigals contain advanced chromatic harmonies almost suggestive of Gesualdo, while his canzonets are light and charming, especially the onomatopoeic *Mentre il cuculo*.

Calata Italian dance going back to the C14, and found in Dalza's 1508 lutebook. Though notated in bars of 2/4 and 4/4 its real metre is 3/2.

Calestani, Vincenzo Early C17 Italian composer. Served at the courts of Ferrara and Pisa, and in 1517 published his *Madrigali ed arie*, including dancesongs and canzonets, many of which are comparable with the work of better known contemporaries such as Caccini. *Damigella tutta bella* is one of the most charming songs of the period.

Calvisius, Sethus (b. Gorsleben über Heldrungen, nr. Weissenfels, 21 Feb 1556; d. Leipzig, 24 Nov 1615) German composer and theorist. He directed music at the Pauluskirche, Leipzig, in 1581, was cantor in Schulpforta in 1582, and cantor at the Thomaskirche in Leipzig in 1594 with responsibility for music in the city churches. As theorist he made Zarlino's writings known in Germany; as composer he was highly revered for some fine Lutheran chorale harmonizations.

Cambio, Perissone (d. ?Venice, *c*1574) Flemish composer. Renowned as a singer, he came to Venice around 1540 as a member of St Mark's choir under Willaert. His compositions include a Mass as well as 3 books of madrigals and one of villanellas which was highly praised at the time, and includes reworkings of pieces by Nola.

Camerata A group of distinguished Florentine literary men, artists, musicians and aristocrats who gathered in the 1570s and 1580s to discuss the revival of ancient Greek music drama. These meetings, which took place at the home of Count Bardi, led to the evolution of a new style of singing that came to be used in opera and monody.

Campion (Campian), Thomas (b. Witham, Essex, 12 Feb 1567; d. London, 1 Mar 1620) English poet and composer. Apart from poetical works, he published 5 books of ayres mainly to his own texts, beginning with a volume compiled jointly with Rosseter (1601), and also wrote masques and occasional music, little of which survives. He was the only English composer to experiment with *musique mesurée* and the first to imitate the Florentine monodists, denouncing intricate counterpoint and naive word painting. As a poet he strove to preserve the true poetic metre even in very expressive songs. He was best at epigrammatic, dance-like pieces with an attractive lyrical melody, in which sense he was the opposite of Dowland.

CE: Ayres in *EL* 1st ser., iv, xiii, 2nd ser., i–ii, x–xi (rev. edn.)

Canali, Floriano (b. Brescia, *c*1550) Italian composer. Organist at S. Giovanni Evangelista in Brescia from 1581 to 1603; published much church music, and also volumes of canzonets and of instrumental canzonas in up to 8 parts.

Canario French C17 dance, similar to the gigue, supposedly imitating a dance of the Canary Islanders.

Cancionero de Palacio Manuscript collection (*c*1500) at the Palace Library in Madrid, containing several hundred Spanish songs for 3 or 4 voices, mostly VILLANCICOS; the principal source for Spanish secular music of the time. Juan del Encina is the composer most heavily represented.

CE: *MME* v, x, ed. H. Anglés

Canis, Cornelius (b. ?Ghent, 1510x20; d. Prague, 15 Feb 1561) Franco-Flemish composer. In 1542 he succeeded Gombert as master of the children in Charles V's chapel in Brussels and Madrid, later becoming *Kapellmeister*. In 1555 he was a canon in Courtrai, and he spent his last years (from 1557) in the service of Emperor Ferdinand I. His motets, Masses and chansons, in anthologies and MSS, are strongly Franco-Flemish in style and especially reminiscent of Gombert.

Cantigas de Santa María Spanish C13 monophonic songs in honour of the Virgin Mary and the miracles she performed. Collected for King ALFON-SO X ('El Sabio'), a lover of poetry and music, they are preserved in 4 MSS at Madrid and Florence, which also contain pictorial representations of instruments and players.

CE: *La Musica de las Cantigas . . .*, ed. H. Anglés (Barcelona, 1943)

Canto carnascialesco Popular strophic Italian song of the late C15, designed for open-air carnival festivities at the Florentine court. The texts were topical, descriptive and full of double meanings; the songs accompanied allegorical scenes or were sung from grotesque street floats.

Cantus firmus A pre-existent melody used as a basis for polyphonic composition; it may be a plainsong, a Protestant chorale, a secular tune or an abstract sequence of notes. The cantus firmus may lie in the tenor, either in notes of longer value than in the other voices or else ornamented and elaborated; alternatively it may be decorated in the treble part, as frequently occurs in the early C15.

Canzona, canzone 1. In Italian poetry, *canzone* is the name for serious lyrical poems between the C13 and C17. Applied in the early years of the C16 to secular vocal pieces set to free poems by Petrarch and others, it was an important forerunner of the madrigal.

2. With the suffix *villanesca* or *alla Napoletana*, equivalent to VILLA-NELLA.

3. An important keyboard or ensemble form in the C16–17, derived from the French chanson (chansons were printed in Italy as *canzone francesi*). Its counterpoint was less severe than that of the ricercar, and it often opened with a dactylic rhythm.

Canzonet, canzonetta Short, light, dance-like vocal piece in late C16 and early C17 written by Italian and later

English madrigalists (Germans like Hassler also imitated the type). The Italian *canzonetta* combined elements of villanella and madrigal; the English canzonet was more complex and polyphonic, though Morley wrote some for only 2 voices.

Capello, Giovanni Francesco (b. Venice; fl. 1610–19) Italian composer; organist at S. Maria delle Grazie in Brescia (1613–19). He published a book of monodies in 1617; his several extant volumes of sacred music place him in the forefront of early Baroque musical experimentalism, in his use of monodic or dialogue writing, quirky and imaginative word setting, and unusually rich instrumental colours. His 1615 Mass may be the first to include an *obbligato* instrumental ensemble.

Capirola, Vincenzo Early C16 Italian lutenist. A nobleman in Brescia, he compiled in 1517 a retrospective manuscript lute tablature, including ricercars and transcriptions of works by composers such as Obrecht and Févin, which contains some of the earliest indications of varied touch.

Cappella Giulia The choir that sang for services in St Peter's, Rome, as distinct from the *Cappella Sistina,* or Papal choir, which sang in the Pope's private (Sistine) chapel.

Capriccio 1. A term sometimes applied to lighter Italian madrigals of the late C16.
2. Italian instrumental piece, usually indistinguishable from the FANTASIA or CANZONA, though in Frescobaldi closer to the TOCCATA, and featuring a particular compositional technique (e.g. *capriccio chromatico*).

Caput Mass A mid-C15 Mass formerly attributed to Dufay but now thought to be English in origin. The cantus firmus consists of the melisma on the final word 'caput' from the Sarum plainsong *Venit ad Petrum.* Ockeghem and Obrecht wrote Caput Masses on the same cantus firmus.

Cara, Marco (b. Venice; d. Mantua, after 1525) Italian composer. He was in the service of the Gonzaga court at Mantua from 1495 to 1525, in which year he was made a citizen of the town. He was Isabella d'Este's favourite composer, and along with Tromboncino was a master of the frottola form, writing over 100 of them, and putting Mantua on the musical map. Many of his works were published by Petrucci. He aimed to provide a light and airy texture appropriate to the frottola texts he set, which could also be successfully performed by voice and lute. His own singing to the lute was praised for its 'mourning sweetness' in Castiglione's *Il cortegiano,* and indeed he raised the frottola to a level where it anticipated the sophistication of the early madrigal.
Frottolas in *IM* 1st ser., i, ed. G. Cesari and R. Monterosso; in *SCMA* iv, ed. A. Einstein

Cardenal see **Peire Cardenal**

Cardoso, Manuel (bp. Fronteira, nr. Elvas, 11 Dec 1566; d. Lisbon, 24 Nov 1650) Portuguese composer. Studied at Evora, one of Portugal's main musical centres, and was choirmaster at the cathedral there until 1588, when he joined the Carmelites in Lisbon and became their choirmaster. He published Masses, Magnificats and Holy Week music, all strongly Palestrinian in style, and was highly esteemed by the Portuguese King João IV.

Carleton, Nicholas C16 English composer. He made keyboard arrangements of vocal pieces and composed one of the earliest known organ duets, found in MS with a similar piece by Tomkins.

Carmen see **Instrumental chanson**

Carmen, Johannes Late C14/early C15 Franco-Flemish composer. He is one of the 3 composers said by Martin le Franc in *Le Champion des Dames* (c1440) to have 'astonished all Paris' with their music before that of Dunstable and Dufay had reached the city (the others were Cesaris and Tapissier). He is known today only by his sacred music, mainly traditional isorhythmic motets, sometimes employing a fast *parlando* style in the upper parts; the text of one motet refers to the Papal schism.
CE: in *CMM* 11/i, ed. G. Reaney

Carol Festive religious song. There was an important repertory in C15 England; they were often in major mode and triple time, with verses punctuated by a burden. The texts were often in the vernacular, sometimes with Latin refrains. A famous example is *Deo gracias Anglia*, which commemorates Henry V's victory at Agincourt in 1415.

Caron Later C15 Franco-Flemish composer, a contemporary of Ockeghem and Busnois. He may have spent at least part of his life in Cambrai, and been a pupil of Dufay. He was highly esteemed by Tinctoris, and composed several Masses and some 20 chansons in an up-to-date style. *Hélas, que pourra devenir* was extremely well known all over Europe, and survives in almost 20 manuscripts.
CE: *IMM* Collected works ser., vi, ed. J. Thomson

Caroso, Fabritio (b. ?Sermoneta, nr. Velletri, 1527x35; d. after 1605) Italian dancing-master. *Il Ballerino* (1581) is an important source of information on C16 dances, containing rules for the art

of dancing and lute arrangements of dance music. An expanded edition, *Nobiltà di Dame*, appeared in 1600.

Carpentras (Genet), Elzear (b. Carpentras, Vaucluse, c1475; d. Avignon, 14 June 1548) French composer. Except for a brief period at the French court, he served the Popes in Rome as singer (from 1508) and *maestro di cappella* (from 1518) until 1526, when overwork and mental fatigue forced him to retire to Avignon at the peak of his career. Despite a long and agonizing illness, he wrote and had published (at his own expense) church music including Masses and a set of Lamentations in an austere style which were dedicated to the Pope and remained in the Papal choir's repertory for many years.
CE: *Collected Works* (*CMM* 58), ed. A. Seay (Rome, 1972–)

Carver, Robert (b. 1487; d. after 1546) Scotch composer and monk. He spent 36 years at the Abbey of Scone (Perthshire) and is Scotland's greatest C16 composer. His church music includes the only British *L'homme armé* Mass, and *O bone Jesu*, a massive 19-part motet.
CE: *Opera omnia* (*CMM* 16), ed. D. Stevens (Rome, 1959–); Works in *MB* xv, ed. K. Elliott

Cascia, Giovanni da see **Giovanni da Firenze**

Caserta, da see under the first name of composers known thus.

Castanets see **Percussion**

Castello, Dario (d. 1656x58) Italian composer. Details of his life are elusive; he seems to have been a Venetian instrumentalist, possibly a musician at St Mark's. He published 2 very popular volumes of sonatas for up to 4 instruments and continuo which apply the new ornamental and dramatic vocal style to instrumental writing; some are scored for contrasted groups such as 2 violins and 2 sackbuts.

Ensemble sonatas in *RRMB* xxiii–iv, ed. E. Selfridge-Field

Castileti see **Guyot**

Castro, Jean de (b. in or nr. Liège, *c*1540; d. ?after 1611) Franco-Flemish composer. Vice-*Kapellmeister* at the Imperial court in Vienna from 1582 and later worked in various German cities. He published a great deal of church music, some conventional madrigals and chansons, and many volumes of secular pieces in which the music follows the poetic metre with great strictness.

Cauda see **Conductus**

Caurroy see **du Caurroy**

Caustun, Thomas (d. London, 28 Oct 1569) English composer. He was a Gentleman of the Chapel Royal in 1552, and contributed Anglican services and anthems to Day's *Certaine Notes* of 1560. The 4-part psalm settings of his in Day's 1563 psalter are more elaborate than the rest of the collection, and include an adaptation of an In nomine by Taverner.

Cavalieri, Emilio de' (b. Rome, *c*1550; d. Rome, 11 Mar 1602) Italian composer. From 1578–84 he organized performances of Lenten music at the Oratorio del Crocefisso at the church of S. Marcello in Rome. In 1588 he became General Inspector of Arts for Ferdinand I de' Medici at Florence.

Along with Peri and Caccini, Cavalieri was in the 1590s responsible for developing the pastoral play with music (dialogue, songs and choruses) and the new style of singing called *stile rappresentativo*, but his main claim to fame is as the composer of an allegori-

cal stage work, *Rappresentatione di anima e di corpo*, performed in Rome in February 1600 at St Philip Neri's oratory of S. Maria in Vallicella. This is less an oratorio (in the musical sense) than a sacred opera whose characters are allegorical figures such as Soul, Body, Intellect, Counsel and so on. Cavalieri claimed it moved his listeners more than the early Florentine operas; in any case it was the first-ever printed musical drama in the new style, and the printed score was the first to use a figured bass. Cavalieri also wrote 3 vocal pieces for the 1589 Florentine *intermedi*, one of which (*O che nuovo miracolo*) became the subject of numerous variations and elaborations.

Cavazzoni, Girolamo (b. Urbino, 1510; d. Mantua, after 1565) Italian organist and composer. The son of M. A. Cavazzoni, he worked as an organist at the Mantuan court, and his organ publications of 1542 and 1543 were among the most important of their time. They show great advances on the work of earlier keyboard composers, containing ricercars in a fully polyphonic imitative style, canzonas based on French chansons, and plainsong-based pieces which make free and skilful use of their Gregorian themes.

CE: *Orgelwerke*, ed. O. Mischiati (Mainz, 1959–61)

Cavazzoni, Marco Antonio (da Bologna) (b. Bologna, *c*1490; d. Venice, after 1570) Italian organist. He held several posts in Venice as organist, and as singer at St Mark's, and was a friend of Willaert, but also spent periods in Urbino, Rome (at the Papal court), Padua (in the service of Cardinal Bembo), Chioggia and Mantua, where he may have succeeded his son Girolamo as organist at S. Barbara in 1565. In 1523 he published an organ book which contains the earliest known use of the term 'ricercar' applied to organ music, and of 'canzona' as an instrumental form. The canzonas are modelled on French chansons, and the ricercars are in an improvisatory style, mixing imitative with chordal and toccata-like passages. Cavazzoni uses varied figurations and rich harmonies and textures, and some pieces seem to require the use of pedals.

Organ works in *CMI* i, ed. G. Benvenuti

Cavendish, Michael (b. *c*1565; d. Aldermanbury, London, 5 July 1628) English composer of noble birth (he was a cousin of Lady Arabella Stuart and lived at court). He contributed to East's and Ravenscroft's psalters, and in 1598 published a volume of lute songs and 5-part madrigals in a simple but graceful style.

Madrigals in *EM* xxxvi, rev. edn.; Ayres in *EL* 2nd ser., vii

Ceballos, Rodrigo de (b. Aracena, nr. Seville, 1525x30; d. Granada, 1591) Spanish composer and priest. Held posts at the cathedrals of Málaga and Córdoba before becoming choirmaster to the royal chapel at Granada in 1561. One of the best Andalusian composers of the period: his church music (all in MS) is often bold and dramatic, and has features in common with Morales and Victoria.

Certon, Pierre (b. ?Melun, *c*1510; d. Paris, 23 Feb 1572) French composer. A *clericus matutinale* (Matins Clerk) at Notre Dame, Paris, in 1529; joined the S. Chapelle as a singer in 1532 and was master of the boys there from 1542 until his death. He was one of the best chanson composers of Janequin's generation, but also wrote Masses, motets and spiritual chansons. His works were widely known in printed anthologies.

Chansons polyphoniques, ed. H. Expert and A. Agnel (Paris, 1967–9)

Césaris, Johannes Late C14/early C15 Franco-Flemish composer. Along with Carmen and Tapissier he is one of the composers who, according to Martin le Franc's *Le Champion des Dames* (*c*1440), 'astonished all Paris' with their music in the years before Dunstable and Dufay were known there. His earlier chansons are in the complex, 'mannered' style of late C14 France, but his later ones are simpler, with more clear-cut melodies, looking forward to the work of Dufay. He also wrote an isorhythmic motet.

CE: in *CMM* 11/i, ed. G. Reaney

Ceterone Bass plucked string instrument, not the same as a chitarrone, but the bass of the CITTERN family. It has a flat back and 8 metal strings stopped on fixed frets, and additional unstopped bass strings; Praetorius mentions a ceterone with 12 courses of strings, the lowest tuned to B♭. It is a useful continuo instrument, and 2 are specified in the 1615 edition of Monteverdi's *Orfeo*, in addition to 2 chitarroni.

Chaillou de Pestain (fl. *c*1316) French editor and/or composer. In 1316 he added some poems and 160 pieces of music to the *Roman de Fauvel*, the violent anti-clerical satire written by Gervaise de Bus between 1310 and 1314. It is not known whether any of these are his own compositions (some have been ascribed to Philippe de Vitry without conclusive evidence for the ascription) but they are very well chosen. They include both monophonic and polyphonic settings of French and Latin texts, some of the polyphonic pieces being in the old conductus style of many decades earlier, and some in a more modern style which looks forward to the *ars nova*.

Chanson French word for song. It applies to secular vocal works with

French text throughout the Middle Ages and Renaissance, especially polyphonic pieces of 1300–1600. (See also INSTRUMENTAL CHANSON.)

Chapel Royal A name sometimes given to the Household Chapel of the English royal court, an institution which played a notable part in the cultivation of sacred music in England.

Chastelain de Coucy (Gui II de Coucy) (b. Coucy, nr. Laon, c1160; d. 1203) Trouvère. A member of a distinguished family, he became Châtelain of his ancestral fortress at Coucy in 1186 (it was destroyed by bombardment in the 1914–18 War). He went on the Crusades of 1190 and 1198 and died on another journey to the East; a C13 poem gives a bizarre but largely untrue account of his life. He was one of the first generation of trouvères, and 15 of his songs survive.

Châtelet see **Guyot**

Chest of viols In C17 England, a set of 6 or more viols (usually 2 each of treble, tenor and bass), kept in a chest with partitions.

Chiavette An Italian term for clef-groupings (see p. 13) in C16 vocal music for 4 or more voices. The two most common groupings were C1 C3 C4 F4 (normal clefs) and G2 C2 C3 F3 (high clefs) in which the clefs were separated by a 5th, a 3rd and a 5th. The combinations could signal transposition up or down so as to keep the actual singing pitch within convenient voice ranges.

Chime bells Set of accurately tuned, tongueless cup bells, usually suspended from a frame and struck with a pair of small beaters. They were much used in the Middle Ages to teach musical theory as well as to accompany plainsong and liturgical drama, and were frequently illustrated. A set could include between 3 and 15 bells, but a diatonic octave was most common.

Chirbury (Chyrbury), Robert (d. c1456) English composer. A member of the Chapel Royal from 1421, he became a chaplain at Windsor in 1455. The Old Hall MS contains four 3-part Mass movements of his, in conductus style, two of which contain remarkable chromaticisms.

Chitarra, chitarra battente, chitarra spagnola, chitarriglia, chitarrino see **Guitar**

Chitarrone Plucked string instrument, essentially a bass lute with a resonant lower register, long fingerboard, and very long neck (up to 7 feet/ 215 cm long). There are 6 double courses of strings, often made of brass, tuned from G upwards and stopped on widely spaced frets, plus 8 unstopped bass strings tuned from F' upwards which have a separate pegbox. Of Italian origin, the chitarrone was much favoured as an accompaniment to the voice by composers such as Caccini, but though unsuited to rapid lute-style figurations it did also develop an extensive solo repertory which exploited its special characteristics; some 40 publications for it appeared in the first half of the C17.

Chorale A Lutheran hymn tune. Its history begins with Luther himself and his musical collaborator WALTER. Chorales became the backbone of much German Protestant music.

Choralis Constantinus The earliest polyphonic cycle of liturgical compositions for the whole ecclesiastical year. Written by Isaac in 1517 and completed after his death by Senfl for the use of Konstanz cathedral, it includes Mass

Propers and items for the Office, all based on plainsong.

CE: see under ISAAC

Ciconia, Johannes (b. Liège, c1373; d. ?Padua, Dec 1411) Franco-Flemish composer. The Johannes Ciconia to whom a biography between 1350 and 1390 is assigned was most probably the composer's father. The son was a choirboy at S. Jean l'Evangeliste, Liège, in 1385. In 1398 he went to Padua, becoming cantor at the cathedral there in 1403–a post he held until his death. His output includes 11 Mass sections, 11 motets and about 20 secular works, mostly settings of Italian texts. His Mass sections belong to the turn of the C15, having similarities with those of Loqueville and the 2 Lantins. The motets can be almost certainly dated 1395–1410; they contain a progressive element in their use of imitation, present even in 2 isorhythmic pieces written for the Bishop of Padua (several of Ciconia's motets are occasional, celebratory pieces). In his Italian works there are late examples of the *ballata*, but the song *O rosa bella*, with its word repetitions, is an entirely forward-looking example of the Burgundian chanson style. His music could be said to bridge the gap between the late C14 and the period of Dufay.

CE: In S. Clercx, *Johannes Ciconia* (Brussels, 1960); in *PMFC*, ed. M. Bent and A. Hallmark (forthcoming)

Cifra, Antonio (b. Terracina, nr. Rome, 1584; d. Loreto, 2 Oct 1629) Italian composer, pupil of G. B. Nanino. Worked at the Roman Seminary and German College before becoming *maestro di cappella* at the Santa Casa in Loreto in 1609. Except for the years 1622–6 when he was *maestro* at St John Lateran, he remained there until his death. One of the most popular and prolific members of the early C17 Roman school, Cifra not only wrote Masses in a Palestrinian style, but was the first Roman composer to adopt, albeit somewhat unimaginatively, the new concertato manner in church music. He published many small-scale motets, some inventive madrigals and 2 volumes of instrumental music.

Cima, Gian Paolo (b. Milan, c1570; d. after 1622) Italian composer. *Maestro di cappella* and organist at S. Celso, Milan, in 1610, he was one of the more important early C17 Milanese instrumental composers. His publications (1606, 1610) include polychoral instrumental pieces, polyphonic ricercars in which the themes are fully developed, and an important early example of a thematically integrated trio sonata for violin, cornett and continuo.

Keyboard works in *CEKM* 20, ed. C. Rayner

Cimello, Tomaso (b. Monte San Giovanni, nr. Frosinone, c1510; d. after 1579) Italian composer. Worked in Rome, but his villanellas of 1545, including a parody of Janequin's *La guerre*, belong to the Neapolitan school. He also published a madrigal book (1548) which contains *note nere* pieces.

Citole A medieval string instrument on which information is very sparse, though there are many literary references to it from the C13 onwards. It has been thought to be an ancestor of the Renaissance CITTERN. Recent research however seems to prove beyond reasonable doubt that it was in fact the medieval instrument hitherto known as the GITTERN.

Cittern Plucked string instrument with pear-shaped body, flat back, movable bridge and fixed frets, played with a plectrum. An attempt to re-create the ancient Greek cithara, it originated in medieval Italy. During the

C16 it had something of a dual personality: as a musicians' instrument it was second in popularity only to the lute, but it also had low-class associations as an instrument strummed on by waiting customers in barbers' shops. Earlier in the century it had between 4 and 6 double courses of strings and the fretting was diatonic, but from about 1570 onwards instruments with more strings and chromatic fretting were made. Praetorius describes several types, including a 12-course instrument with a strong, harpsichord-like tone. It developed an advanced technique, publications for it appeared, and it had roles both as a member of the BROKEN CONSORT and as a clear-toned melody instrument. The bass citern was called a CETERONE.

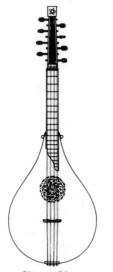

Cittern, 76 cm

Among the cittern's many relatives are the following:

Penorcon An instrument with 9 courses of strings, broader and shorter than the BANDORA but longer than the ORPHARION. It is known only because mentioned by Praetorius.

Poliphant Invented by Daniel Farrant *c*1600, this was an attempt to cross bandora and harp. It had about 40 strings, the bass set being supported on a harp-like frame to one side of the body.

Stump The one surviving piece for this instrument, of which no specimens or descriptions survive, requires 7 fingered courses of strings and 8 unstopped bass strings. It may have been a wire-strung equivalent of the THEORBO.

Clarion Medieval name for the short straight trumpet, usually 2–3 feet/60–90 cm long.

Claro see **Buisine**

Claudin see **Sermisy, Claudin de**

Clausula In music of the Notre Dame school *c*1200, a polyphonic piece using a short melisma of chant as a cantus firmus moving in relatively quick note values against an upper voice in discant style. Such nearly homophonic pieces may have been used by Perotin as substitutes for settings of *organa* by Leonin, but they also existed independently.

Clavichord String keyboard instrument, probably developed during the C14. It applies the keyboard principle to the MONOCHORD, so that the same string produces different notes by means of tangents, operated by the keys, which both stop and sound it. The oldest surviving specimen produces 45 notes from 22 strings, but the proportion of strings gradually increased. Some of the music in the Buxheim Organ Book may be intended for the clavichord, whose quiet tone made it ideal for practice and private recreation.

Clavicytherium Upright harpsichord, probably with gut strings, developed in the C15. The complexity of its mechanism probably contributed to its relative lack of popularity.

Claviorganum Experimental double keyboard instrument, usually combining harpsichord and organ, though other combinations occurred, such as organ and spinet or clavichord, or spinet and regal. It suffered from intractable tuning problems.

Clemens non Papa, Jacobus (b. Middelburg, Walcheren, 1510x15; d. Dixmuide, c1556) Franco-Flemish composer. Lived for a time in Ypres, and acquired the 'non Papa' of his name to distinguish him from a poet there Jacobus Papa. Named as 'singing master' at S. Donatien in Bruges in March 1544, in late 1550 he was a guest of the brotherhood of Our Lady at 's-Hertogenbosch.

Clemens was one of the most important composers of the generation between Josquin and Palestrina. His extensive output consists of 16 Masses, over 230 motets, 159 *souterliedekens* and about 90 chansons. The *souterliedekens* are simple settings of Flemish metrical psalm texts to popular melodies, scored for 3 voices. Clemens' chansons were as popular as they were numerous, being reprinted over many years. But it is in sacred music that he was particularly distinguished. Here his style is smoother than that of Gombert and closer to an Italianate lucidity of harmony, though fairly often dissonant (in sounding resolution notes against suspensions, for example) and occasionally chromatic, as in the motet *Fremuit spiritu Jesus*, where the application of *musica ficta* produces a striking 'modulation'. The fine 4-part motet *Vox in Rama* illustrates the use of the melodic minor second

interval to create a mood of pathos.
CE: *Opera omnia* (*CMM* 4), ed. K. Bernet Kempers (Rome, 1951–76)

Cleve, Johannes de (b. ?Cleve, c1529; d. Augsburg, 14 July 1582) German composer. *Kapellmeister* to the Archducal court at Graz (1544–70) and lived in Augsburg from 1579. He published motets in the traditional Netherlands style of Gombert and others, and composed old-fashioned sacred songs for inclusion in a book of rhyming sermons.

Coclico, Adrianus Petit (b. Flanders, 1499x1500; d. Copenhagen, Sep 1562) Flemish composer and theorist. A long-bearded, gnome-like figure, he was one of the most colourful characters in C16 music. In his treatise *Compendium Musices* of 1552 he made almost certainly unfounded claims to have studied with Josquin and served popes and kings of France. His chequered career did take him to various German cities; his school at Nürnberg failed, and he had to flee the Prussian court at Königsberg after a serious scandal. His motets of 1552, described as MUSICA RESERVATA, attempt a very detailed expression of their texts, but Coclico's lack of technical expertise renders them merely curious.

Sacred music in *EDM* xlii

Codax, Martín C13 Spanish troubadour and jongleur, from Vigo. His 6 songs (discovered in the binding of a C14 MS in 1914) are the earliest known Spanish secular songs that are capable of transcription; their texts are in Galician-Portuguese dialect, and the nonmensural melodies are simple, with some resemblance to Galician folksong and Mozarabic chant.

Coelho, Manuel Rodrigues (b. Elvas, c1555; d. ?Lisbon, after 1633) Portuguese organist and composer. After working at the cathedrals of Badajoz and Elvas, he became in 1603 organist of Lisbon cathedral and a member of the royal chapel. The first important Iberian keyboard composer since Cabezón, he wrote *tientos* in a vividly baroque style in which brilliant figuration predominates over thematic development.

Coinci see **Gautier de Coinci**

Colascione see **Lute**

Colin Muset Early/mid-C13 jongleur, possibly from the Champagne district. A true poet and musician rather than merely a popular entertainer, he raised his status to that of a trouvère. Fifteen of his poems and 8 melodies survive.

Comes, Juan Bautista (b. Valencia, 29 Feb 1568; d. Valencia, 5 Jan 1643) Spanish composer, pupil of Gines Pérez. Held posts as *maestro de capilla* at Lérida cathedral, the Colegio del Patriarca in Valencia and, between 1613 and 1619, and from 1632, at Valencia cathedral; he was second *maestro* at the court in Madrid 1619–29. Much of his surviving church music is polychoral, including a fine *Hodie Christus natus est* for three 4-part choirs; he also wrote sacred *villancicos* in which the verse is sung by a few voices and the refrain by a 6-part choir.

Compère, Loyset (b. ?S. Omer, c1450; d. S. Quentin, 16 Aug 1518) Franco-Flemish composer. A singer in the Sforza family chapel in Milan in 1474–5, and a court chapel singer in Paris in 1486; a prebendary at Cambrai in 1498 and at Douai in 1500; at his death he was a canon at S. Quentin.

Compère's extant outputs consists of 2 Masses and 4 Mass sections, 3 motet cycles, 23 motets and Magni-

ficats, 5 motet-chansons, 49 chansons and 2 frottolas. He was regarded as one of the most prominent of the contemporaries of Josquin Desprez. His *Missa Allez regrets*, based on Hayne van Ghizeghem's chanson, is a notable forerunner of the C16 parody Mass. The motet cycles are in fact designed to be substituted for the correct liturgical items (both Ordinary and Proper) of Masses for certain feasts – hence the label 'substitution Mass' sometimes given them; this custom was unique to the Ambrosian use of Milan. Compère's motet-chansons have a tenor with Latin text glossed by the French words of the upper voices, as in the exquisite *Royne du ciel/Regina caeli*. His secular works document the change from sentimental Burgundian chansons in the fixed poetic forms towards the witty chansons of later French composers. Several were printed in Petrucci's *Odhecaton*.

CE: *Opera omnia* (*CMM* 15), ed. L. Finscher (Rome, 1958–72)

Compline see **Office**

Concertato Generic term for the new style of C17 music for 2 or more voices or instruments with indispensable continuo. It differed from C16 practice in allowing writing for individual soloists or voice-groups within the texture (as in Monteverdi's earliest continuo madrigals of 1605). *Coro concertato* signified a small body of solo singers in distinction to full choir (*cappella* or *ripieno*).

Concerto Before 1650 this term was used for vocal compositions with organ or continuo, e.g. church concertos by the Gabrielis and Banchieri (for double choir) or Viadana (for solo voices in the newer style). Schütz's *Kleine geistliche Konzerte* of 1636 follow the latter usage. The element of opposition implicit in the more recent concerto was less marked, if not actually absent, in the early baroque conception of a concerto.

Conductus Medieval Latin songs, either monophonic or later polyphonic (often *à 2*), mainly with strophic texts. The conductus differed from other genres in its lack of a chant-derived cantus firmus and frequent syllabic writing (though many examples ended with a melismatic phrase known as a *cauda*). Originating as music to accompany liturgical processions, it came to reflect non-liturgical clerical activities – perhaps a clerical equivalent of troubadour song.

Conforti, Giovanni Luca (b. Mileto, Calabria, *c*1560) Italian singer. Sang in the Papal choir from 1580 to 1585 and from 1595 onwards. Especially renowned for his *passaggi* (ornamented versions of vocal lines), he published instructions for devising *passaggi* in 1593 and a volume of ornamented psalms in 1607.

Ricercars and madrigals containing his *passaggi* in *CM* iv, ed. D. Kämper.

Conon de Béthune (b. *c*1160; d. in the East, 17 Dec 1219) Trouvère; son of Robert V of Béthune and an important soldier, politician and diplomat. One of the northern French aristocrats deeply involved in the Crusades, he was a leading figure at Constantinople in that of 1204, and composed 2 Crusade songs, widely disseminated in MS, which are of a higher standard than most of their kind. He wrote an *enueg*, a satire attacking the nobles who misappropriated to their own use funds donated to help the Crusades.

Conseil, Jean (b. Paris, 1498; d. Rome, prob. 11 Jan 1535) French composer who worked in Italy. Sang in the Papal choir from 1513 and became its *maestro di cappella* in 1534. He was

one of the lesser but talented figures of the early C16, and his motets and chansons appeared in anthologies of 1529–59.

Consort C16 and C17 term for an instrumental chamber ensemble, and (in England) for the music written for it. The term is today applied most commonly to the consort of viols. (See also BROKEN CONSORT.)

Consort song A type of English C16 song for voice accompanied by viol consort. Words were sometimes underlaid to the viol parts, offering the option of completely vocal performance; in an instrumentally accompanied performance the voice took the second-highest line, often termed 'the first singing part'.

Continuo see **Basso continuo**

Contractus see **Hermannus Contractus**

Contrafactum A vocal piece with a substituted text, e.g. sacred in place of secular, or vice-versa. A number of early Lutheran chorales are *contrafacta*.

Contratenor C14 and C15 name for the third voice after discantus (top part) and tenor, with a range like the latter but a more angular part. In 4-part writing, there came to be two voices so labelled – the *contratenor altus* and *contratenor bassus*; the name stuck to the former voice.

Conversi, Girolamo (b. Correggio, nr. Modena; fl. 1572–84) Italian composer. In 1584 he was in the service of the Viceroy of Naples. A prolific composer of madrigals, villanellas and light but not scurrilous canzonets; he is represented in *Musica Transalpina*, and composed the popular *Sola, soletta* arranged for instruments in Morley's *Consort Lessons*.

Cooke, John Early C15 English composer. Clerk to the Chapel Royal of Henry V and Henry VI, and is probably the 'Cook' represented in the Old Hall MS by 5 Mass movements and 3 motets. Some of this music is in the 'free treble' style, with an ornamental melody over 2 accompanying parts; other pieces use a chordal style, or alternate sections for 2 and 4 voices. His motet *Ave proles regia* is isorhythmic.

Coperario see **Coprario**

Coppini, Alessandro (b. c1465; d. Florence, 1527) Italian composer, active in Florence (he was probably born there); became a monk, a doctor of sacred theology, and organist of various Florentine churches including S. Lorenzo and SS. Annunziata. He wrote a Mass on Agricola's *Si dedero*, but was most notable as a composer of carnival songs for the Florence of Lorenzo the Magnificent. These are good examples of the current Italian fashion for 4-part homophonic textures varied by repetition, triple-time passages and reduction of voices for imitative sections.

CE: *CMM* 32/ii, ed. F. d'Accone

Coprario (Coperario), John (b. c1575; d. London, Jan x June 1626) English composer. Served at the English court from 1606 to 1626 as lutenist, gamba player and composer, and taught the future King Charles I and also William Lawes. There is no evidence that he travelled to Italy, despite the fact that he Italianized his name from Cooper. He published 2 books of lute songs (*Funeral Teares* and *Songs of Mourning*) and wrote a large number of fantasias and suites for consort, some Italian villanellas, and a treatise *Rules how to compose*. His fantasias for viols show the progress of idiomatic instrumental writing, but more important are his consort suites, both for their novel medium of one or 2 violins with bass viol and organ, and for their development of the concept of the suite: a fantasia plus 2 dance movements.

Lute songs in *EL* 1st ser., xvii

Coranto Originally a C16 dance with jumping movements, with music of lighter texture than the saltarello and with running figures. The C17 Italian *corrente*, in quick triple time, was adopted by Frescobaldi, Scheidt and others.

Cordier, Baude Late C14 French composer, from Rheims. He may be the Baude Fresnel who was harper and *valet de chambre* to Philip the Bold of Burgundy from 1384 until his death in 1397–8, and who travelled to Milan and Avignon. Some of his 10 secular pieces (mostly *rondeaux*) are in the rhythmically complex late C14 French style; others are simpler, with greater emphasis on lyrical melody, in the manner of early Binchois. Of his 2 chansons in the Chantilly MS, one is written in the form of a heart and the other in a circle. His Mass movement in the Apt MS is also in a more C15 style.

CE: in *CMM* 11/i, ed. G. Reaney

Cori spezzati Italian for separated choirs. The term is often used of groups of performers in polychoral Venetian music, spatially separated among the choirstalls and flanking galleries.

Cornago, Johannes (fl. before 1466–73) Spanish composer. Spent many years up to 1466 at the Naples court, and in 1473 was a singer to Ferdinand I of Aragon. He composed church music and secular pieces, including 3 *villancicos* in the *Cancionero de Palacio*.

Cornamuse 1. Reedcap wind instrument whose sound emerges from small holes in a covered bell. No specimens survive, and Praetorius does not illustrate it, merely describing it as a keyless, straight instrument with a cylindrical bore and 9-note compass. The cornamuses heard today are therefore constructed on a purely speculative basis, and do not necessarily bear any resemblance to a C16 instrument. The tone of the cornamuse was said to be softer and sweeter than that of the crumhorn, and its name appears in lists of ensembles used at various courtly entertainments.

2. French term for bagpipe.

Cornet, Pieter (b. c1562; d. after 1633) Dutch organist and composer. Court organist in Brussels 1593–1626; his organ fantasias, dances and variations show the influence of the English virginalists (both Bull and Philips worked in Brussels).

CE: *Collected Keyboard Works* in *CEKM 26*, ed, W. Apel

Cornett, cornetto Wind instrument with cup mouthpiece and finger-holes of gently curved shape and usually made of leather-covered wood (though ivory specimens also exist). Developed, probably in Germany and Austria, from the medieval finger-hole cow-horn, it became the most versatile wind instrument of the period 1500–1650. The combination of brass-style sound-production and woodwind fingering causes formidable technical difficulties, but the cornett can produce both loud, brilliant and soft, singing tone over its compass of some 2 octaves (more in the hands of an expert), and can also negotiate complex ornamentations. It was suitable for every kind of music, indoors and out, sacred and secular, could be used as a substitute for the violin, and was treated as a true virtuoso instrument, as for example in Monteverdi's *Vespers*. The standard cornett was pitched in G,

the cornettino was a small instrument a 4th or 5th higher, and there was an alto cornett in F.

Cornett, 61 cm

Other members of the family are:

Mute cornett A straight cornett with built-in rather than detachable mouthpiece, wider throat and narrower bore. Its soft, sweet tone is ideal for consort playing.

Tenor cornett or **lizard** The length of this instrument in C necessitates the 2 curves which account for its name. Praetorius disliked its sound, and the tenor cornett's wide bore makes it more like the SERPENT, better when blending with voices or in consort than on its own.

Cornettino see **Cornett**

Cornuel (Verjust), Jean (d. 1499) Franco-Flemish singer, possibly also composer. Spent much of his life as an ecclesiastic in Cambrai, but also worked in Köln and Milan and at the Hungarian court under Stockem (probably 1483–90).

Cornysh, William (b. E. Greenwich, c1468; d. Hylden, Kent, ?Oct 1523) English composer. Probably the son of the elder William Cornysh (d. 1502), he entered royal service in 1492 and was a Gentleman of the Chapel Royal from 1496, being Master of the Children there from 1509 until his death. In 1504 he was imprisoned on account of a political pamphlet, but soon returned to favour. He wrote music for court pageants, one of which was performed at the Field of the Cloth of Gold, and a number of secular songs preserved in the Henry VIII MS; his surviving sacred music includes 3 votive antiphons and a Magnificat. This latter work, in 5 parts, displays the extreme vocal exuberance of the Eton Choirbook composers, though preserved in the Caius choirbook; the Eton MS contains the votive antiphons.

Secular works in *MB* xviii, ed. J. Stevens; Magnificat in *EECM* iv, ed. P. Doe

Correa de Arauxo, Francisco (b. ?Seville, 1575x80; d. Segovia, before 13 Feb 1655) Spanish organist and composer, possibly of Portuguese descent. Organist at S. Salvador, Seville (1599–1636) and at the cathedrals of Jaén (until 1640) and Segovia. His *Libro de tientos* (1626) contains more than 60 pieces in a colourful baroque style, with bold dissonances and wayward figurations.

Libro de tientos in *MME* vi, xii, ed. M. Kastner

Corrente see **Coranto**

Corteccia, Francesco (b. Florence, 27 July 1502; d. Florence, 7 June 1571) Italian composer. He spent his life in Florence, as organist of S. Lorenzo in 1531 and director of music to Cosimo I de' Medici from 1539, during which time he wrote the music for many *intermedi*, the first being for Cosimo's wedding in 1539. He published several volumes of madrigals and motets; the *turba* parts for a Passion survive, together with meditative motets to be interpolated. His music for the 1539 *intermedio* included pieces for voice and instruments and a 9-part motet *Ingredere* performed by 24 voices, 4 cornetts and 4 trombones (despite the Latin text this was the earliest 'ceremonial madrigal'). He was one of the first to write *note nere* madrigals, and to bring Neapolitan villanellas to the attention of north Italian musicians.

Motets in *RRMR* vi, ed. A. McKinley

Costeley, Guillaume (b. ?Pont-

Audemer, Normandy, *c*1531; d. Évreux, 1x2 Feb 1606) French composer. By 1560 he was court organist to Charles IX of France, and in 1575 founded the Évreux 'Puy de musique' –an annual prize for composition–in honour of St Cecilia. He wrote over 100 chansons, which continued to be reprinted until 1633, and was the leading chanson composer of the late C16. He belonged for a time to the poet Baïf's circle.

Chansons in *MMRF* iii, xviii–xix

Cosyn's Virginal Book MS collection of English keyboard music dated 1620 and compiled by the organist Benjamin Cosyn (fl. 1620–43). It contains some 90 pieces mostly by Bull, Gibbons and Cosyn himself.

Coucy see **Chastelain de Coucy**

Council of Trent Held in 1545–63, this meeting of the Catholic Church in the Italian Tyrol was decisive for the development of Catholic music. In 1562, under the heading 'Abuses in the sacrifice of the Mass', it directed that dignity should be restored to services, the use of secular melodies outlawed, and the liturgical texts rendered intelligible.

Courtaut Double-reed wind instrument, with narrow cylindrical double bore. It has neither reedcap nor pirouette, and has 6 projecting tubes called 'tetines' to help the player locate the remoter finger-holes, especially those covered by the middle joints of the fingers. It has a basic 9-note compass, and its soft and muffled tone resembles that of the SORDUN.

Cowhorn see **Horn**

Cox (Cockx), Richard C15 English composer. A Mass of his preserved in MS at Brussels contains a troped Kyrie and telescopes the text of the Credo. It dates from c1450 and could be an early example of parody Mass.

Craen, Nikolaus (b. 's-Hertogenbosch; fl. 1504) Franco-Flemish composer. In 1504 a singer at S. Donatien in Bruges. Glareanus esteemed him highly enough to include a 3-part motet in the DODECACHORDON, and he is also represented in Sicher's organ tablature.

Crecquillon, Thomas (b. c1500; d. Béthune, 1557) Franco-Flemish composer. Became director of music to Charles V's chapel at Brussels in about 1544, and was later a prebendary in various Flemish towns–Louvain, Namur, Termonde and finally Béthune. He wrote some 16 Masses, 116 motets, 192 chansons, 5 French psalms and Lamentations. Highly regarded in his own day (much of his music circulated widely in print), he is most distinguished as a chanson composer. Though some of his chansons are in the light and witty French style, many are more serious in tone and written in flowing, imitative 5-part polyphony sometimes involving canon; in this they hark back to the late chansons of Josquin Desprez. In sacred music Crecquillon often matched musical to verbal expression, using harsh dissonances to create tension (the 5-part set of Lamentations shows this well, despite its major mode), but his smooth vocal line and command of sonority are equally impressive.

CE: *Opera omnia* (*CMM* 63), ed. N. Bridgman and B. Hudson (Rome, 1974–); 4-part motets in *IMM* Musicological studies ser., xxxi, ed. H. Marshall

Crema, Giovanni Maria da (fl. 1546) Italian lutenist. Probably belonged to the circle of Francesco da Milano and may have been at the Mantuan court in 1513–15 and in 1522. His lute books of 1546 contain ricercars in both polyphonic and improvisatory style, dances, and transcriptions of pieces by composers such as Josquin, Gombert and Arcadelt.

Crivelli, Giovanni Battista (b. Scandiano, nr. Modena; d. Modena, Mar 1652) Italian composer. He directed music in various Italian cities (at the cathedrals of Reggio and Milan, the Accademia dello Spirito Santo at Ferrara, S. Maria Maggiore at Bergamo), and served at the courts of Munich and Modena. He wrote *intermezzi* and operatic music and was one of the more talented composers of small-scale concertato motets and madrigals, tempering melodic expressiveness with structural subtlety.

Croce, Giovanni (b. Chioggia, c1557; d. Venice, 15 May 1609) Italian composer. A pupil of Zarlino, he joined the choir of St Mark's, Venice, in 1565. He was a priest by 1585, and became vice-*maestro* at St Mark's in 1594 and full *maestro di cappella* in 1603. He was a prolific church composer (he published 15 volumes) who in his late *Cantilene* adopted the concertato idiom, and a versatile madrigalist, contributing to the vogue for madrigal comedy in his *Triaca Musicale*.

Triaca in *CP* iii

Crowd, crwth, bowed lyre Bowed string instrument, bowed successor to the LYRE, whose shape it resembled. In the C11 and C12 it usually had 3 or 4 strings which sometimes included unstopped drones; in some cases the shape of the instrument would cause all the strings to be sounded together. There was a central neck but no fingerboard, the strings being stopped only by finger pressure. Later the crowd acquired a fingerboard and extra strings, and probably came to resemble the comparatively recent Welsh crwth.

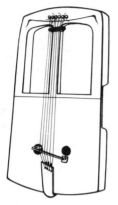

Crowd, 80 cm

Cruce see **Petrus de Cruce**

Crumhorn Reedcap wind instrument with narrow cylindrical bore, which produces a buzzing, slightly nasal tone. Its name, meaning 'curved horn', probably derives from the characteristic pothook shape. Probably developed during the late C15 or very early C16, the crumhorn became the most common reedcap instrument of the Renaissance. Praetorius lists 6 sizes, from soprano to great bass, each with a basic 9-note compass; C16 crumhorns did not have the extra upper keys often added on modern copies. The standard 4-part consort of ATTB crumhorns has a tone similar to that of the REGAL, and is suitable for a wide range of Renaissance dances and other ensemble music. There is surviving music specifically scored for crumhorns by composers such as Corteccia and Schein (*Banchetto musicale*, 1626).

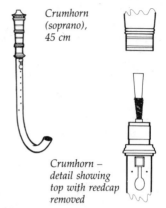

Crumhorn (soprano), 45 cm

Crumhorn – detail showing top with reedcap removed

Crwth see **Crowd**

Curtal or **dulcian** Double-reed wind instrument with widely-expanding conical double bore. A less unwieldy and pleasanter-sounding substitute for

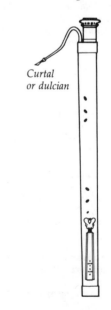

Curtal or dulcian

the bass shawm, it emerged in the mid-C16 and quickly established itself as a band instrument and useful reinforcement to choral bass lines. Praetorius lists 5 sizes, from quint bass (from F' upwards) to soprano, of which the commonest was the bass (C-g') which continued to be used during the baroque period. The first solo for bass curtal, a fantasia requiring virtuoso technique over a 3-octave range, was published in 1638 by Fray Bartolomé de Selma y Salaverde.

Cutting, Francis (fl. 1596) English lutenist and composer. One of the most talented English composers for the lute, especially when writing in a highly ornamented style, he is represented in Barley's tablature of 1596.

Cuvelier, Jean (fl. 1372–84) French composer and poet. He came from Tournai and was 'diseur' to the king of France in 1372. In 1387 he completed his great epic poem, the *Chronique de Bertrand de Guesclin*. His 3 *ballades* in the Chantilly MS are rhythmically extremely complex; 2 of them also use canon.

Cymbals see **Percussion**

D

Da cappella, a cappella The term 'a cappella', though traditionally understood to mean 'unaccompanied choral music', has no historical basis. In 1600–50 'da cappella' signified 'for a full choir without soloists or instrumental *obbligati*' in distinction to CONCERTATO; this did not imply 'unaccompanied' since many such Masses (Monteverdi's, for example) were issued with organ continuo, and in any case the Renaissance polyphony on which such music was modelled (thus in the STILE ANTICO) was itself often supported by organ or instruments.

Dalla Casa, Girolamo (b. c1543; d. Venice, before 12 Dec 1601) Italian composer and cornettist. From 1568 a wind player at St Mark's, with the title 'capo dei concerti nelli organi', he also became leader of the Venice town band in 1584. He published madrigals, motets and 2 volumes of *Il vero modo di diminuir*, which contains very difficult divisions on voice parts of well-known chansons and madrigals.

Dalza, Joanambrosio (fl. 1508) Italian lutenist, working in Milan. In 1508 he published a lute book with transcriptions of frottolas, improvisatory ricercars to be used as preludes to them, and dances. The dances are arranged in miniature suites of a pavane followed by a saltarello and piva which are thematically related to it.

Damett, Thomas (d. before 13 Apr 1437) English singer and composer. The illegitimate son of a gentleman of southern England, he was educated at Winchester College until 1407, and received a dispensation to enter the priesthood. After a period as Rector of Stockton, Wilts., he was a chaplain in the Chapel Royal of Henry V and Henry VI, travelling to the French and Burgundian courts, and held prebends at St. Paul's cathedral and (from 1431) St George's, Windsor. Most of his music survives in the Old Hall MS, including 4 Glorias, 2 each in the treble-dominated and the more chordal style, and an isorhythmic motet.

Danckerts (Dankers), Ghiselin (b. Tholen, Zeeland, 1505x15) Franco-Flemish composer and theorist. A Papal singer from 1535 until 1565 (when he was dismissed as a wealthy, voiceless womanizer); one of the judges in a dispute on musical theory between VICENTINO and Lusitano about which he wrote a treatise. He composed some motets and madrigals in an old-fashioned Netherlands style.

Daniel see **Arnaut Daniel**

Danyel, John (bp. Wellow, nr. Bath, 6 Nov 1564; d. after 1625) English composer and lutenist. Brother of the poet Samuel Danyel, whose works he edited, he had entered royal service by 1612. He is one of the most important composers of lute songs; their emotional power is surpassed only in those of Dowland. The 2 tragic song-cycles *Can doleful notes* and *Grief keep within* are especially fine.

Ayres in *EL* 2nd ser., viii, rev. edn.

Daser, Ludwig (b. Munich, c1525; d. Stuttgart, 27 Mar 1589) German composer. Became court *Kapellmeister* at

Munich in 1552, but was pensioned off in 1559 to make way for Lassus; took up a similar post in Stuttgart in 1572. He published a Passion in 1578, and left MSS of many Masses, motets and German sacred songs, and 2 cycles of Mass Propers.

Motets in *EDM* xlvii

Davy, Richard (b. *c*1467; d. ?Blickling, Norfolk, *c*1516) English composer. Entered Magdalen College, Oxford, in 1483 and became organist and joint choirmaster there in 1490. Probably he was the Richard Davy who was priest and vicar-choral at Exeter cathedral from 1494 to 1507; thereafter he served the Boleyn family at Blickling in Norfolk. His surviving music consists of 7 votive antiphons and a St Matthew Passion in the Eton Choirbook, and one carol. The Passion provides polyphony for the crowd and individual characters other than Christ and the Evangelist in a resourceful and imaginative style, while the votive antiphons illustrate his facility as a composer (one long piece of *c*260 bars was, the Eton scribe tells us, written in a single day).

Daza, Esteban (fl. 1576) Spanish vihuelist. His *Libro de musica* (1576) was the last of the Spanish publications for the vihuela, and contains fantasias, and transcriptions of motets and secular pieces by composers such as Guerrero and Vásquez.

De la Hèle see **Hèle, Georges de la**

De la Rue see **Rue, Pierre de la**

Delattre, Petit-Jean (b. in or nr. Liège; d. Utrecht, 31 Aug 1569) Franco-Flemish composer. Choirmaster to the Bishop of Liège *c*1554, and later probably master of the boys at Verdun cathedral. He published volumes of chansons and Lamentations in 3 to 6 parts, and is represented in anthologies. (He is not the Claude Petit-Jean Delattre who won a prize at the Évreux composition contest in 1576 and died at Metz in 1589.)

Della Viola, Alfonso (b. Ferrara, *c*1508; d. ?Ferrara, *c*1570) Italian composer and virtuoso viol player, who worked at the Ferrara court for many years and wrote music for several dramatic productions there. His recitative-like solos, anticipating long in advance the new style of *c*1600, mark an important stage in the development of dramatic music. He also published 2 volumes of madrigals and made elaborate and heavily ornamented arrangements of polyphonic music for solo viol (the viola bastarda or division viol style).

Della Viola, Francesco (b. beginning C16; d. Ferrara, Mar 1568) Italian composer, possibly related to A. Della Viola. He worked in Modena, Ferrara and possibly Venice before returning in 1559 to the Ferrara court as *maestro di cappella* in succession to Rore. A disciple of Willaert, whose *Musica Nova* he edited in 1558, he published his own 4-part madrigals in 1550.

Demantius, Johannes Christoph (b. Reichenberg [Liberec], Bohemia, 15 Dec 1567; d. Freiberg, Saxony, 20 Apr 1643) German composer. Studied at Wittenberg, and was a cantor at Zittau in 1597, and at Freiberg in 1604. A versatile follower of Hassler, he wrote Lieder, works in the HISTORIA tradition (including a St John Passion) and a number of instrumental collections which contained dances in Polish style and Hungarian 'battle music' for trumpets and drums.

Secular songs in *EDM* Sonderreihe i

Dering, Richard (b. *c*1580; bd. London, 22 Mar 1630) English composer. Educated in England, travelled to Italy probably after 1610, and was converted to Catholicism while in Rome. In 1617 he was organist to the nuns of the English convent in Brussels, and in 1625 he returned to England as organist to Queen Henrietta Maria. He wrote 3 books of motets with continuo, 2 of canzonets and 1 of continuo madrigals, and is represented in many MSS and anthologies. This music shows varying degrees of Italian influence; the continuo madrigals and small concertato motets are very much in the idiom of Grandi or d'India, with wayward modulations and dramatic expression; the *Cantio Sacra* (1618) contains 6-part motets that recall a more conventionally expressive Italian madrigal-like idiom.

Secular music in *MB* xxv, ed. P. Platt; *Cantio Sacra* in *EECM* xv, ed. P. Platt

Descant An English C14 technique of improvising or composing additional parts above or below a plainsong in the middle voice. The outer voices (descant and counter) would move mostly by contrary motion against one another. This is slightly different from the improvised technique of FABURDEN.

Des Prés, Desprez see **Josquin Desprez**

Diabolus in Musica Nickname for the tritone or augmented 4th, regarded as a 'dangerous' interval in early musical theory. Late medieval theorists coined the expression with the solmization rule 'mi contra fa, diabolus in musica'.

Dietrich, Sixt (b. Augsburg, 1492x94; d. St Gallen, 21 Oct 1548) German composer. In 1517 he taught at the cathedral school of Konstanz, and became chaplain to the Holy Cross there in 1522. He keenly supported the Reformation cause and mixed in the Reformers' circles at Basle, Strasbourg,

Ulm and Wittenberg, where he lectured; before Konstanz was overrun by Charles V and reclaimed for Catholicism he fled to St Gallen. Dietrich wrote both Latin music (Magnificats, hymns, motets) for Catholic use and sacred Lieder for the Lutherans, and contributed to Ott's second secular songbook. Like many of his generation (including Senfl) he could write in an earnest and distinguished Franco-Flemish manner, but his chorale settings in Rhaw's 1544 collection are chordal, with regular cadences and little counterpoint, looking forward to a later epoch.

Hymns in *EDM* xxiii; Antiphons in Rhaw, *Musikdrucke*, vii (Kassel, 1964)

Diferencias C16 Spanish term for variations. The earliest examples are by the vihuelists (Narváez and others); Cabezón wrote some outstanding examples for organ.

Dijon see **Guiot de Dijon**

Diminutions, divisions In the C16 and C17, the embellishment of a melody by breaking it into fast figurations. This was often done by a soloist (e.g. voice or viol) against a harmonic background, and was frequently improvised–hence a number of manuals and treatises on the technique by, for example, Ganassi and Bassano.

D'India see **India, Sigismondo d'**

Diruta, Girolamo (b. Diruta, nr. Perugia, *c*1550x60) Italian organist, composer and Minorite monk. A pupil of C. Porta, Zarlino and Merulo, he was probably an organist in Venice until 1593 and was later organist at the cathedrals of Chioggia (1597) and Gubbio (1609). *Il Transilvano*, a 2-volume treatise on how to play and write for the organ, contains pieces by Diruta himself as well as Banchieri, Bellavere and Quagliati.

Discant A note-against-note style in early ORGANUM, as distinct from melismatic writing where the 'organal' (i.e. added) voice sang several notes to a single note of the plainsong. It also applied to improvised counterpoint in note-against-note style, as described by medieval theorists.

Division viol The playing of 'divisions', or rapid and elaborate solo passages, on the bass viol became popular in England in the later C16, and though the term 'division viol' may refer only to the style, it also applies to a slightly smaller version of the normal consort instrument developed with this purpose in mind, and still in use in the mid-C17.

Divisions see **Diminutions**

Divitis, Antonius (b. Louvain, c1475; d. after 1526) Franco-Flemish composer. From 1501 to 1506 worked at churches in Bruges and Malines and visited Spain, and in 1515 was a singer at the French court. 2 of his Masses, on motets by Richafort and A. Agricola, and some Mass movements and motets, were published in anthologies between 1514 and 1549.

Długoraj, Wojciech [Adalbert] (b. Gostyniec, c1550; d. after 1619) Polish lutenist, probably a pupil of Bakfark. Became a lutenist to the King of Poland in 1583, but later had to flee the country after denouncing high treason in influential circles. Besard's tablature of 1603 includes 8 pieces by Długoraj, 6 of which are villanella transcriptions; a number of Polish dances survive in MS.

Dodecachordon The title of an important theoretical treatise of 1547 by GLAREANUS, which enlarged the number of modes from 8 to 12, and contained a judicious and comprehensive commentary on the counterpoint of Josquin Desprez and other early C16 masters.

Dolzaina Probably a reedcap wind instrument with straight cylindrical bore. No specimens survive, but in 1592 Zacconi described the dolzaina as having the compass of a 9th with keys for 2 extra notes, and it probably resembled the CORNAMUSE. The name now applies to a keyless Spanish SHAWM.

Donati, Ignazio (b. Casalmaggiore, Parma, c1575; d. Milan, 21 Jan 1638) Italian composer. His varied career as a choirmaster caused him to travel widely around northern Italy, and he held posts at the Accademia dello Spirito Santo, Ferrara, and the cathedrals of Novara and Milan. He was a most inventive church composer and a pioneer of the small concertato motet, in which he shows both contrapuntal dexterity and melodic charm. Apart from motets, he wrote psalms and Masses and one volume of madrigals.

Donato, Baldassare (b. c1530; d. Venice, beginning 1603) Italian composer, probably a pupil of Rore. A singer at St Mark's, Venice, from 1550, succeeding Zarlino as *maestro di cappella* there in 1590. His humorous villanellas of 1550 were reprinted many times and praised by Burney in his *General History of Music*. He also published madrigals and a volume of motets in up to 8 parts which use Venetian polychoral effects.

Donato da Firenze (da Cascia) (fl. 1370–5) C14 Italian composer. He lived at the Benedictine abbey at Cascia in Umbria, and his surviving music consists of 14 madrigals, a *ballata à 2* and a 3-part *caccia*.

Douçaine Medieval wind instrument of which little is known, despite many literary references to its sweet tone. As described by Tinctoris it was a cylindrical bore reed instrument, probably at tenor pitch and useful for medieval tenor parts, which would fit its 9-note range.

Dowland, John (b. London or Dublin, Dec 1562; bd. London, 20 Feb 1626) English composer and lutenist. In 1579–84 he was in the service of the English ambassador in Paris, and became a Catholic. He graduated in music at Oxford in 1588, and visited the courts of Wolfenbüttel and Kassel in 1594/5, where offers were made for his services. However he went to Italy (Venice and Florence) and then back to England to publish his first songbook and take a Cambridge degree. He was royal lutenist at the Danish court from 1598 to 1606 but frequently took leave of absence in England. In 1612 he was lutenist to Lord Walden, and finally secured the position of royal lutenist that he had sought since his youth.

Dowland was the greatest English composer of the lute AYRE, which succeeded the madrigal as the fashionable genre, and published 5 volumes between 1597 and 1612; he also wrote much solo lute music and published a collection of *Lachrymae* for viol consort and lute in 1605. His lute songs are remarkable for their depth of expression and dramatic declamation of the words. His instrumental music ranges from crisp dance movements to impressively serious pavans, fantasias and 'funerals'; the *Lachrymae* are based on one of his most famous tunes, *Flow my tears*.

CE: Lute ayres in *EL* 1st ser., vols. i–ii, v–vi, x–xii, xiv, rev. edn.; also *MB* vi, ed. T. Dart and N. Fortune; Collected lute music, ed. D. Poulton and B. Lam (London, 1974)

Dowland, Robert (b. ?London, c1591; d. Holborn, London, 28 Nov 1641) English lutenist, son of John Dowland, whom he succeeded as royal lutenist in 1626. His *Varietie of Lute Lessons* (1610) includes more music by continental than by English composers, and contains useful remarks on lute playing by J. Dowland and Besard. His *Musicall Banquet* (also 1610) includes songs in the latest Italian style by Melli and Caccini.

Lute lessons, ed. E. Hunt (London, 1956–8); Songs in *EL* 2nd ser., xx

Dressler, Gallus (b. Nebra an der Unstrut, nr. Weissenfels, 16 Oct 1533; d. Zerbst, 1580x89) German composer. A Protestant, he worked in Jena, Magdeburg and Zerbst as ecclesiastic and schoolmaster, and wrote musical textbooks as well as composing many motets, German songs, and Latin and German psalm settings. These show the influence of Lassus and Clemens, whose music he also used for many examples in his textbooks.

Drum Many types of drum existed in the Middle Ages and Renaissance, usually with thick, low-tension skin heads secured to the shells with ropes. Among the most common were:

Nakers A pair of equal-sized drums, about 8 inches/26 cm in diameter, often slung round the player's waist, and played with 2 sticks. They could probably not be tuned, but virtuoso rhythmic techniques were pos-

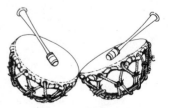

Nakers, 26 cm diameter

sible. Used to great effect by the Saracen army during the Crusades, nakers came to have a function in dances and processions as well as at the wars.

Tabor Most popular of medieval drums, played with a simpler single-stick technique. There was no standard shape or size, but all tabors were cylindrical with 2 heads, one with snares. The tabor could be held in the player's left hand or slung round his waist, and was often associated with the PIPE.

Kettledrums Early C16 successors to the nakers, also of Arabic origin. Their shells, 17 to 30 inches/45 to 75 cm in diameter, were made of metal, and had screws instead of rope tensioning. They could therefore be tuned, to fulfil a harmonic as well as a rhythmic function. They were often suspended one on each side of a horse's back.

Side drum Early C16 successor of tabor, which retained its rope tensioning and flexible size and shape. It provided rhythmic background for dances and marches, and certain special stick techniques were devised for frightening an enemy; it was often associated with the FIFE and with flutes.

Du Caurroy, (François) Eustache (bp. Beauvais, 4 Feb 1549; d. Paris, 7 Aug 1609) French composer, of good family. Singer, and later *maître de chapelle*, to the French kings from 1569, he won prizes at the Évreux composition contests in 1576 and 1583, and was one of those who cultivated the MUSIQUE MESURÉE style in secular music. He was one of the first French composers to use the double-choir style, and his Requiem continued to be sung at the funerals of the French kings until the C18. He also wrote instrumental music, including some 40 fantasias in 3 to 6 parts, many based on French popular songs.

CE: Chansons in *MMRF* xvii; *Oeuvres Complètes* (*IMM* Collected works ser., ix), ed. B. Pidoux (Brooklyn, 1975–   )

Ducis, Benedictus (b. nr. Konstanz, c1490; d. Schalkstetten, nr. Ulm, end 1544) German composer. He was connected with the Reformation and became a pastor at various churches in the Geislingen and Ulm regions. (He was not the same as Benedictus de Opitiis nor Appenzeller, whose works have sometimes been attributed to him.) Ducis appears to have been an irascible character, given to wife-beating, though intellectually a friend to humanism. He composed both florid Catholic music and simpler chorale settings published by Rhaw for Lutheran use; his style is closer to that of Isaac and Dietrich than that of Josquin Desprez, and his use of the cantus firmus is unusually free.

Ductia C13 instrumental dance form; a shorter form of ESTAMPIE.

Dufay, Guillaume (b. ?nr. Cambrai, c1400; d. Cambrai, 27 Nov 1474) Franco-Flemish composer. He became a choirboy at Cambrai cathedral in 1409 and a clerk by 1413/14, and probably studied with Loqueville. He left his homeland after 1414 and in 1420–6 was established in Italy, writing works to commemorate notable events for the Malatesta family at Pesaro. In 1426–8 he was in Bologna and subsequently became a singer in the Papal chapel choir, which at that time included many distinguished north Europeans. During leave of absence in 1433–5 he paid the first of several visits to the court of Savoy. When the Pope fled to Florence in 1435 Dufay followed, composing a motet for the dedication of Brunelleschi's famous cathedral there in 1436. Most of the remainder of his life Dufay spent at Cambrai, apart from another period at Savoy (1452–8); he was canon of the cathedral and for some time master of the *petites vicaires*. His mature Masses date from these years.

Dufay's works include 8 Masses and some individual or paired Mass movements, motets and other liturgical pieces such as hymns, and some 70 chansons, together with a few Italian songs. Not only does this versatility stand out in the C15, but the remarkable change of style between his early and late works in all genres proclaims him to be the bridge between the Middle Ages and the Renaissance, and the composer who formed a Renaissance musical language. In music for the Mass his works show the progress from single and paired movements towards a concept of the cyclic Ordinary of the Mass unified by a cantus firmus and also 'motto openings' to each section; a concept already existing in English Masses of this period. In motets the change was from severe isorhythmic style redolent of the previous century towards a homogeneous texture, as in the remarkable late piece, *Ave Regina caelorum*, with its bold use of C minor chords. The chansons, mainly in *rondeau* form, at first show a mixture of older French with Italian and English elements. They are mainly for 3 voices whereas the sacred music came to use 4.

CE: *Opera omnia* (*CMM* 1), ed. H. Besseler (Rome, 1951–66)

Dulcian see **Curtal**

Dulcimer Medieval struck string instrument; basically a struck psaltery, which it resembled in its trapezoidal shape. Its open metal strings, originally diatonically tuned, were struck with a pair of hammers, giving the sweet sound implied by its name; compass and number of strings varied widely. It came into use in the C15, and though not in serious use after the C16 survived as a folk instrument.

Dump, domp An early type of English or Irish song of lamenting character. An early C16 piece called *My Lady Carey's Dompe* belongs to the genre.

Dunstable, John (b. *c*1380; d. 24 Dec 1453) English composer, also mathematician and astronomer. It is possible that he served the Duke of Bedford, Regent of France, as musician in Paris from 1422–35. The fact that so much of his music survives in Continental sources suggests that his fame was widespread. He was undoubtedly one of the greatest English composers in this period of transition from the Middle Ages to the Renaissance, not an innovator so much as one who refined existing techniques, though the 'contenance Angloise' – 'English sweetness' – attributed to his style by the contemporary French poet Martin le Franc was extremely influential among Continental masters such as Dufay. 55 works survive that are normally considered to be by Dunstable, including 2 complete Masses (one isorhythmic) and several paired and single Mass sections, a large number of motets, and 2 secular songs. The complete Masses are among the first ever unified Mass settings; the non-isorhythmic *Missa Rex seculorum* was attributed to both Dunstable and Power. Of the motets, the most complex in structure are the isorhythmic ones, often written for special occasions, in which not only the tenor but also the other voices are organized to a predetermined rhythmic scheme; a fine example is *Veni sancte Spiritus/Veni creator*, where plainsong appears in the top part from time to time as well as in the tenor. Other motets carry the plainsong, gracefully paraphrased, in the top part throughout. These include hymn settings like *Ave maris stella*, whose polyphonic verses alternated with the original plainsong. The motets in free style, not dependent on plainsong, contain Dunstable's most euphonious music and illustrate best the smooth consonance and triadic melody that characterise the English style.

CE: *MB* viii, ed. M. Bukofzer, rev. M. Bent and others

Durante, Ottavio (fl. 1608) Italian composer, of a noble family. Originally from Rome, he lived in Viterbo, and was one of the first composers to apply the monodic style to sacred music. His *Arie devote* of 1608 contain virtuoso coloratura passages.

E

East, Michael (b. London, c1580; d. Lichfield, 1647x48) English composer, probably the son of Thomas East. Choirmaster of Lichfield cathedral in 1618; published 6 volumes of anthems, madrigals and instrumental consort music.

Madrigals in *EM* xxix–xxxi[b], rev. edn.

East, Thomas (b. c1535; d. London, before 17 Jan 1609) English music printer, who printed the music published by Byrd and later Morley under their privileges; his first production was Byrd's *Psalmes, sonnets and songs* of 1588. In 1592 he issued a collection of 4-part psalm tunes including contributions by many composers, among them leading figures such as Dowland and Farnaby. The composer Michael East may be his son.

Eccard, Johannes (b. Mühlhausen, 1553; d. Berlin, late 1611) German composer. In 1571–3 he sang in the Munich court chapel and studied with Lassus; in 1577–8 he served the Fugger family at Augsburg, and in 1580 was appointed vice-*Kapellmeister* at the Königsberg [Kaliningrad] court, taking charge of the music there in 1586. He spent his last years as electoral music director in Berlin. Eccard was one of the most important composers of Lutheran song, second only to Lechner in his day; he wrote some 250 sacred and secular songs, some published jointly with those of J. a Burck. He was a distinguished follower of Lassus, showing an element of restrained counterpoint in what was in reality a decorated homophonic idiom,

and in his expressive writing looked forward to the baroque age; indeed his songs were still being printed as late as 1644.

Edwards, Richard (b. Yeovil, c1522; d. London, 31 Oct 1566) English composer and poet. Became Master of the Children of the Chapel Royal in 1561, and wrote 2 plays for them. His 5 surviving songs, of which the most famous is *In going to my naked bed*, show the influence of the Franco-Flemish style on English music before the arrival of the Italian madrigal.

Encina, Juan del (b. Salamanca, 12 July 1468; d. Laón, ?after 29 Aug 1529) Spanish composer, playwright and courtier. He entered the Duke of Alba's service in 1492 as master of ceremonies, writing both text and music for plays that were performed at the court. When in 1498 he failed to get a musical post at Salamanca cathedral he went to Rome to seek the aid of the Spanish Pope Alexander VI, who gave him a benefice there; he became a priest in 1519 and held various ecclesiastical posts in Málaga and Laón. Encina was the principal contributor to the *Cancionero de Palacio*, a songbook of c1500 containing courtly love-songs in *villancico* form. Some of his pieces were for occasional use, and some intended to be sung at theatrical productions; indeed, by uniting popular and artistic elements, he broke new ground in the field of Spanish secular drama.

CE: *L'opera musicale*, ed. C. Terni (Messina, 1974); *Villancicos* in *MME* v, x, xiv, ed. H. Anglés

Ensalada Spanish term for potpourri or 'mish-mash'; applied to C16 Spanish QUODLIBETS of humorous character, or to longer cycles of pieces on devotional themes which served a moralising purpose (presenting, for instance, allegorical conflicts between sin and salvation).

Erart see **Jehan Erart**

Erbach, Christian (b. Gau-Algesheim, nr. Mainz, 1570; bd. Augsburg, 14 June 1635) German composer. From 1596 he held various posts as organist, including those of cathedral and town organist, in Augsburg, and through his pupils had much influence on German music of the time. He published canzonets and motets and wrote much organ music, including Venetian-style toccatas, ricercars (some of which could be regarded as embryonic fugues), and an interesting *canzona chromatica*, based on a descending chromatic theme.

Organ works in *DTB* iv/2; also *CEKM* 36, ed. C. Rayner

Ernoul le Vieux Troubadour. His *Lai de l'Ancien et du Nouvel Testament* consists of 23 sections, each a concise summary of a passage of the Bible.

Eschenbach, Wolfram von see **Wolfram**

Escobar, Pedro de (d. Seville, 1513x14) Spanish composer. Choirmaster at Seville cathedral in 1507; one of the best Spanish composers of church music in the reign of Ferdinand and Isabella. His music, though simple and rather old-fashioned in style, has great intensity. (A certain amount of confusion exists regarding his works, as there were a number of composers called Scobar or Escobar in Spain at that time.)

Songs in *MME* v, x; Mass in *MME* i

Escobedo, Bartolomé (b. Zamora, c1515; d. Segovia, before Nov 1563) Spanish composer. A Papal singer from 1536 to 1541 and 1545 to 1548; worked at the court of Castile until 1552 and then became *maestro de capilla* in Segovia. He was a friend of Morales and probable teacher of Victoria. His music includes two 6-part Masses, one being for Philip II's coronation, and some motets. One of the judges in a dispute on musical theory between VICENTINO and Lusitano, he declared that Vicentino's theories had been completely demolished.

Escribano, Juan (b. c1480; d. Rome, 7 Oct 1557) Spanish composer. Sang in the Papal choir 1507–39, and was one of the Spanish composers most highly regarded in Rome. His small amount of surviving music, including motets and several sets of Lamentations, is of high quality.

Escurel see **Jehannot de l'Escurel**

Esquivel, Juan (b. Ciudad Rodrigo, c1565; d. after 1613) Spanish composer. He was *maestro de capilla* at Ciudad Rodrigo from before 1608 until at least 1613. He published volumes of Masses, motets and other liturgical music; most of his Masses make extensive use of canon, but the *Missa batalla*, like Victoria's *Missa pro Victoria*, is based on Janequin's *La guerre*.

Estampie An important medieval instrumental dance-form, at first vocal (the C12 *Kalenda maya* is an example with words added). Like the vocal LAI, it consisted of a number of sections, each repeated, though perhaps with different endings.

Eton Choirbook An important MS of English liturgical music from the end of the C15, preserved in Eton College Library. The surviving parts of the MS include Magnificats, votive antiphons and a Passion setting (by Davy); the principal composers represented are Browne, Wylkynson and Cornysh, and the music is often in a brilliant, florid style, in 4 or more parts.

CE: *MB* x-xii, ed. F. Harrison

Eustachio Romano see next entry

Eustachius de Monte Regali (b. ?Mondovì, Piedmont, or Montreal, S. France; fl. 1514–20) French composer. Probably the Eustachius who sang in the Cappella Giulia at the Vatican in 1514; in 1520 he directed music at Modena cathedral. He wrote psalms, antiphons and hymns, and several frottolas to texts of high literary quality. Not to be confused with Eustachio

Romano, a Roman gentleman who published an excellent collection of duos in Rome in 1521, one of the earliest printed books to contain nothing but instrumental ensemble music.

Romano's duos in *MRM* vii, ed. H. David

Évreux see **Puy d'Évreux**

Exce(s)tre (fl. 1393–4) English composer. A member of the Chapel Royal from 1393, and holder of a prebend at St Stephen's, Westminster, from 1394; one of the older composers represented in the Old Hall MS, which contains three pairs of Mass movements by him. One Gloria carries a plainsong cantus firmus in the treble.

F

Faburden Improvised polyphonic elaboration of chant recitation in C15 England. The 3 parts were probably derived by singing 3rds or 5ths below the plainsong (itself transposed up a 5th) in the 'MEANE' or middle part, while a high part moved in parallel 4ths above the 'meane'. Later composers sometimes used the lowest part in preference to the actual plainsong as a cantus firmus; hence the phrase 'on the faburden'. (See also BURDEN.)

Faidit see **Gaucelm Faidit**

Faignient, Noel (b. Cambrai, c1540; d. Antwerp, 1598) Franco-Flemish composer. Lived in Antwerp (where he may have been a shopkeeper) from at least 1561 until 1577, and became *Kapellmeister* to the Duke of Brunswick in 1580. In 1568 he published a volume of madrigals, chansons and motets which show the influence of Lassus; further pieces appeared in anthologies.

Falsobordone Improvised or notated 4-part harmonization of recitation chants in Italy, c1480–1620, used mainly in psalms in alternation with plainsong. As in Anglican chant, the reciting chord was declaimed in speech rhythm, leading to a metrically notated cadence. Monteverdi occasionally used *falsobordone* in his madrigals as a 'new' declamatory device.

Fancy see **Fantasia**

Fantasia, fantasy Instrumental piece of C16 and C17 in contrapuntal style. Freer than the ricercar, it consisted of workings of several contrasting imitative points, perhaps interspersed with more chordal passages. In English consort music the term 'fancy' was used.

Farina, Carlo (b. Mantua, c1600; d. prob. Massa, Tuscany, c1640) Italian composer and violinist; one of the earliest violin virtuosos – at the courts of Dresden and Köln in the 1620s, and later in Italy–who made many advances in violin technique. These new developments can be seen in his 5 volumes of sonatas and other pieces à 2–5; his *Capriccio stravagante* contains probably the first examples of instructions to play *pizzicato* and *col legno*, and of the use of harmonics.

Farmer, John (b. c1560) English composer. Organist of Holy Trinity (now Christ Church) cathedral, Dublin, between c1595 and c1599, but otherwise lived in London. His madrigals of 1599 are unassuming but attractive, and he supplied many competent 4-part psalm settings for East's psalter, and instrumental music for anthologies by Simpson and Rosseter.

Madrigals in *EM* viii

Farnaby, Giles (b. c1565; d. London, 25 Nov 1640) English composer. He came of a musical family and graduated at Oxford in 1592, though he probably lived in London. He wrote psalms and motets and published some canzonets, but is most notable for his virginal music, 52 pieces of his being included in the Fitzwilliam Virginal Book. There are fantasias, dances and variations and a number of 'genre-pieces'–a type Farnaby seemed to make his own, heading them with fanciful titles like 'His Humour' and 'Farnaby's Dreame'. The first of these gives a whimsical picture of his character, mixing playful melody with chromaticism and jibing at earnest contrapuntal elaboration.

Keyboard works in *MB* xxiv, ed. R. Marlow; Canzonets in *EM* xx, rev. edn.

Farrant, Richard (b. *c*1530; d. Windsor, 30 Nov 1580 or 1581) English composer. Held various posts at the Chapel Royal and St George's, Windsor, as well as being involved with the Blackfriars theatre, and composing music for and directing dramatic entertainments at court and plays staged by his choirboys. His consort songs are among the few pieces of Elizabethan stage music to survive; he also wrote some dignified Anglican church music, though the anthem *Lord for thy tender mercy's sake*, often attributed to him, is not in fact his.

Consort songs in *MB* xxii, ed. P. Brett

Faugues, Guillaume (or **Vincent**) C15 Franco-Flemish composer; much admired by Tinctoris, and mentioned in Compère's *Omnium bonorum plena*. Of his 3 surviving Masses, one is based on the basse dance, that on *L'homme armé* is probably the earliest entirely canonic setting, and that on *Le Serviteur*, formerly ascribed to Ockeghem, is an early example of the parody Mass.

CE: *IMM* Collected works ser., i, ed. G. Schuetze (Brooklyn, 1961)

Fauvel, Roman de see **Roman de Fauvel**

Fauxbourdon 1. A C15 Continental method of creating an unwritten middle part to 2 existing voice parts by writing a line in parallel 4ths with the highest part. It may have been devised by Dufay, in the Communion of whose *Missa Sancti Jacobi* it occurs, and was most often used in hymn settings.

2. Continental adaptation of English FABURDEN, though with the plainsong transposed up an octave in the top part.

Fawkyner, John Later C15 English composer. He was rector at Horncastle in the 1490s, and a contributor to the Eton Choirbook; his 2 pieces in it are in a most elaborate and highly-decorated style.

Fayrfax, Robert (bp. Deeping Gate, Lincolnshire, 23 Apr 1464; d. St Albans, 24 Oct 1521) English composer. Became a Gentleman of the Chapel Royal around 1497, and graduated in music at Cambridge in 1501, taking a doctorate there in 1504 for his Mass *O quam glorifica*; in 1511 he was awarded the first doctorate in music conferred by Oxford.

Fayrfax's surviving output contains 6 Masses, 2 Magnificats, 9 votive antiphons and a number of secular partsongs. He is the most important figure in English sacred music between the Eton Choirbook composers (*c*1500) and Taverner, and his works show a gradual decline in florid writing compared to those of the Eton composers, with less brilliance of vocal scoring and rhythmic complexity. His style shows discrimination and restraint, as in the fine votive antiphon *Aeterne laudis lilium*, though Fayrfax could display technical and notational intricacy, as in the Mass he submitted for his Cambridge doctorate. His Masses use cantus firmus technique in a variety of ways; in the *Missa Albanus* a fragment of plainsong is treated as an ostinato, appearing backwards, inverted and even both simultaneously.

CE: *Collected Works* (*CMM* 17), ed. E. Warren (Rome, 1959–66)

Fayrfax MS Collection of English

secular vocal music of c1500, including love songs, satirical and political songs, and some especially fine religious pieces (Passion carols) by Browne, Cornysh and Davy.

Felsztyna, Sebastian z (b. Felsztyn, Galicia, c1485; d. after 1543) Polish composer and theorist. After studying in Kraków from 1507 to 1509 he held ecclesiastical posts at Felsztyn and Sanok and was probably also a singer at Przemyśl cathedral. He published a collection of Gregorian chants, an interesting description of the musical organization of Przemyśl cathedral, treatises on singing, and, in 1522, a volume of 4-part hymns which are the earliest Polish 4-part music, and lack technical accomplishment. He was probably the teacher of Lwówczyk (Leopolita).

Ferabosco, Domenico (b. Bologna, 14 Feb 1513; d. Bologna, Feb 1574) Italian composer, father of A. Ferrabosco 1. Singer and (from 1547) *maestro di cappella* at S. Petronio, Bologna, he may be identical with the Domenico Ferabosco who sang in the Papal choir from 1551–5 (when he was dismissed for being married) and was later *maestro* at a Roman church. He published a volume of madrigals in 1542 and contributed others to anthologies; *Io mi son giovinetta* was especially popular and is the basis of a Mass by Palestrina.

Feragut, Beltrame (fl. 1409–39) French composer, probably from Avignon. His motet *Excelsa civitas* was written for the enthronement of a Bishop of Vicenza in 1409; from 1425 to 1430 he was *maestro di cappella* at Milan cathedral (in succession to Matheus de Perusio) and in 1439 he was a singer at 2 churches in Florence. His surviving Mass movements, motets and *rondeau* are in a style closely akin to that of Dufay's early works.

Ferrabosco, Alfonso 1 (bp. Bologna, 18 Jan 1543; d. Bologna, 12 Aug 1588) Italian composer, son of D. Ferabosco. He served Elizabeth I of England from 1562, but earned royal disfavour by being involved in a murder case and overstaying his leave in Italy (perhaps to pursue his reputed activities as a secret agent); in 1578 he broke his pledge of lifelong service by entering the employ of the Duke of Savoy (and abandoning his young children to the care of an English colleague). His published madrigals date from this later period, but while in England he did much to interest native musicians in Italian music, and though a conservative in style he is the composer most generously represented in *Musica Transalpina*. He also wrote instrumental pieces and church music whose style is closer to that of his friend Byrd than to his Continental contemporaries.

Ferrabosco, Alfonso 2 (b. Greenwich, ?1572; bd. Greenwich, 11 Mar 1628) English composer, son of A. Ferrabosco 1. He was a viol player at the royal court in 1604 and teacher to Prince Henry and later Prince Charles (the future Charles I). In 1626 he succeeded Coprario as composer of the King's Music. He published ayres, wrote songs for Ben Jonson's masques in 1605–9, and contributed 3 anthems to Leighton's *Teares*. His excellent viol music includes about 50 fancies and dance pieces.

Ayres in *EL* 2nd ser., xvi

Ferretti, Giovanni (b. Ancona, c1540; d. Loreto, after 1609) Italian composer. From 1575 he was *maestro di cappella* at Ancona cathedral and from 1580 to 1582, and 1596 to 1602, at the Santa Casa in Loreto. He published 1 volume of madrigals and 7 of *canzoni alla Napoletana* in 5 and 6 parts, which started the vogue for the canzonet and later influenced the English madrigalists.

Festa, Costanzo (b. Villafranca, Turin, c1480; d. Rome, 10 Apr 1545) Italian composer. He served the d'Avalos family on Ischia around 1510 and then seems to have studied with Mouton in Paris. In 1517 he entered the service of the Papal chapel in Rome as a singer, remaining there until his death. He was one of the few native Italians in the choir, which was at this time dominated by musicians from northern Europe.

Festa's surviving output includes 4 Masses, more than 40 motets, 30 hymns, 13 Magnificats, litanies for double choir, and a large quantity of madrigals. He was one of the principal composers (and again one of the few native Italians) in the generation of early madrigalists. Though one volume of his madrigals is for 3 voices, the majority are for 4, and are characteristic of the early madrigal in their combination of imitative and chordal writing. Festa took up the fashion for *note nere* madrigals (i.e. with black notes, thus faster crotchet movement). Where he wrote for 5 voices, his style sometimes harked back to the chansons of Josquin; some such madrigals are written for very low voice ranges, suggesting solo performance with instrumental support. Festa contributed 2 ceremonial madrigals to the Duke of Florence's wedding entertainment in 1539. He was a distinguished sacred polyphonist, skilfully varying his writing between pervading imitation, non-imitative counterpoint and chordal passages.

CE: *Opera omnia* (*CMM* 25), ed. A. Main and A. Seay (Rome, 1962–   )

Festa, Sebastian (b. Villafranca, Turin; d. Rome, 31 July 1524) Italian composer, probably a brother or cousin of C. Festa; contributed motets and secular pieces to anthologies, the latter music providing one of the most important links between frottola and madrigal.

Févin, Antoine de (b. ?Arras, c1473; d. Blois, 1511x12) Franco-Flemish composer. Spent his last years as singer to Louis XII at Orléans and Blois. Glareanus dubbed him a 'happy imitator of Josquin'; certainly his church music (9 Masses, one Requiem, nearly 20 motets, Lamentations and Magnificats) was widely printed, and some of his Masses parody Josquin motets. Another is based on his own attractively airy 4-part motet *Sancta Trinitas*.

Fiddle Bowed string instrument. The name can be used generically for any medieval bowed instrument, but is also applied to one particular type. This is entirely different from the REBEC, usually having a flat back and oval or waisted shape, and a neck quite distinct from the body. The number of strings varied, but Jerome of Moravia gives three 5-string tunings; the lowest string could be a lateral drone. A common method of bowing was to sound several strings at once. Playing position varied; the fiddle could be held on

Fiddle, 66 cm

the shoulder, across the body, or between the knees (large fiddles played this way are sometimes called 'medieval viols'), and both long and short bows were used. The fiddle was the most important bowed instrument in medieval court music, suitable for any kind of music and cultivated by both professionals and amateurs. By 1500 it closely resembled the violin in appearance, except that the fingerboard was often fretted.

Fife 6-holed transverse flute with very narrow bore, giving a shrill sound. Its associations were chiefly military; Praetorius mentions 2 sizes, with lowest notes e' and g' and a range of 1½ octaves. Contemporary names for it include Zwerchpfeif and Schweitzerpfeif.

Figured bass see **Basso continuo**

Filippo da Caserta (Filipoctus, Philippot) Late C14 Italian composer and theorist. Originally from Caserta, near Naples, he was in Avignon in the 1380s but worked in Italy. He may be the 'Philippot' who was at the Aragon court in 1420. His 6 pieces to French texts in the Chantilly MS show that, though an Italian, he had absorbed the essentials of the late C14 French school; his *cacce* and *ballate* are simpler and more characteristically Italian.
CE: in *CMM* 53/i, ed. W. Apel

Finck, Heinrich (b. Bamberg, 1444x45; d. Vienna, 9 June 1527) German composer. A member of the Polish court chapel at Kraków, and a good singer; in 1482 matriculated at Leipzig University; travelled in Poland, Hungary and Germany, and in 1510 became *Kapellmeister* at the Stuttgart court chapel. This was dissolved in 1514, after which he visited Augsburg and Innsbruck (possibly as a composer to Maximilian I) and was working at

Salzburg cathedral in 1524. In his last year he directed music at the Imperial court chapel at Vienna.

Finck was one of Germany's most notable composers at a time when Germans had yet to make their mark on European music. He wrote at least 4 Masses, some motets and other liturgical works, and many Lieder; it is on these last that his reputation rests. Their melodies (in the tenor part) are mostly his own rather than borrowed; he surrounds them with a most resourceful contrapuntal texture in which the top voice has its own melodic quality, and in which dissonance is an important element (his greatnephew Hermann Finck praised his talent and learning but said his style was 'hard'). One of his Masses is noteworthy for its rich 6- and 7-part writing.
Secular works in *EDM* lvii

Finck, Hermann (b. Pirna, nr. Dresden, 21 Mar 1527; d. Wittenberg, 28 Dec 1558) German composer, greatnephew of Heinrich Finck. Taught at the university of Wittenberg from 1554 and became its organist in 1557. He published a few German songs and Latin motets, but is chiefly important for the 5-volume *Practica Musica*, a comprehensive treatise on many aspects of the art of music. In particular he praised Gombert as the greatest master of imitative composition, and condemned the current ornamental German organ style as noisy and amorphous.

Firenze, da see under the first name of composers known thus.

Firmin Le Bel see **Le Bel**

Fitzwilliam Virginal Book The most extensive collection of English virginal music, *c*1600; it contains 297 pieces by almost every composer active in the field, and was copied by Francis Tregian while he was in prison in 1609–19.

CE: *FVB*

Flageolet Wind instrument. The name seems to have been used indiscriminately in the Middle Ages for any wind instrument with a whistle mouthpiece, irrespective of the number of its finger-holes. (The more recent instrument of this name, popular during the Baroque, which had 2 thumb-holes and a special mouthpiece, was not invented until the early C17.)

Flecha, Mateo 1 (b. Prades, 1481; d. Poblet, Tarragona, 1553) Spanish composer. Taught music to the daughters of Charles V, and composed *ensaladas*, which were gathered together and published by his nephew in 1581.

Las ensaladas, ed. H. Anglés (Barcelona, 1955)

Flecha, Mateo 2 (b. Prades, 1530; d. La Portella, Catalonia, 20 Feb 1604) Spanish composer, nephew of Flecha 1. Entered the service of Maria of Hungary, consort of Maximilian II, later becoming her chaplain and travelling to Italy, Vienna and Prague; became Abbot of Tihany in Hungary in 1568, and (on his return to Spain in 1599) of La Portella. He published madrigals and a Compline and motet collection, and included *ensaladas* by himself and others in the 1581 volume of his uncle's pieces, which appeared in Prague.

Flute, Transverse 6-holed, side blown wind instrument with cylindrical bore and 2-octave range. It could be made of many materials, including glass and ivory as well as wood. In the Middle Ages it replaced the panpipes and was especially popular with the Minnesingers. In the Renaissance the name was often applied indiscriminately to flute and recorder, and they are to some extent interchangeable, the transverse flute with its tiny mouthhole being much the more difficult to play in tune. Praetorius describes alto, tenor and bass sizes, the tenor with its compass over 2 octaves from d' being the most versatile. Like the recorder, the flute had more respectable associations than some other Renaissance wind instruments; it was used in consorts, and in dramatic music has a special connection with seascapes.

Fogliano, Giacomo (b. Modena, 1468; d. Modena, 10 Apr 1548) Italian composer. Organist at Modena cathedral between 1489 and 1497, and from 1504; published a volume of madrigals in 1547; his frottolas, madrigals, *laude* and organ ricercars appeared in anthologies between 1504 and 1551. Much of his music shows the influence of Josquin, and his organ style is less advanced than that of M. A. Cavazzoni.

Fogliano, Lodovico (b. Modena, end C15; d. Modena, c1538) Italian theorist, brother of G. Fogliano. Sang in the Papal chapel in 1513–14 and was later choirmaster at Modena cathedral. His treatise *Musica theorica* (1529) came close to propounding just intonation; he also wrote psalms and a quodlibet containing several Italian popular tunes.

Folia Famous late C16 and C17 melody and bass pattern used in Spain and Italy; either both of these, or just

Transverse flute, 94 cm

the bass, were used as the basis for variations.

Folia

Folquet de Marselh (b. ?Marseilles, *c*1155; d. Toulouse, 25 Dec 1231) Troubadour and ecclesiastic. The son of a merchant, he was brought up in Marseilles. His activity as a poet and musician covered the years 1179–93; in 1195 he and his wife and sons embraced the religious life, and in 1201 he became Abbot of the Cistercian house at Toronet en Provence. He was Bishop of Toulouse from 1205, and founded the university there. His 19 surviving poems reflect his great learning, being full of devices such as abstract metaphors and clever aphorisms; Dante esteemed him worthy of a place in Paradise. 13 of his melodies survive; he is reputed to have said that 'a verse without music is a mill without water'.

Folz, Hans (b. Worms, 1435x40; d. Nürnberg, Jan 1513) German Meistersinger. He attempted to break down the rigid system of 'tones' (melodies) which constricted the Meistersingers' work, but could do nothing to halt the style's ultimate demise.

Fontaine, Pierre (b. Rouen, after 1380; d. *c*1450) Franco-Flemish composer. Having been a choirboy at Rouen, he was a member of the Burgundian court chapel between 1404 and 1420, and from 1428; between 1420 and 1427 he was a Papal singer, and was once more at the Burgundian court from *c*1430 to 1447. His chansons are in the new simple style of the early C15 and show his talent for writing attractive melodies and for providing music appropriate to melancholy texts; *J'ayme bien* has an instrumental contratenor marked 'trompette' in one source. He may be the composer of the piece ascribed to 'Fonteyns' in the Old Hall MS.

Fontana, Giovanni Battista (b. Brescia, late C16; d. Padua, 1630) Italian violinist; one of the early violin virtuosos who composed sonatas for 1 or more violins and continuo (posthumously published), constructed as mosaics of many short contrasted sections.

Ford, Thomas (b. *c*1580; bd. Westminster, 17 Nov 1648) English lutenist and composer. Originally in the service of Prince Henry of Wales (d. 1611), he was one of the King's musicians in 1626. His *Musick of Sundrie Kindes* (1607) contains dances as well as lute songs in a graceful rather than intensely expressive style; however, his anthem *Miserere my maker* uses advanced chromaticism to create a penitential atmosphere.

Songs in *EL* 1st ser., iii, rev. edn.

Forest, John Early C15 English composer. 2 motets of his are in the Old Hall MS, but much more survives in Continental sources such as the Trent Codices. His music contrasts declamatory and melismatic passages; the conflict of rhythms between the various voices gives his music a restless quality.

Formes fixes Generic name for the medieval poetic forms (e.g. *rondeau*, *ballade*, *virelai*) which determined the musical shape of polyphonic French chansons up to around 1500, when they were abandoned in favour of freer musical forms.

Forrest-Heather partbooks The largest and most comprehensive MS source of English festal Masses in the early C16. It was begun at Cardinal College (now Christ Church), Oxford, under Wolsey during Taverner's time there (1526–9), and contains his festal Masses and those of many of the best English composers of the day.

Forster, Georg (b. Amberg, c1510; d. Nürnberg, 12 Nov 1588) German composer and doctor. Studied at Heidelberg with Lemlin and became a medical student at Ingolstadt in 1531; in 1534–9 he was in Wittenberg in Luther's circle; after qualifying he practised as a doctor in various German cities. He wrote a book of motets and psalms, but–more significantly–edited a monumental collection of German songs, the *Frische teutsche Liedlein* in 5 volumes (1539–56). These contain his own works as well as those of many composers associated with Heidelberg, and chart the development of the Lied from 4- to 5-part writing, and from the medium of solo voice with instruments to that of the vocal consort with all parts having text underlaid.
 F. t. Liedlein in *EDM* xx, lx, lxi

Fossa, Johannes de (d. Munich, 1603) German composer, probably of Netherlands descent. *Unterkapellmeister* at the Munich court from 1569, he succeeded Lassus as *Kapellmeister* in 1594 and is probably identical with the Jean des Fosses who had been a singer to the Duke of Savoy in 1557. His Mass *Si du malheur* was based on a chanson by Lassus.
 CE: *RRMR* xxviii–ix, ed. E. Ennulat

Fournival see **Richard de Fournival**

Francesco da Milano see **Milano**

Franchois de Gembloux Early C15 Franco-Flemish composer. A chaplain at the Burgundian court in the early C15; unlike many of his Franco-Flemish contemporaries he stayed in his native land rather than seeking his fortune in Italy. His style in some ways marks the transition between those of the late C14 and early C15; one of his isorhythmic motets opens with an unusual and impressive trumpet-like introductory passage, and the popularity of 2 of his Gloria/Credo pairs is attested by their appearance in several different sources. He also composed chansons, and is represented by one piece in the Buxheim Organ Book.

Francisque, Antoine (b. S. Quentin, c1570; bd. Paris, 5 Oct 1605) Franco-Flemish lutenist; in Cambrai in 1596, but later worked in Paris. His lute tablature *Le Trésor d'Orphée* (1600) contains preludes and fantasias and examples of many different types of dance.

Franck, Melchior (b. Zittau, c1580; d. Coburg, 1 June 1639) German composer, possibly a pupil of Demantius. Sang at Augsburg under Gumpelzhaimer and was court *Kapellmeister* at Coburg from 1603 until his death. He published chorale settings, motets, secular Lieder and instrumental music, which all show the influence of Hassler and the Venetian polychoral style.
 Instrumental music in *DDT* xvi

Franco of Cologne (fl. mid-C13) Theorist, who gave his name to 'Franconian notation' through a treatise of c1260, *Ars cantus mensurabilis*, which is the major source of information on the newly established system of mensural notation.

Frauenlob see **Heinrich von Meissen**

Frescobaldi, Girolamo (b. Ferrara, ?12 Sep 1583; d. Rome, 1 Mar 1643) Italian composer. He studied in Ferrara with Luzzaschi. From 1604 onwards he was based in Rome, first as organist and singer at the Congregazione S. Cecilia, in 1607 as organist at S. Maria in Trastevere, and from 1608 almost until his death as organist of St Peter's. His absences included a visit to Brussels with the Papal Nuncio in 1607-8, a brief spell as Mantuan court organist in 1615, and a longer one as ducal organist at Florence, 1628-33. So great was his renown that Froberger, court organist at Vienna, was given leave to study with him in 1637-41.

Frescobaldi was not only a formidable player of both organ and harpsichord, he was a noted improviser and the founder of a new style of organ music, welding elements characteristic of the organ schools of Ferrara, Naples and Venice. His works range between strict Renaissance forms and sophisticated original structures. His toccatas make dramatic contrast between chordal and fugal sections, his ricercars show great resource in their ever inventive counter-subjects to given themes. Chromaticism, variation techniques and rubato playing are all present. Frescobaldi's output apart from keyboard music includes Masses, motets, secular music and ensemble canzonas.

CE: *Opere complete*, ed. O. Mischiati and L. Tagliavini (Milan, 1976–   ); *Orgel-und Klavierwerke*, ed. P. Pidoux (Kassel, 1950-4); Keyboard music also in *CEKM* xxx, ed. W. Shindle; *Arie musicali* in *MD* iv, ed. H. Spohr

Friedrich von Hûsen (d. in the East, 6 May 1190) Minnesinger. A friend of the Archbishop of Mainz and secretary to the Emperor Frederick I; died in the Third Crusade. One of the early Minnesingers, he did much to extend French influence on German song by writing German texts, which fit the music perfectly (*contrafacta*), to songs by troubadours such as Guiot de Provins and Bernart de Ventadour; none of his own melodies survive.

Frottola A type of poetry and music which flourished at the north Italian courts, especially Mantua, *c*1480-1525. The term, though strictly a specific poetic form, was also used as a generic designation for Italian secular songs to various other poetic forms (canzona, oda, strambotto). The most noted composers of frottolas were Cara and Tromboncino; the main sources for them are the 11 volumes Petrucci published in 1504-14. Their style was simple and chordal, usually *à 4*, the phrase lengths being determined by the lines of the poem; though all parts were texted, the words fitted the upper part most exactly, suggesting performance by voice and instruments.

Frye, Walter (d. before 5 June 1475) C15 English composer who belonged to the Guild of St Nicholas in London from 1457. A number of his songs and the motet *Ave Regina caelorum* became very popular in northern Europe in the late C15, single lines from them providing cantus firmi for works by Josquin, Obrecht and Tinctoris. The motet itself was clearly depicted in 3 Continental pictures of the time. 3 cantus firmus Masses survive; in them Frye uses head motives (motto themes appearing at the beginning of each movement) with little imitative writing.

CE: *Collected works* (*CMM* 19), ed. S. Kenney (Rome, 1960)

Fuenllana, Miguel de (b. Navalcarnero, nr. Madrid, *c*1525; d. ?Valladolid, 1585x1605) Spanish lutenist and composer. Blind from birth, he became a consummate virtuoso on the vihuela, and served at the Spanish court in the 1560s. His principal collection of music for the vihuela, *Orphénica lyra* (1554), was dedicated to King Philip II and represents perhaps the high point of this repertory. It contains many transcriptions of polyphony by a wide range of Continental masters – Morales, Guerrero, Gombert, Josquin, Willaert – and fantasias of his own; in fact the latter are often paired with the transcriptions from which they take their musical inspiration. His vihuela writing is in a free polyphonic style, with much dissonance and adroit contrapuntal procedure. The volume also contains some accompanied solo songs.

CE: *Orphénica lyra*, ed. C. Jacobs (London, 1978)

Full anthem see **Anthem**

G

Gabrieli, Andrea (b. Venice, c 1520; d. Venice, 1586) Italian composer. He may have been a pupil of Willaert at St Mark's, Venice, where he was a singer in 1536. Towards 1550 he was in the composer RUFFO's circle and may have sung at Verona cathedral; sometime in the 1550s he became organist at S. Geremia, Venice. He succeeded Merulo as second organist at St Mark's in 1564, and became first organist in 1584. He travelled north of the Alps, visiting the courts of Munich (where he met Lassus) and Graz, and receiving the patronage of the Fugger family at Augsburg. He taught a number of Germans, including Hassler and Aichinger.

Andrea Gabrieli's output includes a large number of madrigals and some lighter secular pieces, Masses, Penitential Psalms and motets, and keyboard music. He developed in his motets the polychoral style of Willaert and his predecessors, using 2 or more groups of voices and instruments of varying ranges as in the splendid Magnificat for 3 choirs, and even in less ambitious works shows an acute sense of vocal sonority. Though some were written for ceremonial use, most of his madrigals were aimed at both professional and amateur singers, and had wide appeal. In keyboard music he developed the canzona and ricercar as idiomatic instrumental forms.

CE: *Orgelwerke*, ed. P. Pidoux (Kassel, 1952–9)

Gabrieli, Giovanni (b. Venice, c1556, d. Venice, 12 Aug 1612x13) Italian composer, nephew of A. Gabrieli with whom he studied. His uncle's travels gave him the chance to become known abroad, and he served in 1575–9 under Lassus at the Munich court, having a madrigal published in 1575 in a collection of music by Munich composers. By 1584 he had become a temporary organist at St Mark's, Venice, and soon succeeded his uncle as second organist there–a post he held for the rest of his life, though in his last years illness forced him to employ a deputy. In later life he became a famous teacher, attracting many pupils from northern Europe. The most notable of these was Schütz, who studied with him from 1609 to 1612.

Though his organ music and madrigals occupy a distinguished place in their respective repertories, the most distinctive part of his output consists of large-scale ceremonial music for St Mark's, whether motets for important church and state occasions or instrumental music for the talented church orchestra which played a notable part in the basilica's music. These works were issued in 3 large collections; 2 volumes of *Symphoniae Sacrae* (1597 and 1615) and one of *Canzoni e sonate* (1615). In them he gradually transformed the Venetian polychoral style with its blocks of equally balanced performers (as in his uncle's music) into a more baroque concept of solo voices, instruments, full choir and continuo. This he did by specifying which instruments were to be used and which passages were to be sung by soloists and by tutti, and further by distinguishing the musical style of each. At the same time he devised coherent musical structures, often involving refrains, to weld together these diverse sonorities. All this is well illustrated in the motet *In ecclesiis* (perhaps his masterpiece) for 4 soloists, 4-part choir, 3 cornetts, viola, 2 trombones and organ. That Gabrieli was capable of a madrigalian intensity of expression is evident from a smaller work like *Timor et tremor*. There is emotional intensity rather than mere ceremonial pomp in some of the instrumental canzonas, too, together with brilliant instrumental writing.

CE: *Opera omnia* (*CMM* 12), ed. D. Arnold (Rome, 1956–)

Gace Brule (b. ?Nanteuil-les-Meaux, Seine et Marne, *c*1159; d. 1212x13) One of the earliest trouvères, and among the most famous poets of the period. For a time at the court of Marie de Champagne, he may have gone on one or more Crusades. 69 of his poems, for which 57 melodies survive, were widely disseminated in MS. Some of his melodies show the influence of Gregorian chant.

Gacien Reyneau French composer, from Tours. Served John I of Catalonia and Aragon (reigned 1350–96), whose court at Barcelona was heavily dependent on Avignon for its music and musicians; represented in the Chantilly MS.

Gafori, Franchino (b. Lodi, 1451; d. Milan, 1522) Italian theorist, composer and humanist. His most notable work, *Practica musicae* (1496), contains rules of counterpoint, a theory of mensural proportions, and a statement about the semibreve being equivalent to the 'pulse beat of a quietly breathing man'.

CE: *Collected musical works* (*CMM* 10), ed. L. Finscher (Rome, 1955–)

Gagliano, Marco da (b. Gagliano, Tuscany, 1 May 1582; d. Florence, 25 Feb 1643) Italian composer. Became a priest at S. Lorenzo, Florence, and director of music there in succession to his teacher, Luca Bati, in 1608; succeeded to the post of court musical director 3 years later, but retained his ecclesiastical connections as a canon and, in 1614, Apostolic Protonotary (a senior Curial secretary at the Vatican). In 1607 he founded the Accademia degli Elevati, and wrote his first opera *Dafne* for the Gonzaga court at Mantua, where it was performed the following year.

Gagliano was one of the most important early opera composers – he wrote several apart from *Dafne* which do not survive complete. He also wrote an oratorio, 6 books of 5-part madrigals, a volume of *Musiche* (monodies, secular duets and trios) and a quantity of sacred music including 38 motets. In *Dafne* he supplements the recitative of Peri and Caccini with arias and polyphonic choruses, giving a more varied whole. In the song *Valli profonde* he uses an arresting variety of moods to produce one of the finest monodies of the early Baroque. Gagliano's madrigals are more conventional, however, and his church music is distinctly old-fashioned.

Galilei, Vincenzo (b. S. Maria in Monte, nr. Florence, *c*1520; bd. Florence, 2 July 1591) Italian composer and theorist, father of Galileo Galilei the astronomer. He studied with Zarlino in Venice and with Girolamo Mei, a philosopher, in Rome. He was a capable lutenist, publishing a treatise on lute playing (*Fronimo*), but is better known as a champion of Greek music who condemned modern music, especially the conventional madrigal, and as spokesman of the Florentine Camerata in the writings of his *Dialogo* of 1581.

Contrapuncti in *SCMA* viii, ed. L. Rood

Galliard (Gagliarda) C16 dance of Italian origin in moderately fast triple time, with exaggerated leaps. Attaingnant published the first music for it; after 1550 the galliard was usually an after-dance to the PAVANE, on whose music it would sometimes be based.

Galliculus (Hähnel), Johannes (b. Dresden, c1490; d. Leipzig, c1550) German composer. Matriculated at Leipzig University in 1505 and lived in the city from 1520–50. An important early Protestant composer, he was a pupil of Isaac. His church music, which shows the influence of Josquin, includes 2 Protestant Easter Masses (in Latin) using both plainsong and Lutheran melodies, motets, and a through-composed Passion.
CE: *IMM* Collected works ser., viii, ed. A. Moorefield

Gallus see **Handl**

Gamut In medieval theory, the lowest note of the musical compass (G); a contraction of 'gamma-ut' (see SOLMIZATION). The term was later applied to the entire compass.

Ganassi, Silvestro (b. Fontego, nr. Venice, 1492) Italian musician. In 1535 he published the earliest known recorder tutor (*Opera Intitulata Fontegara*) and in 1542 a treatise on playing the viol (*Regola Rubertina*).

Gardane, Gardano Firm of Venetian music printers. Antonio Gardane (1509–69), an emigrant from France, set up the business in 1537 as a rival to that of SCOTTO; his son Angelo continued it until his death in 1610. The firm used the Italian spelling Gardano from 1557.

Gascongne, Mathieu (fl. 1518–?1529) French composer. A priest at Cambrai in 1518, probably served King Francis I, and composed Masses, motets and chansons, some published in anthologies. His style is closer to that of his Franco-Flemish than his French contemporaries, and, unlike theirs, his chansons and a Mass on de la Rue's *Pourquoi non* are in a serious vein.

Gastoldi, Giovanni Giacomo (b. Caravaggio, nr. Milan, c1550; d. 1622) Italian composer. He sang in the Gonzaga court chapel in Mantua in 1581 and the following year succeeded Wert as choirmaster there. He remained in Mantua, working with the young Monteverdi, until 1609 when he was appointed choirmaster at Milan cathedral. His output consists of 12 volumes of sacred music (Masses, motets, Vespers and Compline collections), 10 of secular works (madrigals and *balletti*) and 1 of canzonas. He is best known as the writer of the 5-part *Balletti* of 1591, which became the prototype of the English ballett of Morley and Weelkes, though Gastoldi's are generally in a quite simple homophonic style with fa-la endings to certain phrases, and a regular rhythmic structure.
Balletti, ed. M. Sanvoisin (Paris, 1968)

Gaucelm Faidit (b. Uzerche, Corrèze, c1170; d. 1230) Troubadour. Travelled to Italy and went on the Fourth Crusade. 70 of his poems and 14 melodies survive; his *planh,* or lament, for Richard I of England is the only surviving example of this type of troubadour song written on the death of a friend or patron.

Gautier de Coinci (b. Coinci, Aisne, 1177x78; d. Soissons, 25 Sep 1236) Trouvère and monk. Entered the Benedictine house of S. Médard at Soissons in 1193, and rose to become Prior at Vic-sur-Aisne in 1214 and Grand Prior at

Soissons in 1233. His *Miracles de Notre Dame* consists of legends of the Blessed Virgin rendered into *c*30,000 verses and interspersed with 37 songs which may well be *contrafacta* of secular pieces.

Geigenwerk Form of mechanized hurdy-gurdy (see SYMPHONY) with a keyboard which brings the strings into contact with the wheels which sound them; the wheels are activated by a treadle mechanism. Invented *c*1570, it was capable of some dynamic variations and also of imitating other instruments.

Gembloux see **Franchois de Gembloux**

Gemshorn Medieval whistle instrument made out of animal horn and therefore having a tapering conical bore. Its sweet, thin tone must have been known by the mid-C15 when the name began to be used for an organ stop; Virdung's treatise *Musica getuscht* (1511) illustrates a gemshorn with 4 finger-holes. It had probably fallen into disuse by the mid-C16.

Gero, Ihan (Jehan) (fl. 1541–56) Franco-Flemish composer, not to be confused with Jean Le Cocq. He worked in Italy and was highly esteemed as a madrigalist. As well as his own 5 volumes of madrigals and pieces in anthologies, he wrote all but 2 of the madrigals in the collection published by C. Festa in 1541; his work is notable for skilful manipulation of rhythms and use of word painting.

Gervaise, Claude (fl. 1550) French composer. Worked in Paris, possibly in the service of King Francis I; published a volume of chansons in 1550, but is best known for his *Danceries*, books of dances mostly edited from the work of other composers.

Dances in *MMRF* xxiii

Gesius, Bartholomäus (b. Müncheberg, nr. Frankfurt an der Oder, 1562; d. Frankfurt an der Oder, Aug 1613) German composer. After studying theology in Frankfurt he worked as cantor at Müncheberg, served the Freiherr von Schönaich, and became cantor of the Marienkirche in Frankfurt in 1593. He composed

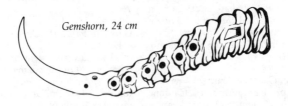

Gemshorn, 24 cm

Genet see **Carpentras**

Gerle, Hans (d. Nürnberg, 1570) German lutenist; also a lute and viol maker. In the 1530s he issued one of the more important German lute tablature books.

sacred music of every kind required by the Lutheran church, including Passions, psalm settings, sacred songs and congregational hymns; his style belongs to the C16 rather than the early C17, and shows the influence of Lassus.

Gesualdo, Don Carlo (b. Naples, c1560; d. Naples, 8 Sep 1613) Italian composer. Born of a noble Neapolitan family (he became Prince of Venosa), he probably studied music with P. Nenna. Temperamentally he was given to excess, and the sensational murder of his first wife and her lover in 1590 was one of the great C16 musical scandals. His second marriage, to Eleonora d'Este, gave him contacts with the musical circle of Ferrara and the poet Tasso whom he befriended.

Gesualdo's output consists of 6 volumes of 5-part madrigals, published from 1594; 2 books of motets and 1 of responsories; and a few keyboard works. Though from the south, he is linked by his visits to Ferrara and his friendship with Tasso with the 'mannerist' madrigalists of northern Italy. Wayward harmonies in his earlier madrigals develop, in his later ones, into wild and passionate juxtapositions of fast and slow motion, and of total and extremely chromatic harmony. These violent contrasts seem to reflect Gesualdo's neurotic personality; from a stylistic viewpoint his harmonic experiments are more the ultimate outcome of C16 harmonic vocabulary than prophetic of the music that was to come; it was only in the eccentricity of his melodic lines that some monodists followed him.

CE: *Sämtliche Werke*, ed. W. Weismann and G. Watkins (Hamburg, 1957–67)

Gherardello da Firenze (Gherardellus, Ser Gherardello) (d. 1364) Italian composer. 16 of his works, mainly madrigals and *ballate*, are found in the Squarcialupi Codex, along with a portrait of him. He was one of the most important C14 Italian composers contemporary with Landini, and is especially famous for his *caccia, Tosto che l'alba*. His Gloria and Credo show the influence of the French style of Machaut.

CE: in *CMM* 8/i, ed. N. Pirrotta; in *PMFC* vii, ed. W. T. Marrocco

Ghiselin (alias Verbonnet), Jean (b. c1455; d. ?Bergen op Zoom, c1511) Franco-Flemish composer. A singer in Florence in 1492–3, he then worked at the Ferrara court until at least 1503 (and may have been responsible for Josquin's going there) and in 1508 was a singer in Bergen op Zoom. He published a volume of Masses (based on chansons by such composers as A. Agricola and Ockeghem) in 1503, and his motets occur in anthologies; his style has features in common with that of Obrecht.

CE: *Opera Omnia* (*CMM* 23), ed. C. Gottwald (Rome, 1961–8)

Ghizeghem see **Hayne van Ghizeghem**

Giacobbi, Girolamo (bp. Bologna, 10 Aug 1567; d. Bologna, Feb 1629) Italian composer. Spent his whole career at S. Petronio, Bologna, as chorister, adult singer and (from 1604) *maestro di cappella*. He was one of the first opera composers in Bologna, and his *Andromeda*, given in Salzburg in 1618, may have been the first opera to be performed outside Italy. He also published church music, including psalms for up to 5 choirs, and large-scale motets.

Gibbons, Orlando (bp. Oxford, 25 Dec 1583; d. Canterbury, 5 June 1625) English composer. The son of a musical family, he became a choirboy at King's College chapel, Cambridge, in 1596 and matriculated from there in 1598. He was appointed organist at the Chapel Royal in 1605, a post he held until his death. He graduated in music at Cambridge in 1606 and took an Oxford doctorate in 1622. Other posts he held included those of court virginalist and organist of Westminster Abbey (in 1623).

Gibbons' output comprises a set of madrigals published in 1612, about 40 anthems, a full service, a verse service, sets of psalms and hymn tunes, many keyboard works (fantasias, preludes, dance pieces, variations) and a number of consort pieces (fantasias, In nomines, etc.). Gibbons' best-known music is found in his anthems, which show impressive contrapuntal writing in the full anthems and a style varying between the staid and the deeply-felt in the verse anthems. His madrigals, with their ethical, serious texts, really belong to the tradition of English song rather than the Italianate madrigal. Though he was a renowned keyboard virtuoso, Gibbons' keyboard music is also marked by restraint and seriousness; the *Earl of Salisbury Pavan and Galliard* is one of the finest works by any English virginalist. Consort music provided a further outlet for his contrapuntal skill and feeling for musical structure.

CE: Church music in *TCM* iv; Verse anthems in *EECM* iii, xxi, ed. D. Wulstan; madrigals in *EM* v, rev. edn.; keyboard music in *MB* xx, ed. G. Hendrie

Giles, Nathaniel (b. ?Worcester, c1558; d. Windsor, 24 Jan 1633) English composer. Organist of Worcester cathedral from 1581; became organist and choirmaster at St George's, Windsor, in 1585, and also Master of the Children of the Chapel Royal in 1597. In 1600 he took over the Blackfriars theatre and in collaboration with Ben Jonson ran a successful children's company there. He composed Latin church music as well as Anglican anthems and services, and contributed to Leighton's *Teares*.

Anthems in *EECM* xxiii, ed. J. Bunker Clark

Gillebert de Berneville Mid-C13 trouvère, who had become famous by 1260, and was frequently present at tournaments and other grand entertainments given by the nobility of Flanders. He had connections with the Arras trouvères, and left 32 poems and 15 melodies.

Gilles le Vinier (b. 1190; d. 13 Nov 1252) Trouvère, brother of Guillaume le Vinier. A canon of Lille and official at Arras in 1225, and canon of Arras in 1234; 10 of his songs survive.

Gimel see Gymel

Gintzler, Simon (b. prob. South Tyrol, c1490; d. after 1550) Austrian lutenist. By 1547 he had been for many years in the service of the Cardinal Prince Bishop of Trent. In that year he published a lute book containing pieces in an Italianate style, and richly imitative ricercars which almost suggest organ rather than lute writing. He is also represented in anthologies of Gerle and Phalèse.

Lute pieces in DTO xxxvii

Giovannelli, Ruggiero (b. Velletri, c1560; d. Rome, 7 Jan 1625) Italian composer. A pupil of Palestrina, whom he succeeded in 1594 as *maestro di cappella* at St Peter's, Rome, he also held similar posts at S. Luigi dei Francesi, the German College and, from 1614, the Sistine Chapel. His many books of madrigals, villanellas and canzonets were much reprinted, but he is in fact more notable for his church music, most of which survives in MS, though he did publish 2 volumes of motets.

Giovanni da Firenze (da Cascia) C14 Italian composer, from Cascia in Umbria. He was organist at Florence cathedral and reformed the musical establishment there sometime in the first half of the C14; he also served at the courts of Milan and of Mastino della Scala, tyrant ruler of Verona, between 1329 and 1351, where he was involved in musical competitions. One of the first Italian *trecento* composers to achieve widespread fame and one of the earliest represented in the Squarcialupi Codex, he composed mainly madrigals in 2 parts, often to sensuous and amorous texts. However he did also write 2 exciting *cacce*, *Per larghi prati* and the especially fine *Con bracchi assai*, which describes a quail hunt.

CE: in *CMM* 8/i, ed. N. Pirrotta

Giovanni Maria da Crema see Crema

Gittern Plucked string instrument; possibly a medieval ancestor of the guitar, and also known as the *guitarra latina*. The name gittern has been applied to an instrument with flat back and waisted shape resembling the fiddle; its fingerboard was usually fretted and the usual number of strings was 4, though 3 and 5 were also possible. However, recent research has suggested that this name was in fact applied to the medieval instrument hitherto known as the MANDORA – a plucked instrument with rounded back and sickle-shaped pegbox closely resembling the rebec. The gittern was especially popular in the C14, and many pictures of and literary references to it survive, but during the C15 its popularity declined. In the C16 the name refers to a small 4-course guitar, quite distinct from the medieval gittern.

Gittern and plectrum, 74 cm

Giustiniana 1. A setting of lyrical poetry by, or in the style of, the Venetian poet and politician Leonardo Giustiniani (d. 1446).

2. A humorous Venetian type of 3-part VILLANELLA poking fun at stuttering, lustful old men.

Glareanus, Heinrich (b. Mollis, Glarus, June 1488; d. Freiburg im Breisgau, 28 Mar 1563) Swiss theorist and humanist. In 1547 he published the DODECACHORDON, in which he propounded the theory of 12 church modes.

Glogauer Liederbuch A German MS song collection of c1480, the first to be written out in partbooks. The Lieder, in 3 or 4 parts, are equally divided between sacred and secular texts, and there is also a quantity of pieces apparently for instrumental ensemble –perhaps the earliest such collection to survive.

CE: *EDM* iv, viii, ed. H. Ringmann and J. Klapper

Godebrye see Jacotin

Godric, St (b. Walpole, Lincolnshire, c1069; d. Finchale, nr. Durham, 1170) English sailor, hermit and composer. Spent his early life as a sea-captain, and possibly also a pirate, before becoming a hermit and eventually settling in a cave by the river Wear, where he had mystical visions. His 3 songs, said to have been dictated by angels, are the earliest surviving post-Conquest vernacular English songs, and their melodies are strongly influenced by plainsong.

Goliards Wandering students or young clerics (C10–13) who wrote Latin secular poems with music, including the famous *Carmina Burana*. The subject matter ranges from chaste love lyrics to obscene drinking songs.

Gombert, Nicolas (b. c1500; d. ?Tournai, c1556) Franco-Flemish composer. Probably a pupil of Josquin Desprez, he entered the service of Charles V's chapel as a singer in or before 1526, and within a few years had become master of the boys, a post he still held in 1537 and which gave him many opportunities to travel abroad, especially to Spain. Around 1540 he was sentenced to a period of exile on the high seas for gross indecency, but he earned his release by composing his 'swan song'–perhaps a set of Magnificats. He later held a canonry at the cathedral of Tournai, where he spent the last few years of his life.

Gombert was one of the leading figures of the generation between Josquin and Palestrina. He wrote some 10 Masses, about 160 motets, 8 Magnificats and 60 chansons; the tally of his sacred works shows the general ascendancy of the motet over the Mass at this period. The Masses themselves demonstrate the modern trend towards the parody technique. One of the great polyphonists of the Renaissance, Gombert wrote in a consistently polyphonic style, based on imitative entries for each phrase of text, without variations of texture or chordal passages. He tended to avoid cantus firmus and canonic treatment, and his music is on the whole severely modal, lacking in Italianate tonal feeling. His harmonies are often dissonant, and his melodic lines planned for striking musical effect rather than clear verbal declamation.

CE: *Opera omnia* (*CMM* 6), ed. J. Schmidt-Görg (Rome, 1951–75)

Gorzanis, Giacomo (b. Apulia [=province of Puglia], c1525; d. ?Trieste, after 1575) Italian lutenist. He was blind and lived in Trieste, and his 4 published lute-books, in an elaborate virtuoso style, contain transcriptions of Neapolitan songs, and many dances, including saltarellos on all 12 semitones. The dances are often arranged as miniature suites, in groups such as passamezzo-padovano-saltarello, and make much use of variation techniques.

Gosswin, Anton (b. in or nr. Liège, 1535x46; d. June 1597xOct 1598) Franco-Flemish composer. A singer at Munich under Lassus in 1568, he was appointed court *Kapellmeister* at Landshut in 1569, and returned to Munich in 1570, becoming organist at the Peterskirche in 1577. In 1580 he became *Kapellmeister* to the Bishop of Freising, whom he accompanied to Bonn in 1584. 4 of his 7 Masses are on models by Lassus, and he published skilful 3-part reworkings of Lassus' 5-part German songs, as well as his own motets and madrigals.

Goudimel, Claude (b. Besançon, c1514; d. Lyons, 28x31 Aug 1572) French composer. Probably lived in Paris and worked as a collector and adviser to Du Chemin, a Parisian publisher who issued his chansons. He was converted to Protestantism in about 1560, and travelled round various Huguenot centres. It was in one of these, Lyons, that he was killed by fanatical anti-Protestants in the aftermath of the St Bartholomew's Day massacre. Before his conversion he wrote 5 Masses, 3 Magnificats and some motets for Catholic use; he also made some motet-like settings of Genevan psalm texts. However, he is chiefly noted for his later 4-part settings of the entire Genevan Psalter, designed for home use, in which the melody is in the top voice or the tenor, with straightforward chordal harmonization, sometimes decorated.

CE: *IMM* Collected works ser., iii, ed. L. Dittmer and P. Pidoux (Brooklyn, 1967–74)

Graduale Latin name for a liturgical book containing the music for all the chants of the Catholic Mass.

Grandi, Alessandro (b. ?1575x80; d. Bergamo, 1630) Italian composer. He was not born in Sicily, as some reference works state. Perhaps a pupil of Giovanni Gabrieli, he became choir-master at the Accademia della Morte in Ferrara in 1597, and held the same post at the Accademia dello Spirito Santo there in 1604–14. In 1616 he directed music at Ferrara cathedral. The next year he became a singer and in 1620 vice-*maestro* at St Mark's, Venice, under Monteverdi, and from 1627 till his death of the plague he directed music at S. Maria Maggiore, Bergamo.

Grandi was one of the most talented north Italian composers of the early years of the C17. His main contribution was to church music in the new concertato style: he published 11 volumes of motets, many of them exceptionally popular, 3 volumes of psalms, and 5 Masses; his secular output contained 2 books of concertato madrigals and 4 of solo cantatas and arias. He was a master of melody, as is evident from his arias and solo motets; in the former he developed the art of strophic variation over a repeating bass line. His concertato motets show superb control of texture and expressive pathos, and the motets 'with symphonies' published in the 1620s, employing an *obbligato* pair of violins, afforded novelties of structure and influenced Schütz.

Grazioso da Padova (d. *c*1400) Italian composer, known only by a Gloria and Sanctus in *ballata* style which show the influence of late C14 Italian secular music.

Greaves, Thomas (fl. 1604) English lutenist and composer. Apparently in the service of Sir Henry Pierrepoint, he published (in 1604) a volume of madrigals and lute songs, some of which are very fine.

Songs in *EL* 2nd ser., xviii; Madrigals in *EM* xxxvi, rev. edn.

Grefinger, Wolfgang (b. Krems, nr. Vienna, prob. *c*1480; d. after 1525) Austrian composer and organist. An outstanding pupil of Hofhaimer, he was organist at St Stephen's, Vienna, in 1505, and was probably Hungarian court organist from 1515 to 1525. His sacred songs in a simple, chordal style survive in anthologies and MSS, and he is represented in Sicher's organ tablature.

Gregorian chant see **Plainsong**

Greiter, Matthias (b. Aichach, nr. Augsburg, *c*1495; d. Strasbourg, 20 Dec 1550) German composer. A priest and singer at Strasbourg cathedral until the Reformation, he became a Protestant and stayed on to direct congregational singing (which greatly impressed Calvin). However, in 1549 he returned to the Catholic Church. His psalm tunes were much admired, and some appeared in Calvin's 1539 psalter; he also composed sacred songs and motets on German texts.

Grenon, Nicholas (d. 1456) Franco-Flemish composer. He is first heard of at the Burgundian court in 1385, was a canon at S. Sepulcre in Paris in 1399, and was master of the boys at Laon cathedral in 1403. In 1408 and from 1421–4 he was at Cambrai cathedral, latterly as music master; in 1412 he was in the service of the Duke of Berry, from 1413 to 1421 he was at the Burgundian court again, and from 1425 to 1427 he was a member of the Papal choir in Rome and in charge of its boys. In 1427 he returned to Cambrai as canon at the cathedral; though heard of in Bruges in 1437 he seems to have remained largely in Cambrai for the rest of his life. His chansons and isorhythmic motets are a link between the late C14 style and that of Dufay in their rejection of rhythmic complexity and cultivation of a simple melodic line and syllabic declamation.

Grimace Late C14 French composer. He may have been connected with Avignon, but did not adopt the rhythmically very complex style of the other Avignon composers of the period; the style of his 3 *ballades*, 1 *rondeau* and 1 *virelai* recalls Machaut. His best known work, *À l'arme à l'arme*, uses fanfare-like motifs to illustrate the warlike imagery of its text.

Grocheo see **Johannes de Grocheo**

Grossin, Estienne (fl. 1418–21) French composer, possibly from the diocese of Sens. He was a chaplain at S. Merry in Paris in 1418, and a matins clerk at Notre Dame in 1421. His *Missa trompette* (settings of the Kyrie, Gloria, Credo and part of the Sanctus) has passages of contratenor marked 'trompette', probably intended for the slide trumpet; his chansons have a delicate expressiveness.

CE: in *CMM* 11/iii, ed. G. Reaney

Ground A musical phrase repeated over and over again in the bass, with varied superstructure. It can be a simple 4-note figure (the descending tetrachord) or a more extended paragraph. Found in various types of vocal and instrumental music from c1580 onwards, it provided a useful method of unifying extended set pieces in opera or liturgical compositions. 'Ground' was the term used in England, *basso ostinato* the Italian equivalent. (See also PASSAMEZZO, ROMANESCA, RUGGIERO.)

Guami, Francesco (b. Lucca, c1544; d. Lucca, 30 Jan 1602) Italian composer, brother of G. Guami. A sackbut player at the Munich court from 1568 to 1580, court *Kapellmeister* at Baden Baden in 1588, and later worked as *maestro di cappella* at churches in Udine, Venice and Lucca. He published 3 volumes of madrigals and one of instrumental ricercars.

Guami, Gioseffo (b. Lucca, c1540; d. Lucca, c1612) Italian composer, brother of F. Guami. Probably a pupil of Willaert, he worked at the Munich court from 1568–79, and was first organist at St Mark's, Venice, 1588–91. Later he became organist of Lucca cathedral, and was the teacher of Banchieri. He published motets, canzonas and 3 volumes of madrigals, and was represented in many anthologies.

Guédron, Pierre (b. in or nr. Châteaudun, nr. Orléans, c1565; d. ?Paris, 1620x21) French composer. A singer to Cardinal de Guise in 1583, when he won a composition prize at Évreux; joined the royal chapel as a singer in 1590, became master of the children in 1599, and in 1601 succeeded LE JEUNE as royal chamber composer (his son-in-law Boësset succeeded him in 1613). The only French composer of his time whose music shows any knowledge of contemporary Italian developments, he composed *récits* – expressive and declamatory solos with chordal lute accompaniments – and music for many court entertainments. He published 6 volumes of *airs de cour*.

Guerrero, Francisco (b. Seville, 4 Oct 1528; d. Seville, 8 Nov 1599) Spanish composer; a pupil of his brother Pedro and (briefly) of Morales. He directed music at Jaén cathedral in 1546–8, and was a singer at Seville cathedral in 1550. In 1554 he succeeded Morales as choirmaster at Málaga cathedral, but he returned to Seville the following year to direct the music there. He travelled to Rome in 1581–4 and made a pilgrimage to the Holy Land in 1588–9.

Unlike his compatriots, Morales and Victoria, Guerrero was taught and worked entirely in Spain. His style is less intense than theirs, but alongside a gentle lyricism he displays a superb mastery of contrapuntal device, which places him among the great Spanish polyphonists. He published 17 Masses, 2 Requiems, 4 books of motets, volumes of psalms, Magnificats, Vespers music and Passions, and a collection of spiritual madrigals to Spanish texts. The spiritual madrigals reflect a Counter-Reformation fervour; though intended for a secular context, their texts are devotional *contrafacta*.

CE: *Opera omnia* in *MME* xvi, xix and further vols., ed. V. Garcia and M. Querol (Barcelona, 1955–   )

Gui II de Coucy see **Chastelain de Coucy**

Guido d'Arezzo (b. Arezzo, *c*992; d. *c*1050) Italian theorist, teacher and choir trainer. A Benedictine monk, he invented SOLMIZATION syllables and the HEXACHORD, which enabled musicians to describe a note in any position on the diatonic scale. These descriptions were charted on a diagram of a human hand (the 'Guidonian hand') as an aid to sight-singing. He was also reputed to be the inventor of the stave, drawing lines of different colours to represent different pitch levels.

Guillaume de Machaut see **Machaut**

Guillaume le Vinier (b. *c*1190; d. 1245) Trouvère, brother of Gilles le Vinier. A priest at Arras, he left more than 30 poems, for most of which melodies survive.

Guiot de Dijon Early C13 troubadour. His Crusade song *Chanterai por*

mon coraige achieves a measure of unity by skilful use of repetition.

Guiot de Provins (b. *c*1145; d. after 1208) Trouvère. In the service of the Dukes of Champagne in Provins, and may have gone to the Holy Land on one or more Crusades. His 6 surviving songs date from *c*1180; later he became a Cluniac monk and wrote 2 satires on contemporary morals.

Guiraut de Bornelh (b. ?Boureix, Dordogne, *c*1138; d. *c*1215) Troubadour. He was at the court of Alfonso II of Aragon, and went on a Crusade. His contemporaries called him 'Master of the Troubadours' and Dante ranked him second only to Arnaut Daniel. Only 4 of his melodies survive: his 'alba' or dawn song *Reis glorios* became very famous and is exceptionally beautiful.

Guiraut Riquier (b. Narbonne, *c*1230; d. 1292) The last of the troubadours, surviving the Albigensian Crusade and the wars which effectively destroyed the cultured Provençal society which had supported them; he wrote that though song should be joyful, he was oppressed by sorrow and had come into the world too late. For some years after *c*1260 he lived in Spain, under the patronage of Alfonso X, and a letter of his to Alfonso, dealing with troubadours and jongleurs, still survives. He left a large number of songs, many with religious texts.

Guitar Plucked string instrument; one of the 3 main types of plucked instrument, the others being lute and cittern. It has a waisted shape, flat back, gut strings and frets, and no movable bridge. The C16 guitar was light and shallow, about half the size of the modern classical instrument, with 4 double courses of gut strings. By 1600 the guitar was very popular all over

Europe, and had a wide repertory, largely of lighter music, notated in tablature. It was often associated with the cittern. In the early C17 a 5-course instrument known as the 'chitarra spagnola' became standard, and the 4-course guitar was called 'chitarrino'. A small high-pitched guitar was called a 'chitarriglia', and 'mandola' was an ambiguous name for several small types of guitar. Other varieties of the instrument include:

Chitarra battente 5-course metal-strung guitar with fixed metal frets, played with a plectrum.

Bandurria A small instrument shaped like a rebec and played with a plectrum; it normally had 3 courses of strings, but 4- and 5-course instruments were also possible.

Gumpelzhaimer, Adam (b. Trostberg, Bavaria, 1559; d. Augsburg, 3 Nov 1625) German composer. He may have studied briefly with Lassus, and also in Italy. Except for a short period in Stuttgart, he was teacher and cantor at the S. Anna *Gymnasium* in Augsburg from 1581 until his death. In 1595 he published a modernized version of Faber's *Compendium Musicae*, with examples taken from the music of contemporary German composers, which remained a standard textbook in southern Germany until the late C17. He composed psalms and sacred songs, and motets which use poly-choral effects.

Selected works in *DTB* x/2

Gussago, Cesario (b. Ostiano, nr. Brescia, c1550) Italian composer and priest; in 1599 Vicar-General of the Order of S. Gerolamo in Brescia, and in 1612 organist of S. Maria delle Grazie. He published instrumental sonatas in up to 8 parts, and large- and small-scale motets and psalms.

Guyot (Castileti, Châtelet), Jean (Johannes) (b. Châtelet, nr. Liège, 1512; d. Liège, 11 Mar 1588) Franco-Flemish composer. Studied at Louvain, probably visited Italy, and except for a period at the Imperial court in 1563–4 was from 1545 a chaplain and precentor in Liège, first at St Paul's church and then at the cathedral. His Mass, motets, chansons and 12-part arrangement of Josquin's 6-part *Benedicta es* survive in anthologies and MSS; the 4-part chansons are charming, but those in 8 parts seem more weighty then their slight texts justify.

Gymel, Gimel A late medieval term for 2-part harmony with many parallel 3rds, possibly English in origin. In English Tudor church music the term denotes the temporary division into 2 sections of the singers on one voice part, to create variety of vocal scoring.

H

Hähnel see **Galliculus**

Halle, Adam de la see **Adam de la Halle**

Handl (Gallus), Jakob (b. Reifnitz, Carniola [Ribnica, nr. Ljubljana], 15 Apr x 31 July 1550; d. Prague, 18 July 1591) Austrian composer of Slovene descent. Sang in the monastery of Melk in 1568 and in the Vienna court chapel in 1574; choirmaster to the Bishop of Olmütz [Olomouc] 1579–1585, and lived thereafter in Prague as organist at S. Johann. The Emperor Rudolf II gave him a privilege to print music; he issued 11 books of church music (*Opus musicum*) including 16 Masses, 2 Passions and a cycle of music for the liturgical year. His double-choir motets show that he had grasped the essentials of the current Venetian style, while his smaller pieces show an imitative Franco-Flemish idiom (the well-known *Ecce quomodo moritur justus*, however, is an eloquent homophonic piece). Occasionally he uses striking chromaticism (as in *Mirabile mysterium*). His *Moralia* of 1590 were simple Latin madrigals.

Opus musicum and Masses in *DTO* xii, xxiv, xxx, xl, xlviii, li–ii, xciv–v, cxvii, cxix; *Moralia* in *RRMR* vii–viii, ed. A. Skei

Harant z Polžic, Kryštof (b. Burg Klenau [nr. Klatovy], nr. Plzeň, 1564; d. Prague, 21 June 1621) Bohemian composer and nobleman. Educated at the archducal court at Innsbruck from 1576 to 1584, travelled to the Holy Land in 1598–9 and published a book about the journey, containing interesting in-formation about local folk music. He also visited Spain. By 1618 he had declared himself a Protestant and he joined the Hussites as an artillery commander in their attack on Vienna; he was executed after the Battle of the White Mountain. He had kept an excellent musical establishment in his ancestral castle, and though an amateur composed some competent church music in late C16 style, including a Mass on Marenzio's *Dolorosi martir*, and arrangements of Czech religious songs.

CE: *Werke*, ed. J. Berkovec (Prague, 1956)

Harp Plucked string instrument. It was much used in the Middle Ages both as an expressive solo instrument and to accompany monophonic songs, but its repertory was improvised or memorized and no notation system existed. It was of strong triangular construction, and its strings could be of metal, gut, or even twisted hair; there could be any number from 6 or 7 up to

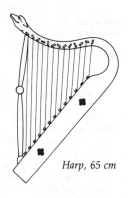

Harp, 65 cm

about 25, and metal strings might be plucked with the nails to give a harsh, brilliant tone. By the late Middle Ages 2 distinct types had emerged: the massively-constructed Irish harp with metal strings, and the lighter Gothic harp with gut strings. During the Renaissance the harp yielded its supremacy among plucked instruments to the fully chromatic lute, but a chromatic double harp with 2 rows of strings was developed in the C16, and by 1600 the triple harp had been invented; this had 3 rows of strings and a range of 4½ octaves, and became a useful continuo instrument in the early Baroque.

Harpsichord Plucked string keyboard instrument, developed during the C15. Its action is essentially a mechanization of the PSALTERY; depressing a key causes the string to be plucked by a long plectrum or 'jack'. No contrasts of tone or dynamics are possible, but touch and articulation are vital, and C16 instruments may have had a second set of strings at 4-foot pitch to give added brilliance. The harpsichord normally had one manual and a 4-octave compass; there were important schools of harpsichord-making in early C16 Italy and later C16 Flanders.

Hartman von der Aue Late C12/early C13 Minnesinger. He belongs to the period when the art of the Minnesingers was at its height and wrote a famous narrative poem *Der arme Heinrich*.

Harzer see **Resinarius**

Hasprois, Johannes Simon (d. *c*1428) French composer. In the service of Charles V of France in 1380, and of the Avignon Pope Benedict III in 1403. His earlier chansons are in the florid style characteristic of late C14 Avignon composers, though their use of melodic sequences shows an Italian touch. His later music is however in a markedly simpler style.

CE: in *CMM* 11/ii, ed. G. Reaney

Hassler, Hans Leo (bp. Nürnberg, 26 Oct 1564; d. Frankfurt, 8 June 1612) German composer, from a famous musical family. He studied with Andrea Gabrieli in Venice in 1584–5. From 1586 he was employed by the Fugger family in Augsburg as organist, working for a time at the church of S. Moritz, and (in 1600) being head of the town band. He was the chief town musician at Nürnberg in 1601–8 and achieved the title of Imperial chamber organist in 1602. In 1608 he served as organist at the Dresden court of Saxony. (He was also a businessman with many interests.)

Hassler was the first German to study in Italy, and his style is tinged with a strong Venetian element. He wrote Masses and motets (though he seems to have been a Protestant) and published Italian *canzonette* and madrigals, and German Lieder often in the Italian manner. In his church music he was influenced by Lassus, whereas his Italian secular music shows his thorough familiarity with the up-to-date style of Vecchi and Marenzio. The specifically Venetian influence is felt most in his double-choir madrigals and Lieder. His best Lieder collection is the 1601 *Lustgarten*, with its dance songs and instrumental INTRADAS for consort.

CE: *Sämtliche Werke*, ed. C. Crosby (Wiesbaden, 1961–) (Vols. i, iv–vi = *DDT* ii, vii, xxiv–v)

Haucourt (Acourt, Johannes de Alte Curie) Late C14 French composer. His style, originally very florid and rhythmically complex in the manner characteristic of the period, later became simpler, with a greater emphasis on lyrical melody. The only work ascribed to 'Alte Curie' is an exceptionally intricate ballade *Se doit il plus* in the Chantilly MS.

CE: in *CMM* 11/ii, ed. G. Reaney

Haussmann, Valentin (b. *c*1570; d. 1611x14) German composer. Worked as organist and town official in Gerbstädt (near Halle) but also travelled widely in Germany and Poland. He published 11 volumes of secular songs and German and Polish dances for instrumental ensemble, and also helped the spread of Italian music in Germany by publishing German-text editions of music by such composers as Marenzio, Vecchi and Gastoldi (works by Morley also received this treatment).

Instrumental works in *DDT* xvi

Hayne van Ghizeghem (b. ?Ghizeghem, nr. Aalst, *c*1445; d. before 1495) Franco-Flemish composer. In 1457 he was studying with Constans d'Utrecht at the court of Burgundy, at which he became a singer and 'valet de chambre' in 1467. He also joined the army under Charles the Bold; the last reference to him occurs in 1472. Hayne was highly respected by his contemporaries. His output was of chansons—about 20 in all—of which some were printed by Petrucci in the earliest volumes of published music. His *De tous biens plaine* was possibly the most famous chanson of its age; its tenor was used as a cantus firmus for motets, Masses and chanson elaborations by many composers.

CE: *Opera omnia* (*CMM* 74), ed. B. Hudson (Rome, 1977)

Heinrich von Meissen (Frauenlob) (b. Meissen, 1250; d. Mainz, 29 Nov 1318) Minnesinger. Called Frauenlob because in a contest with another Minnesinger he championed the use of 'Frau' rather than 'Weib' as the word for a lady. One of the last Minnesingers, he can be seen as in many ways a forerunner of the Meistersingers: his songs have a certain stiffness that became characteristic of the Meistersingers. Comparison of his music with that of Adam de la Halle shows how far German music at that time lagged behind French; he himself seems to have believed that the Golden Age of culture was over and nothing but decline lay ahead.

Heinrich von Mügeln (Müglin) (b. Mügeln, nr. Dresden; d. after 1369) German poet and composer. Worked in Prague, Budapest and Vienna; wrote chronicles in Hungarian and an important allegorical poem, *Der meide Kranz*, and also made translations of the psalms. He devised a melodic formula (the 'Langer Ton') of the Meistersingers, who regarded him as one of the fathers of their art; 9 of his melodies survive.

Hèle, Georges de la (b. Antwerp, 1547; d. Madrid, 19 Feb 1587) Franco-Flemish composer. Served Philip II of Spain from 1560–70, and after a period as choirmaster at S. Rombault in Malines and in Tournai returned to Madrid as *maestro de capilla* in 1580. He won motet and chanson prizes at the Évreux composition contest in 1576, and published a volume of Masses (1578) which are parodies of motets by such composers as Josquin, Rore and Lassus.

CE: *Collected Works* (*CMM* 56), ed. L. Wagner (Rome, 1972–   )

Hellinck, Lupus (b. diocese of Utrecht, *c*1496; d. Bruges, ?14 Jan 1541) Franco-Flemish composer. His musical life was spent in Bruges, as choirboy at S. Donatien, choirmaster at Notre Dame in 1521–3, and succentor at the former church from 1523 onwards. He wrote some fine Masses and motets (his *Panis quem ego dabo* was parodied by Palestrina), Dutch songs, and 11 chorale settings included in Rhaw's 1544 collection. Though a priest, he seems to have had secret sympathy with the Reformation.

Henestrosa see **Venegas de Henestrosa**

'Henry, Roy' ('Roy Henry') King of England (probably Henry IV) and composer. There are 2 pieces ascribed to him in the Old Hall MS, and though this was written out during the reign of Henry V (1413–22), the pieces are in an old-fashioned style more characteristic of the reign of Henry IV (1399–1413), who was himself skilled in and fond of music.

Henry VIII (b. Greenwich, 28 June 1491; d. London, 28 Jan 1547) King of England (from 1509) and composer. As well as composing church music and songs himself, he made his court a centre of musical culture, encouraging foreign musicians to work there, introducing the Franco-Flemish style of church music, and building up an enormous collection of musical instruments. He was also responsible for the English Reformation. The Henry VIII MS is a collection of music used at the court which contains some of Henry's own works.

Works in *MB* xviii, ed. J. Stevens

Heredia see **Aguilera de Heredia**

Hermann, the Monk of Salzburg Late C14 Minnesinger and composer. Suggested identification of him with Johannes Rossus II, Abbot of the Benedictine monastery at Salzburg 1364–75, or with the Prior Hermann living in 1424, now seems implausible, but it appears likely he was in contact with the brilliant and hedonistic court of Archbishop Pilgrim of Salzburg (d. 1396) (one of his songs is a versified love-letter to the most beautiful of

the Archbishop's ladies). His secular music shows a fusion of the styles of the later Minnesingers and of Alpine folksong; most of his songs are monophonic, but he also made some primitive attempts at polyphonic songs, which however had little influence on German music. 3 of his polyphonic pieces are marked 'gut zu blasen' ('good for blowing'), which suggests the use of wind instruments, and the lower part (restricted to 2 notes) of *Der Nachthorn* is in fact marked 'der Pumhart' (? = Bombard). His 40 or so German sacred songs are mainly settings of translations of psalms and sequences; his music continued to be popular into the C16, and is found in such sources as the *Lochamer Liederbuch* and Paumann's tablatures.

Hermannus Contractus (b. 18 July 1013; d. 24 Sep 1054) German theorist and Benedictine monk. His letter notation of plainsong did not find favour owing to GUIDO D'AREZZO's improvements of pitch notation. He wrote some fine sequence and antiphon melodies, including the solemn Marian antiphon chants *Alma redemptoris* and *Salve Regina*.

Hesdin, Nicolle des Celliers d' (d. Beauvais, 21 Aug 1538) French composer. Master of the boys at Beauvais cathedral; his Masses (including one formerly attributed to Willaert) and delightful chansons appeared in anthologies from 1529 onwards.

Hesse, Landgrave of see **Moritz**

Hessen, Paul and **Bartholomäus** (fl. 1555) German editors, brothers, who published in 1555 an enormous collection of over 500 dances for instrumental ensemble (no complete source of which survives).

Hexachord A 6-note diatonic scale with semitone in the middle (e.g. C-D-E-F-G-A) forming the basis of medieval theory on scales. In the pure diatonic scale there were 2 hexachords, on C and G; a third, on F required a B flat. The system was first described by Guido d'Arezzo, who names the 6 notes of a hexachord by the vocables ('voces musicales') ut re mi fa sol la, after the initial syllables of the first 6 lines of the hymn to St John the Baptist. This was because the plainsong melody (probably by Guido) begins each line one note higher than the previous one. (See also SOLMIZATION.)

Heyborne (alias **Richardson**), **Sir Ferdinando** (b. *c*1558; d. Tottenham, Middlesex, 4 June 1618) English composer. A pupil of Tallis and a member of the royal household until 1611, he composed virginal music including 8 pieces in the Fitzwilliam Virginal Book.

Hilton, John 1 (d. Cambridge, Mar 1608) English organist and composer, perhaps father of John Hilton 2. Singer and then assistant organist at Lincoln cathedral before becoming organist at Trinity College, Cambridge, in 1594. He contributed a madrigal to the *Triumphs of Oriana* and composed anthems and organ pieces.

Hilton, John 2 (b. Oxford or ?Cambridge, 1599; bd. London, 21 Mar 1657) English composer. In 1628 he was organist at St Margaret's, Westminster. His 3-part *Ayres* of 1627 (in the style of Morley) was the last English madrigal publication; he also published a collection of glees and catches, *Catch as Catch Can*, in 1652, and composed anthems and an elegy on the death of William Lawes.

Historia C16 and C17 Lutheran musical setting of a Biblical story, developed from the Catholic singing of the Passion. Its text would be taken from one Gospel or compiled from all 4; the Passion narrative was the most common subject, the next most common being the Resurrection. Of the 3 types of *historia*, the responsorial, derived from the Catholic Passion, survived the longest; individual characters were represented by solo voices. The through-composed type set the entire text polyphonically, perhaps with varied voice-groupings to mark off passages of narration and of speech. Schütz's Easter *Historia*, in which only the Evangelist has solo recitation, exemplifies a mixed type.

Hocket In medieval polyphony, the breaking up of a melodic line between 2 voices in rapid alternation within a motet. Machaut's *Hoquetus David* shows the application of the term to an independent instrumental piece using the technique.

Hofhaimer, Paul (b. Radstadt, nr. Salzburg, 25 Jan 1459; d. Salzburg, 1537) Austrian composer and organist. It is possible that he studied with Lapicida and worked at Frederick III's court at Graz before becoming court organist to Archduke Sigismund at Innsbruck in 1480. When the Emperor Maximilian took over the court 10 years later, Hofhaimer remained. He became an adviser on organ building and travelled widely, living at Passau in 1502–6 and 1519–21, and at Augsburg in 1508–18. From 1522 onwards he was organist at Salzburg cathedral. He was knighted by the King of Hungary at a royal wedding at the Hungarian court in 1515.

Hofhaimer was widely renowned as an organist, and his keyboard music (of which little, alas, survives) shows a new freedom and idiomatic quality of writing even in liturgical pieces like the fine *alternatim Salve Regina*. He is also important as a composer of German songs, which date from c1500 and are therefore among the earliest in this rich period of the Lied. Melodies lie in the tenor, and the music proceeds often in short phrases rather than a smooth flow; *Meins traurens ist* is a touching example of Hofhaimer's lyricism.

CE: Lieder and keyboard pieces in *DTO* lxxii

Hofweisen German court tunes used as tenor in the early C16 polyphonic Lied. Their words differ from those of popular song, leaning towards the moral or the didactic. Their verse structure is formal, often following the BARFORM, as also is their melody, which often favours the Ionian mode on F.

Holborne, Anthony (d. ?London, 1602) English lutenist and composer. A gentleman in the service of Elizabeth I, he published a volume of 5-part dances in 1594. His *Cittharn-Schoole*, published by his brother William in 1597, contains pieces for cittern alone, cittern and bass viol, and 3-part consort.

CE: *Complete Works*, ed. M. Kanazawa (Cambridge, Mass., 1967–73)

Hollander, Christian Janszone (b. Dordrecht, 1510x15; d. Innsbruck, 1568x69) Franco-Flemish composer. Choirmaster at S. Walburga, Oudenarde, from 1549 to 1557; sang at the Imperial court until 1564, when he moved to the archducal court at Innsbruck. His employers thought highly of his compositions–German songs and motets which show accomplished use of the mature Franco-Flemish polyphonic style.

Hooper, Edmund (b. Halberton, Devon, c1553; d. Westminster, 14 July 1621) English composer. Became master of the children of Westminster Abbey in 1588, and organist there in

1606, and from 1604 was a Gentleman of the Chapel Royal. He contributed to East's psalter and Leighton's *Teares*, and wrote some intensely expressive anthems.

Horn Wind instrument with cup-shaped mouthpiece and cylindrical bore, originally derived from animal horn. The medieval cowhorn usually had 3 finger-holes, producing a 6-note compass; other types, such as the decorative oliphant, made from an elephant tusk, had no finger-holes. Circular hunting horns seem to have been in use by the later C14 (according to Froissart, such instruments were used to terrifying effect by the Scottish soldiers), but the modern type of coiled metal horn without finger-holes did not develop until the later C16. At this time makers began to experiment with different forms of coil; surviving C16 horn music is limited to hunting-calls, but Mersenne does refer to 4-part horn consorts.

Hornpipe Reedpipe with a horn at each end, the larger acting as a bell and the smaller as a mouthpiece enclosing a single reed. The earliest type of

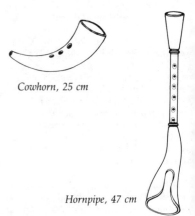

Cowhorn, 25 cm

Hornpipe, 47 cm

reedcap instrument, it played an important part in medieval music-making, but had gone out of use by the time of Praetorius.

Horwood, William (d. 1484) English composer. A singer at Lincoln cathedral in 1470 and choirmaster there from 1477, he is known by 4 pieces in the Eton Choirbook (one is incomplete) and another incomplete piece in a York MS. He is one of the earliest Eton composers, and his style is distinctly old-fashioned with some harsh dissonances and little use of imitation.

Hoyoul, Balduin (b. ?Liège, 1547x49; d. Stuttgart, 26 Nov 1594) Franco-Flemish composer. Worked as chorister, adult singer and (from 1589 in succession to his father-in-law Daser) *Kapellmeister* at the Württemberg court in Stuttgart. A pupil of Lassus, he published motets in up to 10 parts and German chorale motets, and left more church music in MS.
    Chorale motets in *RRMR* xxiii, ed. D. Politoske

Hucbald (b. ?diocese of Tournai, *c*840; d. S. Amand-en-Puisaye, nr. Auxerre, 20 June 930) French theorist and monk of the abbey of S. Amand. The most important writer on music between Boethius and Guido d'Arezzo though not, as once thought, the composer of the earliest notated polyphony. His treatise *De harmonica*

institutione links the scale ranges of the ancient *tonoi* to the modes, while his *Commemoratio brevis* contains the earliest notated forms of the plainsong psalm tones.

Hume, Tobias (d. 16 Apr 1645) English composer. An army officer, he was a fine player of the bass viol 'lyra-way' (see LYRA VIOL) and in 1607 published a volume entitled *Practicall Musicke* which contains mainly pieces for consorts of bass viols, or of bass viols and plucked instruments. Some of his works have such titles as 'My mistress hath a pretty thing', or 'Tickle me quickly', and he asks for unusual effects such as hitting the string with the back of the bow (a very early *col legno*). Originally merely eccentric, he ultimately went mad.

Hurdy-gurdy see **Symphony**

Hûsen see **Friedrich von Hûsen**

Hymn A song of praise with text in strophic, rhyming form. Latin hymns formed part of the OFFICE in the Roman rite; their chant melodies date from the C11 onwards. From the C13 polyphonic settings developed, often for ALTERNATIM performance (including, later, the ORGAN HYMN). Palestrina and Victoria were among the Renaissance polyphonists who composed cycles of Vesper hymns for the ecclesiastical year.

I

Il Verso see **Verso**

Improperia Chants for the Catholic Good Friday liturgy, sung during the veneration of the cross. Also known as 'Reproaches', they set passages from the Prophets and other short texts including the 'Trisagion', an antiphonal alternation of Greek and Latin acclamations. Palestrina, Victoria and other C16 polyphonists set them in simple 4-part homophony.

In nomine English C16/17 cantus firmus piece for consort or keyboard usually based on the plainsong antiphon 'Gloria tibi trinitas'. The title is taken from the words 'in nomine Domini' in the Benedictus of Taverner's Mass upon 'Gloria tibi trinitas', where the cantus firmus is stated complete. A keyboard transcription of this Taverner Benedictus in the MULLINER BOOK represents the earliest surviving source of the In nomine tradition.

'In nomine' cantus firmus

India, Sigismondo d' (b. Palermo, 1580; d. Modena, 1629) Italian composer. Much of his life from 1601 was spent in the employ of the ducal court of Savoy, though he lived in Florence in the first decade of the C17, visited Parma and Piacenza thereafter and

was at Modena in 1623–4. He published 3 volumes of motets, 8 of madrigals and 2 of villanellas, but he was most notable as a follower of the Florentine monodists, issuing 5 books of *Musiche* for 1 or 2 voices and continuo, and introducing into the solo madrigal some radical experiments in chromatic writing new to that medium (though well-tried, of course, in polyphonic composition). His *O dolcezze amarissime* is one of several powerful and distinctive songs, and his longer laments rival Monteverdi in their expressive inventiveness.

Madrigals in *CMI* x, ed. F. Mompellio; *Musiche* in *IM* 1st ser., iv, ed. F. Mompellio

Infantas, Fernando de las (b. Córdoba, 1534; d. Rome or ?Paris, after 1609) Spanish composer, priest and nobleman. Philip II sent him to Rome in 1571 to publish his church music and while there he persuaded Philip to ask the Pope to suspend work on a revised *Graduale*. His works include 3 volumes of motets, mostly based on plainsong and making much use of canon, and a volume of 100 canons *à 2–8* all on the same chant. He seems to have stopped composing after taking orders in 1584.

Ingegneri, Marc'Antonio (b. Verona, *c*1536; d. Cremona, 1 July 1592) Italian composer. A pupil of Ruffo and Rore, he directed music at Cremona cathedral from at least 1581; it was in that city that Monteverdi studied with him. He published 10 books of sacred music and 8 of madrigals. Though he showed himself fairly conventional in the former, the madrigals were in the modern manner after Rore; Monteverdi considered them to belong to the SECONDA PRATTICA.

Responsories in Palestrina, *Werke*, xxxii

Instrumental chanson Early Renaissance instrumental composition, usually in 3 parts, developed in Italy from French vocal chansons in the *formes fixes*. Such pieces abandoned the repetition schemes associated with vocal settings of the poetic forms and became, for a time around 1500, purely instrumental music.

Intabulation C15–17 arrangement of vocal music for keyboard or lute. The derivation from 'tabulatura' (tablature) indicates a change from separate parts to a score-like notation. In the process of arrangements original parts might be omitted or differently distributed and the texture enriched by ornamentation.

Intermedio C15/16 Italian (especially Florentine) court musical entertainment introduced between the acts of a play, significant as one of the forerunners of opera. Among the most notable were those performed in Florence in 1589 at the festivities for the marriage of the Grand Duke of Tuscany with Christine of Lorraine, with music–madrigals, *sinfonie*, ballets with instrumental accompaniment–by several composers including Cavalieri, Malvezzi, Marenzio and Peri.

Intonatione C16 Italian organ prelude, used in the liturgy to set the mode for the ensuing vocal item. Andrea Gabrieli wrote a set of such pieces.

Intrada C16/17 instrumental entry-piece, festive in character and homophonic in style. HASSLER included some fine 6-part examples in his 1601 *Lustgarten*.

Isaac, Heinrich (b. *c*1450; d. Florence, 26 Mar 1517) Franco-Flemish composer. His early life is obscure, but he went sometime after 1480 to Florence, where Lorenzo the Magnificent made him organist at the cathedral and at S. Giovanni. He is known to have visited the court of Innsbruck in 1484, but returned to Florence where he taught Lorenzo's sons. Lorenzo's death in 1492 was soon followed by the downfall of the Medici, and by 1497 Isaac had become court composer to Emperor Maximilian I. He made many journeys (to Konstanz, the Saxon court, and repeatedly back to Florence), and finally pleaded to be dismissed so that he could return to Italy in 1514.

Not only one of Josquin Desprez' greatest contemporaries, Isaac was also the most versatile, many-sided musician before Lassus, writing about 10 Masses and 25 motets, the monumental CHORALIS CONSTANTINUS, 25 German Lieder, some Italian carnival songs and frottolas, and untexted chansons or instrumental pieces. The Lieder belong with those of Heinrich Finck and Hofhaimer, with a tenor melody, though of the several settings of *Innsbruck ich muss dich lassen* one is canonic and another has the tune in the top part of a beautiful harmonization. The Italian songs are either lyrical or boisterous, showing how well he assimilated the Italian manner. Isaac's church music is a masterly compendium of contrapuntal resources.

CE: *Opera omnia (CMM* 65), ed. E. Lerner (Rome, 1974–   ); *Choralis Constantinus* in *DTO* x, xxxii, and ed. L. Cuyler (Ann Arbor, 1950); Masses in *MD* vii–viii, ed. M. Staehelin; Secular works in *DTO* xxviii, xxxii

Isorhythm A term of recent (C20)

origin, denoting a major structural principle in motets of the period 1320–1450; it derived from rhythmic schemes in the ARS ANTIQUA motet and was applied especially to cantus firmus parts. The principle involved the re-iteration of a scheme of rhythmic values (*talea*), sometimes in dimi-nishing proportions (e.g. 3:2:1). (The melodic passage constituting the cantus firmus was known as the *color*). Where rhythmic repetition is also applied to the upper parts, the procedure is known as 'total isorhythm', examples of which are to be found in some of Dunstable's motets.

J

Jachet of Mantua (real name **Jacques Colebault**) (b. Vitré, Brittany, 1483; d. Mantua, c1559) French composer. Probably came to Italy between 1513 and 1515, and worked for Sigismondo d'Este at Ferrara in 1517. In 1524 he moved to Mantua, joining Bishop Ercole Gonzaga's chapel in 1526 and becoming *maestro di cappella* at Mantua cathedral from 1539. He should not be confused with JACHET BERCHEM. He wrote many volumes of church music, including a joint publication with Willaert of Vespers psalms for double choir (1550).

CE: *Collected Works* (*CMM* 34), ed. P. Jackson and G. Nugent (Rome 1971–)

Jacopo da Bologna (fl ?c1340–55) Italian composer, also said to be a virtuoso player of the harp. He served at the courts of Mastino della Scala in Verona (where he was involved in a contest with Giovanni da Firenze) probably between 1340 and 1345, and at the Visconti court in Milan, possibly from 1345 to 1355. One of the earlier C14 composers who helped to give the Italian *trecento* style its impetus, he was the teacher of Landini and wrote a treatise on notation as well as composing c35 surviving pieces, most of which are madrigals (though he also composed motets and a *caccia*). One of his best known works is the madrigal *Fenice fù* which as well as being a lyrical setting of its text also contains much use of imitation. His *Non al suo amante* is the only surviving Petrarch setting from the C14. The text of another madrigal implies the view that singing should be smooth and sweet, not loud and raucous.

CE: in *CMM* 8/iv, ed. N. Pirrotta; *The Music of Jacopo da Bologna*, ed. W. T. Marrocco (Berkeley, 1954)

Jacotin (real name **Jacob Godebrye**) (d. ?Antwerp, prob. 24 Mar 1529) Franco-Flemish composer; from 1479 to 1528 a singer at Notre Dame in Antwerp. His motets and expressive chansons appeared in anthologies from 1519, but it is not certain that all the music ascribed to 'Jacotin' is in fact his, as other composers also used this name.

Ján z Lublina see **Lublina**

Janequin, Clément (b. ?Châtellerault, nr. Poitiers, c1485; d. Paris, ?end Jan 1558) French composer. Active at Bordeaux in 1529, and in about 1532 worked in Anjou, and was choirmaster at Angers cathedral; he also studied at the university there. In 1548 he was a curate at Unverre (near Chartres); he was a protegé of Cardinal de Guise, the patron of Erasmus, Marot and Rabelais. In 1555 he was a singer at the royal chapel and later 'composer in ordinary', but Henri II's coffers were emptied by war so that, far from profiting from this employment, Janequin died a pauper in the Latin Quarter of Paris.

Janequin's success lay in his enormous reputation throughout Europe as a composer of chansons: he wrote 280, mostly *à 4*, and stands at the head of the 'Paris school' whose chansons Attaingnant published. These works embody the most original manifestations of the French Renaissance in their wit, charm and lyricism, varying in texture from chordal to imitative, and having characteristic 'pattering' declamation. Many tell a story, but Janequin's most celebrated pieces are the descriptive or 'programme' chansons (e.g. *La guerre, Le chant des oiseaux*) in which onomatopoeic effects create a realistic atmosphere. He also wrote spiritual chansons and French psalm settings.

CE: *Chansons polyphoniques*, ed. A. T. Merritt and F. Lesure (Monaco, 1965–9)

Japart, Jean (Johannes) (fl. 1500) Franco-Flemish composer. A singer at the Ferrara court in about 1500; 16 of his chansons were published by Petrucci. He was especially skilled at reworking other composers' melodies, sometimes several at once, and liked to add enigmatic verbal mottoes to his pieces.

Jaufre Rudel (b. ?Blaize, Gironde, c1120; d. c1147) Troubadour. Went on the Crusade of Louis VII and may have died either in the East or on the journey home. He is the hero of Rostand's *La Princesse lointaine*, though the story on which this is based is probably apocryphal. He left 4 surviving melodies.

Jeep, Johann (b. Dransfeld, nr. Hanover, 1581x82; d. Hanau, 19 Nov 1644) German composer. Studied in Italy; *Kapellmeister* to the Hohenlohe court at Weikersheim (near Würzburg) 1614–35; cathedral organist and *Kapellmeister* at Frankfurt from 1637 and *Kapellmeister* in Hanau from 1642. He published some psalms and sacred songs, but his most important work is the 2-volume *Studentengärtlein* (1605, 1613) which initiated a tradition of simple strophic secular songs for students.

Studentengärtlein in *EDM* xxix

Jehan Bodel (b. ?1165; d. Beaurain, Feb x Mar 1210) Troubadour from Provence, who lived and worked in Arras. His extant works include the text of a *Jeu de St Nicolas*, possibly to be sung to existing tunes, which ends with a Te Deum; 5 *pastourelles* for which music does survive, and a fine 'congés' in which he says farewell to home and friends when leaving to minister to lepers in a hospital.

Jehan Bretel (b. c1210; d. 1272) Trouvère. The son of an artisan whose family had been in Arras from 1170, he was one of the most famous members of the Confrérie des Jongleurs d'Arras and was chosen as 'Prince du Pui d'Arras'. One of the most prolific writers of JEU-PARTIS, he left some 90 of these, as well as 7 songs for which no melodies survive.

Jehan Erart (b. c1205; d. 1258x9) Trouvère, connected with Arras. Almost all of his 25 poems, for which music survives, were widely disseminated in MS.

CE: *Songs* (*CMM* 67), ed. T. Newcombe (Rome, 1975)

Jehannot de l'Escurel (d. Paris, 1303) French poet and composer. Worked in Paris, where he was executed for an unknown offence. All but one of his 34 surviving pieces are monophonic; the exception is *À vous douce debonaire*, a 3-part *rondeau* in conductus style after Adam de la Halle which closely resembles some of the music of the ROMAN DE FAUVEL, whose source is the same manuscript. His monophonic pieces, found in an alphabetically arranged but incomplete songbook, follow the ideas of PETRUS DE CRUCE as to melody and notation, and use the *formes fixes* of *rondeau, virelai* and *ballade*, showing that these were well established by c1300.

Jenkins, John (b. Maidstone, 1592; d. Kimberley, Norfolk, 27 Oct 1678) English composer. An able player of the viol and lute, he served at the courts of King Charles I and King Charles II, and in the 1660s was house tutor to Lord North and later to Sir Philip Wodehouse at Kimberley in Norfolk. Though he wrote some songs, catches and vocal pieces for the theatre, his reputation rests on his consort music – over 100 fantasias à 2–6, 2 In nomines and many suites. His long life spanned a great era of English consort music, and his works show that he kept abreast of changes of taste and style, from the conventional fantasia (which in his hands reached high artistic perfection without radical innovation) to the suite and trio sonata, which included the violin as well as viols. He was at times fond of exploiting the virtuoso capabilities of violin and bass viol in brilliant divisions.
CE: *Consort Music*, ed. R. Nicholson and A. Ashbee (London, 1971–8); also in *MB* xxvi, ed. A. Ashbee, xxxix, ed. D. Peart

Jerome of Moravia (fl late C13) Bohemian priest and theorist, who taught at the Dominican priory of S. Jacques in Paris. His *Tractatus de musica*, written between 1272 and 1304, contains copies of treatises by earlier theorists (including FRANCO OF COLOGNE, whom Jerome claimed to have met). It describes notational practices going back 100 years and gives information on the performance of chant and on various musical instruments of the time.

Jeune, Claude le see **Le Jeune**

Jeu-parti A form of song popular with the troubadours and trouvères, taking the form of a dialogue between 2 poets (alternating stanzas) on some aspect of courtly love.

Jig English C16 dance. The word also refers to clowns in English comedies.

Joachim a Burck see **Burck**

João (John) IV (b. Villa Viçosa, 19 Mar 1604; d. Lisbon, 6 Nov 1656) King of Portugal (from 1640). Though the well-known motets ascribed to him may not in fact be his work, he was a well-trained musician, writing a defence of modern music and collecting a huge library (destroyed in the Lisbon earthquake of 1755) of music by all the leading late C16 and early C17 composers.

Jobst von Brandt see **Brandt**

Johannes de Alte Curie see **Haucourt**

Johannes de Grocheo Theorist working in Paris around 1300. His treatise *De musica* is a wide-ranging study of music from the standpoint of physics, according to the Greek and Arabic traditions, rather than mathematics. In it he classified musical genres and described certain current forms (*rondeau*, *estampie*, *ductia*).

Johannes de Limburgia (fl. 1408–30) Franco-Flemish composer. Worked at churches in Liège in 1408–19, was succentor at S. Jean l'Evangeliste there in 1426, and in Italy c1430, perhaps in Venice, or Vicenza and/or Padua, for which cities he wrote motets. Like Arnold and Hugo de Lantins he stands out among his contemporaries by virtue of the large number of his surviving works – about 50, including a Mass Ordinary in the Trent Codices.

Johannes (Jean) de Muris (b. diocese of Lisieux, c1295; d. ?Paris, after 1351)

French theorist and teacher at the Sorbonne; a colleague of Philippe de Vitry and writer of many theoretical works including the *Ars nove musice*.

Johannes de Sarto   C15 Franco-Flemish composer. Originally a priest from Liège, he became a member of the Papal choir in Rome. His motet *O quam amabilis* stands comparison with the works of Dunstable and Dufay, and his ornamental writing for upper voices recalls the style of the former.

John of Afflighem   ?Flemish monk of English origin, active in the early C12. His treatise *De arte musica* (*c*1100–21) is one of the theoretical sources which deals with organum and early polyphony.

John IV of Portugal see **João IV**

Johnson, Edward (fl. 1592–4) English composer. In the service of Sir Thomas Kytson of Hengrave Hall in the 1570s, and may have provided music for the Queen's visit to Lord Hertford in 1591; took the Cambridge B.Mus. degree in 1594. He contributed to East's psalter and the *Triumphs of Oriana*, and 3 keyboard pieces by him are in the Fitzwilliam Virginal Book.

Johnson, John (b. *c*1540; d. London, 1595)   English lutenist and composer; lutenist to Elizabeth I from 1581 until his death. Some of his music survives in MS at Cambridge.

Johnson, Robert 1 (b. Duns, *c*1470; d. 1554)   Scotch composer and priest. Accused of heresy, he fled to England before the Reformation and may have been a chaplain to Anne Boleyn, possibly setting her lament 'Defyled is my name'. He wrote Latin church music in both old-fashioned and modern imitative styles, and also some early Anglican music. He is represented in the Mulliner Book.

Johnson, Robert 2 (b. ?*c*1582; d. London, 1633)   English lutenist and composer. A royal lutenist from 1604, he composed instrumental music for masques, and songs in dramatic style for plays by Shakespeare and others produced by the King's Men. He is represented in Leighton's *Teares* and Simpson's and Brade's consort anthologies.

CE: *Complete Works for Solo Lute*, ed. A. Sundermann (London, 1972); Ayres in *EL* 2nd ser., xvii

Jones, Robert 1 (fl. 1530) English composer; member of Henry VIII's chapel. He contributed a Mass and Magnificat to the Peterhouse partbooks, and songs to Wynkyn de Worde's songbook of 1530.

Jones, Robert 2 (b. *c*1577; d. after 1615)   English lutenist and composer; ran a school in London, and in 1610 collaborated with Rosseter to present plays at the Whitefriars theatre. He published 5 volumes of simple and melodious lute songs, and one of madrigals, and contributed to the *Triumphs of Oriana* and Leighton's *Teares*.

Ayres in *EL* 2nd ser., iv–vi, xiv–xv; Madrigals in *EM* xxxv[a]

Jongleur   Early medieval variety entertainer, skilled in dancing, acrobatics and juggling as well as music, who would display his accomplishments to paying audiences on any social level. When both highly talented and lucky enough to serve the nobility he could attain the distinctive social standing and repute of the minstrel.

Josquin Desprez (Des Pres) (b. S. Quentin, *c*1440; d. Condé, 27 Aug 1521)   Franco-Flemish composer. He was a singer at Milan cathedral from 1459 to 1474, and in the latter year sang in the private chapel of the Sforza family. Between 1476 and 1479 he was in the service of Cardinal Ascanio Sforza, whom he accompanied to Rome. He sang in the Papal chapel choir in Rome from 1486–99, and directed music at the Este court in Ferrara in 1503–4. His later years were spent back in his homeland as prebendary of Cambrai, and resident provost of the chapter at Condé. Before 1515 he seems also to have had some connection with the French court of Louis XII.

Josquin's output consists of about 20 Masses, 100 motets and 75 secular pieces; it stands out even above that of his very distinguished generation and marks him as the central figure of the High Renaissance. One factor in the spread of his fame and influence was the rise of music printing; the Venetian printer Petrucci was the first to disseminate his Masses. These represent his more conservative side; they show his superb craftsmanship and illustrate the various compositional methods of his day, especially the emergence of the parody and paraphrase Mass styles. They culminate in the beautiful *Missa Pange lingua* based on the plainsong hymn of that name, whose utterance becomes distinctly plangent at the closing 'dona nobis pacem'. It is this expression of mood that is foremost in Josquin's motets, which are among the first to attempt to convey in music the inner meaning of the words; thus he often selected texts with expressive possibilities. His style reflects formal balance and symmetry of articulation in its use of the device of pervading imitation, which Josquin standardized, and of sequence. Structural procedures like canon and ostinato occur in his motets, as indeed in the secular works, but they are always most artfully concealed. In chansons, Josquin freed the music from the old FORMES FIXES, enabling it to express a much greater variety of mood than ever before through new methods and textures.

CE: *Werken*, ed. A. Smijers and others (Amsterdam, 1922–69)

Judenkünig, Hans (b. Schwäbisch Gmünd, 1455x60; d. Vienna, 4 Mar 1526) German virtuoso lutenist, who may have invented the peculiarly complex tablature used in early German lute books. His tablature book of 1515 is the first German publication for lute, and his *Underweisung* of 1523 contains dances and preludes in a pseudo-polyphonic style, many based on popular tunes.

Lute works in *DTO* xxxvii

K

Kapsberger, Johannes Hieronymus
(b. *c*1575; d. Rome, *c*1661) German
lutenist and composer. He had the reputation of a virtuoso performer on
lute, theorbo and chitarrone, and was
working in Venice in 1604 and Rome in
1610, where he was in favour at the
Papal court. He published music for
lute and chitarrone, villanellas, madrigals, *arie passeggiate* (i.e. with diminutions), motets in the modern style,
double-choir church music, and dances.
He also composed dramatic music and
an oratorio.

Kerle, Jacobus de (b. Ypres, 1531x32;
d. Prague, 7 Jan 1591) Franco-
Flemish composer. From 1555 he was
in Italy, in a church post at Orvieto;
from 1562 he served the Archbishop of
Augsburg in Rome during the closing
stages of the Council of Trent. He was
active at Ypres in 1565–7, but then took
over the choir of Augsburg cathedral,
moving on to a Benedictine abbey in
Kempten in 1575. Again he returned to
Flanders, as canon of Cambrai in 1579,
but he went back to Germany in 1582 as
choirmaster to the Elector of Köln; later
that year he took up his last post, as an
Imperial court chaplain in Prague. His
published music included 8 volumes of
motets and Vespers music and one of
Masses. The *Preces* commissioned by
the Cardinal of Augsburg in 1562 are in
a lyrical, uncomplicated Palestrinian
style and may well have influenced the
fathers of the Council of Trent not to
abandon polyphony in church music.

Selected works in *DTB* xxvi

Kirbye, George (b. ?*c*1565; d. Bury St
Edmunds, Oct 1634) English composer; lived in Suffolk in the retinue of
Sir Robert Jermyn. A contributor to
East's and Ravenscroft's psalters, he
published madrigals, many in a serious and Italianate style, in 1597. He
owned many volumes of music by his
leading Italian contemporaries.

Madrigals in *EM* xxiv, rev. edn.

Kit or **pochette** Bowed string instrument. It developed from the rebec during the C16, and was originally a small,
boat-shaped instrument; in this form it
was the *'violino piccolo alla francese'* required in Monteverdi's *Orfeo*. (In the
C17 it gradually became more like a
miniature violin in appearance, and in
the C18 was much used by dancing-
masters, continuing the rebec's association with dance music.)

Kleber, Leonhard (b. Wiesensteig bei
Göppingen, nr. Stuttgart, *c*1495; d.
Pforzheim, 4 Mar 1556) German
organist and composer. Possibly a
pupil of Hofhaimer, he studied in
Heidelberg and worked as organist
in Horb, Esslingen and (from 1521)
Pforzheim; he was a much esteemed
teacher. His MS tablature of 1524 contains his own preludes in a thoroughly
idiomatic and varied organ style, and
transcriptions of sacred and secular
pieces by composers such as Josquin,
Obrecht, Brumel and Senfl.

Kortholt Reedcap wind instrument
with cylindrical double bore. Not to be
confused with the CURTAL, it is essentially a COURTAUT or SORDUN with a
reedcap; it was something of a rarity
even in the C16. Praetorius illustrates
only the bass kortholt, but modern

makers have added 3 higher sizes to make a complete consort.

Kortholt (alto), 42 cm

Kotter, Hans (b. Strasbourg, c1480; d. Bern, 1541) German organist and composer. He studied with Hofhaimer from 1498 to 1500, was organist at the Saxon court at Torgau until 1508, and then held posts at Freiburg im Breisgau and Fribourg (Switzerland)– from whence he was expelled, after imprisonment and torture, as a Protestant in 1530. From 1534 he was a schoolmaster in Bern. His organ book, compiled between 1513 and 1522, contains the first German dances for organ, transcriptions of pieces by Hofhaimer, Josquin, Isaac and others, and 10 preludes of his own in a not entirely idiomatic style.

Kugelmann, Hans (b. ?Augsburg; d. Königsberg [Kaliningrad], late July x early Aug 1542) German composer and trumpeter. From 1518–23 he served at the Imperial court; he then went to the Prussian court at Königsberg as composer, and after plotting to secure his predecessor's dismissal, became *Kapellmeister* in 1536. He published a book of 3-part German and Latin sacred songs in 1540, intended for schools and other institutions with untrained singers.

1540 *Concentus novi* in *EDM* Sonderreihe ii

L

La Grotte, Nicolas de (b. *c*1530; d. *c*1600) French composer. From 1562 he was organist to the Duke of Anjou (later Henri III). In 1569 he published a volume of Ronsard settings in a simple and melodious homophonic style which anticipates the *air de cour*. He collaborated with Le Jeune on music for the *Balet comique de la Royne* in 1583, published a book of *airs de cour* in 1583, and also wrote some instrumental music.

La Rue, Pierre de see **Rue, Pierre de la**

Lai, leich The most extended of the medieval French poetic and musical forms developed by the trouvères and later also by the German Minnesingers, with poems of 60, 100 or even more lines arranged in irregular paired stanzas. It was the genre which survived longest as a solely monophonic composition; Machaut composed 19 extant examples.

Lambe, Walter (b. Salisbury, 1450x51) English composer. A scholar at Eton in 1467; served at St George's Chapel, Windsor, as clerk, joint and full choirmaster in 1479–84, and again as clerk from 1492-9. One of the leading composers represented in the Eton Choirbook, he composed votive antiphons which contain brilliant vocal display as well as imaginative counterpoint; his *O Maria plena gratia* is the longest work in the manuscript.

Lambert de Sayve see **Sayve**

Lamentations Settings of the Lamentations of Jeremiah sung at Matins (Tenebrae) on the Thursday, Friday

and Saturday of Holy Week in the Roman rite. In plainsong the verses and their introductory Hebrew letters are sung in a simple recitation tone. In the C15–17 they were set polyphonically, often in an elegiac (even lugubrious) style contrasting syllabic setting in the verses with flowing melismatic writing for the Hebrew letters (e.g. settings by Tallis, Whyte, Lassus and Victoria).

Lamento Mournful or elegiac music. In C17 Italian monody and opera it described a self-contained piece expressing despair at the death of a loved one; Monteverdi's *Lamento d'Arianna* (1608) was the first example.

Landi, Stefano (b. ?Rome, *c*1590; d. Rome, 28 Oct 1639) Italian composer. In early life a choirmaster at Padua, in 1624 he moved to Rome as *maestro* at S. Maria dei Monti, and joined the Papal choir in 1629. He was the first Roman opera composer and one of the creators of the baroque cantata. His works include 6 books of *arie* and 3 other secular collections, a Mass, psalms, canzonas, and 2 operas (one of which was *Il Sant'Alessio*).

Landini, Francesco (b. 1325x35; d. ?2 Sep 1397) Italian composer and organist, blind from an early age. He was organist at S. Lorenzo in Florence between 1369 and 1396, and in 1379 was paid 9 *solidi* for writing 5 motets—an extremely rare record of payment to a composer. Landini was the most celebrated musical personality of the *trecento*; his 155-odd extant works are nearly all *ballate*, in which he excelled. In these smoothness of sound rather than dissonant asperity is evident; Landini's technical prowess can be seen in the canonic madrigal *De! dimmi tu*. He was a brilliant player of several instruments, especially the portative organ, and at the same time a distinguished poet, writing some of the texts he set and being awarded poetic honours in Venice. His music not only represents about a quarter of all the Italian *trecento* music known to have survived, but is preserved in many diverse sources, from Florence and elsewhere.

Lanier (Lanière), Nicholas (bp. London, 10 Sep 1588; d. Greenwich, 24 Feb 1666) English composer, singer and painter; descendant of a French family of musicians settled in England since the mid-C16. A royal musician from 1604, he became in 1626 the first holder of the title 'Master of the King's Musick'; after the Civil War deprived him of his post he seems to have lived much abroad, until reinstated by Charles II. He provided music for court entertainments, including the 1617 masque *Lovers Made Men* – the first appearance of the Italianate *stile recitativo* in England. This is lost, but some songs and occasional pieces survive in MS.

Songs in *EL* 2nd ser., xxi; *MB* xxxiii, ed. I. Spink

Lantins, Arnold de (fl. 1428–32) Franco-Flemish composer, possibly brother or cousin of Hugo de Lantins and possibly from the Liège district. He was in Venice in 1428, and was a member of the Papal choir in Rome for a few months in 1431–2. His *Verbum incarnatum* Mass with troped Kyrie is one of the earliest cyclic Masses unified by a head motif; it is in an Italianate style with chanson-type texture. His *c*30 surviving works also include 2 fine motets using texts from the Song of Songs, and some 14 chansons, many of

which are in a melancholy vein and of great beauty. The popularity of his work is implied by its wide dissemination in MS.

Lantins, Hugo de (fl. 1420–3) Franco-Flemish composer, possibly brother or cousin of Arnold de Lantins and possibly from the Liège district. He was in Italy by 1420, when he wrote music for a wedding in the Malatesta family; he also worked in Venice in or after 1423, in Rome, and on the Adriatic coast of Italy. His chansons and motets were widely disseminated in MS; his style shows an unusually large amount of imitation, seeming to anticipate the developments of the later C15. His chansons are generally more cheerful than those of Arnold, though he too set sorrowful texts in an appropriate manner.

Lapicida, Erasmus (b. ?late C15; d. Vienna, 19 Nov 1547) Possibly a German composer. He may have been at the Heidelberg court around 1510, and later had German Lieder published by Rhaw and Forster. On the other hand Italian sources (e.g. prints by Petrucci) include frottolas and Lamentations by a composer of this name. He dedicated a motet to the King (Ferdinand I) in 1536, and in 1545 revealed to him that he was a 'poor, old, sick priest'.

Lappi, Pietro (b. Florence, *c*1575; d. Brescia, 1630) Italian composer; *maestro di cappella* at S. Maria delle Grazie, Brescia, from 1593 onwards. His output was entirely of sacred vocal music except for one book of instrumental canzonas, doubtless a token of his contacts with the flourishing Brescian school of instrumental players. Though a book of Masses (1613) contains works in both old and new styles, he tended to be rather traditional in his sacred music.

Lassus, Orlandus (b. Mons, 1532; d. Munich, 14 June 1594) Franco-Flemish composer. While a choirboy at S. Nicolas in Mons, he was twice abducted and carried abroad for the sake of his voice; the third time this happened he chose not to return and at the age of 12 entered the service of the Viceroy of Sicily. While in Italy in 1544–5 he visited Milan and Naples; in 1551 he became choirmaster at St John Lateran in Rome. In 1554 he returned to the north to supervise his first publications at Antwerp, and in 1557 he became a singer in the court chapel of Duke Albrecht V of Bavaria in Munich. Within 5 years he was appointed *Kapellmeister* there, remaining in this position for the rest of his life, though travelling widely within Germany and to Italy, France and the Netherlands. His reputation was such that in 1574 he received The Knighthood of the Golden Spur from the Pope; however, his later years at Munich were dogged by failing health and depression resulting partly from the unwholesome religious rigours imposed upon the court by the Jesuits.

Lassus enjoyed great fame and influence from very early in his career, but even more remarkable were his sheer industry and his cosmopolitanism; his vast output covered practically every type of vocal music that existed in C16 Europe. His secular music comprises some 200 Italian madrigals and villanellas, 146 French chansons and 93 German Lieder; though he did not speak these 3 languages equally fluently, his letters often contain a hilarious mixture of them, and of Latin too (some of his Latin motets are in fact secular–drinking songs and the like). His sacred works are much more numerous: up to 70 Masses, over 500 motets, 100 Magnificats and many other liturgical works (Passions, hymns, Nunc dimittis settings, Office music). Despite the bold chromaticism

of some early works, Lassus was never a radical. His sacred music is characterised by a flawless contrapuntal technique and feeling for sonority, and above all by a concern for the declamation of the words in a rhetorical manner with sharply contrasted musical figures. His tremendous musical range encompassed at one end the expressive profundity of the 7 *Penitential Psalms* and at the other the racy wit and humour of light chansons and villanellas.

CE: *Sämtliche Werke*, ed. F. X. Haberl and A. Sandberger (Leipzig, 1914–27, repr. 1968–   ); *Neue Reihe*, ed. S. Hermelink and others (Kassel, 1956–   )

Lauda Italian vernacular devotional hymn in popular religious life. The C13 monophonic *laude* were sung by Franciscans and Franciscan communities. In the C14 and C15 many religious poems, written to be sung to secular song melodies, were called *laude*. In the C16 a vast repertory of polyphonic *laude* developed, using a chordal style derived from the FROTTOLA or VILLANELLA; such pieces were sung at the prayer meetings of the Oratorians.

Lawes, Henry (b. Dinton, Wiltshire, 5 Jan 1596; d. London, 21 Oct 1662) English composer, perhaps a pupil of Coprario. Joined the service of the Chapel Royal in 1626, and also held a court post which as a Royalist he lost during the Commonwealth. He was the most prolific song composer in England at that time (he left over 430 songs), sensitive to the feeling and diction of the poems he set. His best songs were of the serious and declamatory type, in an expressionistic rather than melodious style. His masque music is important; at Milton's request he wrote music for *Comus*, performed at Ludlow Castle in July 1634; he also acted in it. He wrote music for plays by Herrick and Cartwright, and also 2 books of psalms for private devotions.

Songs in *MB* xxxiii, ed. I. Spink

Lawes, William (bp. Salisbury, 1 May 1602; d. Chester, 1645) English composer; brother of Henry Lawes and a pupil of Coprario. Played in Charles I's private chamber music and fell in the Civil War while fighting on the Royalist side. Like his brother he wrote songs and some theatrical music, though he is much more notable as a consort composer; in this field his output includes 'Royal consorts', ayres for viol and organ, some impressive suites for up to 6 viols and organ, trio sonatas, and – uniquely – harp consorts, which also contain brilliant writing for the division viol. Lawes' style was highly individual, rich in unpredictable melody and colourful harmony.

Consort pieces in *MB* xxi, ed. M. Lefkowitz

Layolle, François de (b. ?Florence, 4 Mar 1492; d. ?Lyons, c1540) French composer. Brought up in Florence; a pupil of Bartolomeo degli Organi, and worked as a singer and organist at the church of SS. Annunziata until 1518. By 1521 he had settled as organist at the Florentine church in Lyons, but his madrigals are distinctively Italian in style. He also wrote church music; his work was published in Moderne's anthologies.

Le Bel, Firmin (b. Noyon, Picardy; d. Rome, 27 x 30 Dec 1573) French composer. In 1540 he was *maestro di cappella* at S. Maria Maggiore in Rome and probably taught Palestrina there; *maestro* at S. Luigi dei Francesi from 1545–61, and subsequently a Papal singer until 1565. Only a little sacred music by him survives.

Le Cocq (Gallus), Jean (fl. 1514–43) Franco-Flemish composer. Prob-

ably a Papal singer in 1514, he accompanied Willaert to the Ferrara court in 1522 and was *maestro di cappella* there until 1541. He published motets and a collection of madrigals (including works by other composers), and his chansons, in a motet-like style, appeared in anthologies.

Le Heurteur, Guillaume (fl. 1530–45) French composer. In 1545 he was choirmaster and canon at S. Martin in Tours. He published a volume of motets (now lost); his motets, Masses, and chansons (in some of which he pokes fun at his clerical colleagues) appeared in anthologies from 1530 onwards.

Le Jeune, Claude (b. Valenciennes, 1528x30; bd. Paris, 28 July 1600) French composer. Connected with Huguenot circles in Paris in the 1560s; master of the children at the court of François d'Anjou in 1582, and by 1596 had been raised to the position of royal chamber composer. He was the main writer of chansons in MUSIQUE MESURÉE according to the poet Baïf's theories, and was second only to Goudimel as a composer of vernacular psalm collections.

Works in *MMRF*, xi–xiv, xvi, xx–xxii

Le Maistre, Mattheus (b. Roclenge-sur-Geer, nr. Liège, c1505; d. Dresden, before Apr 1577) Franco-Flemish composer. Court *Kapellmeister* at Dresden from 1554 to 1568, and published sacred and secular songs and Protestant church music. Hermann Finck thought him one of the best composers of the time, but his style remained generally conservative. He may have been the 'Mathess Nidlender' who was working at the Munich court in 1552.

Le Petit, Ninot Early C16 French composer. His chansons provide a link between the old cantus firmus and new Parisian styles; he may be the Le Petit who appears in various Petrucci anthologies.

Le Roy, Adrien (b. Montreuil-sur-Mer, nr. Étaples, c1520; d. Paris, 1598) French publisher and lutenist. From 1551 he ran the firm of Le Roy and Ballard in partnership with his brother-in-law Robert Ballard, whose productions included many volumes of chansons and *airs de cour*. Le Roy had great skill in arranging vocal music for the lute, and his *Instruction . . .* (reprinted 1574) describes how to do this, using Lassus' chansons as examples, as well as giving instruction in playing.

Lute music in *CLF* i–iii

Le Vinier see **Guillaume** or **Gilles le Vinier**

Lebertoul, François Early C15 French composer, associated with Cambrai; his 5 surviving pieces–a Latin *ballade* and 4 French chansons–are found in an Oxford MS.

CE: in *CMM* 11/ii, ed. G. Reaney

Lechner, Leonard (b. Etsental, S. Tyrol [Alto Adige], c1553; d. Stuttgart, 9 Sep 1606) German composer of Austrian origin. Till 1570 he was a choirboy at the court chapels of Munich and Landshut under Lassus and Ivo de Vento. Born a Catholic, he was converted to Protestantism in early manhood and settled in Nürnberg, where he wrote many German songbooks for school use. In 1584 he directed music at the Hohenzollern court at Hechingen, but soon fled to Tübingen after quarrels (probably religious). In 1595 he joined the Stuttgart court as a singer and, though in failing health, later became *Kapellmeister*.

The Austrian Lechner was Lassus' most distinguished pupil and a great creative force in German music. He published 7 books of German Lieder

(160 in all) and 5 of church music–motets, Masses, Magnificats and Pentitential Psalms; his many works in manuscript include a St John Passion. While his Latin polyphony is traditional in style, the German songs fuse the Italianate villanella with refrain forms. Some of the later ones have religious texts; their music is among the finest written to any German religious words during the C16, and combines fervour with intense madrigalian expression. Lechner's St John Passion (1594), in 4-part polyphony throughout, is equally impressive, with dramatic touches despite the undifferentiated musical texture.

CE: *Sämtliche Werke*, ed. K. Ameln (Kassel, 1954–)

Legrant, Guillaume (fl. 1419–46) French composer. He was a Papal singer in 1419, and was working in Rouen in 1446. His Mass movements, composed in the 1420s, are among the earliest compositions to distinguish between solo and choral vocal sections; they use a highly distinctive chromatic manner which did not find favour with other composers. His chansons are in a plain and straightforward Burgundian style.

CE: in *CMM* 11/ii, ed. G. Reaney

Legrant, Johannes Early C15 French composer, of whose life nothing is known. Three of his Mass movements and 5 chansons, including the especially vivacious *Entre vous*, survive.

CE: in *CMM* 11/ii, ed. G. Reaney

Leich see **Lai**

Leighton, Sir William (b. Shropshire, c1560; d. before 1617) English poet and composer. A Gentleman Pensioner of Elizabeth I and James I, he published 2 volumes of poetry but is best known for the *Teares and Lamentations of a Sorrowful Soule* (1614), a collection of 54 psalms and hymns for 4 or 5 voices, some with lute, which he compiled while in prison for debt. Eight of the pieces are by Leighton himself; the rest are the work of leading English composers of the day, such as Byrd and Wilbye.

Teares in *EECM* xi, ed. C. Hill

Lemlin, Laurentius (b. Eichstätt, *c*1495; d. ?1549) German composer. Studied at Heidelberg, and was a singer and later *Kapellmeister* at the court chapel there. He taught Forster, who included many of Lemlin's songs in his collections, and also Jobst von Brandt, Othmayr and Zirler; his motets also appeared in anthologies.

Leonin Late C12 French composer, probably Precentor of Notre Dame in Paris. He was probably the composer who developed the contrast between melismatic writing and discant in 2-part *organa* for Graduals and Alleluias, and in processional Office responsories, often proceeding from one style to the other. (In *organum* the plainsong tenor is unmeasured, in discant measured.) The sustained tenor of the *organum* sections supports brilliant runs and melodic sequences, while in the discant sections the long-short rhythms of the duplum (upper voice) over each note of the tenor give a dance-like lilt. Though his settings are also impressive in their length, they are nevertheless shorter than those of Perotin, of whom Leonin was a precursor.

Leopolita see **Lwówczyk**

L'Estocart, Pascal de (b. Noyon, Picardy, before 1540) French composer. A prizewinner at the Évreux composition contest in 1584, he travelled much in Italy and Switzerland, worked briefly at the ducal court in Nancy, and was in the service of the Abbot of Valmont. He set both Protestant and Catholic translations of the psalms, and also published motets and sacred chansons; his style is strongly influenced by the Italian madrigal.

Sacred chansons in *MMRF* x–xi

L'Héritier, Jean (b. prob. *c*1480; d. after 1541) French composer. *Maestro di cappella* at S. Luigi dei Francesi in Rome in 1522, and director of music to the Cardinal de Vermont at Avignon in 1540–1. His church music and chansons appeared in anthologies from 1519 onwards; one Mass of his was included in Lassus' 1588 collection.

CE: *Opera omnia* (*CMM* 48), ed. L. Perkins (Rome, 1969)

L'homme armé C15 popular song used as a cantus firmus in polyphonic Masses from Dufay to Palestrina and beyond.

L'homme armé

Liebert (Libert), Reginaldus Early C15 Franco-Flemish composer, who may have been choirmaster at Cambrai cathedral in 1424. His most important work is a Lady-Mass for the period between the Purification and Easter, which includes Proper as well as Ordinary and in some movements sets the correct plainsong in the top part in a decorated style. He also wrote 2 chansons, including the melancholy *Mourir me voy*.

CE: in *CMM* 11/ii, ed. G. Reaney

Limburgia see **Johannes de Limburgia**

Lira da braccio Bowed string instrument. It developed a separate identity from the fiddle in the late C15 and was similar in size to the modern viola, with 7 strings, 2 being drones off the fingerboard. Primarily a chordal instrument, it was much favoured in early C16 court circles, especially for improvising polyphonic accompaniments to the player's own singing; there were virtuoso players at Ferrara and Milan.

Lirone, lira da gamba Bowed string instrument, result of cross between lira da braccio and bass viol. It had an ornamental outline, broad neck and flattish bridge, with between 9 and 14 stopped strings and a number of drone strings as well. Most common in Italy between about 1550 and 1650, it could play 4–6 note chords in accompaniments, and for solos it also employed chordal technique. Alessandro Striggio 1 was famed for his amazing virtuosity on this instrument.

Liturgical drama Early medieval plays representing Biblical stories which were added to the official liturgy. They developed from simple question-and-answer dialogues sung before the Introit at Mass on certain great feasts (e.g. the C10 *Quem quaeritis* Easter trope), or from the dramatic chanting of the Passion, and came to include action and scenic representation, as in the C12 *Play of Herod*, sung at the end of Matins. The musical element consisted of chant, possibly with improvised counterpoint and instrumental participation.

Lizard see **Cornett**

Lloyd, John (b. ?c1480; d. London, 3 Apr 1523) Welsh composer and priest. A priest at the Chapel Royal in 1505, he served the parish of Munslow (Salop) for some years before accompanying Henry VIII to the Field of the Cloth of Gold in 1520, and then making a pilgrimage to the Holy Land. His *O quam suavis* Mass is based on a very long chant, and the arrangement of notes in the tenor can only be determined by solving some complex numerical puzzles.

Lobo, Alonso (b. Borja, nr. Saragossa, *c*1555; d. Seville, 5 Apr 1617) Spanish composer. *Maestro de capilla* at Toledo cathedral from 1593 and Seville cathedral from 1603. He published a volume of Masses and motets in a Palestrinian style in 1602, and left more church music in MS.

Lôbo, Duarte (bp. Alcáçovas, nr. Evora, 19 Sep 1565; d. Lisbon, 24 Sep 1646) Portuguese composer. Studied in Evora and was *maestro de capilla* at the Portuguese court from at least 1594 to 1639. One of Portugal's best polyphonists, he had an international reputation, publishing several volumes of church music at Antwerp. His style has features in common with that of Victoria, but is less intense.

Sacred works in *Composicoes polifónicas*, ed. M. Joaquim (Lisbon, 1945)

Lochamer Liederbuch A German MS song collection of *c*1452–60 copied in or near Nürnberg and containing mostly monophonic Lieder (though some are polyphonic). The MS also contains Paumann's *Fundamentum Organisandi*.

CE: *DTB* new ser., Sonderband ii, ed. W. Salmen

Longaval, Antoine de (Jean à la Venture) (b. ?Longueval, Somme; d. after 1523) Franco-Flemish composer. A singer at the French court from 1507, he was *maître de chapelle* there from 1517 to 1523. Petrucci published some of his motets in 1519, and a Passion attributed to him survives in MS at Rome. It is polyphonic throughout, based on chant formulas used in Holy Week, and is one of the first through-composed Passions, though setting not one complete Gospel narrative but extracts from all 4 Gospels.

Longnecked lute see **Lute**

Loqueville, Richard de (d. Cambrai, before 25 June 1418) Franco-Flemish composer. He served Duc Robert de Bar as a harp player (1407–10), then becoming master of the boys at Cambrai cathedral, where he remained until his death and was presumably the teacher of Dufay. His Mass movements, which do not use plainchant, are among the earliest compositions since *organum* to make a distinction between choral and solo polyphony and are stylistically very similar to the early Masses by Dufay. His chansons are good examples of the simple style favoured by those early C15 composers who rejected the complexities of the Avignon school.
CE: in *CMM* 11/iii, ed. G. Reaney

Lorenzo da Firenze (d. before 1385) Italian composer; worked as a music teacher at various Florentine churches 1350–70. The authors he drew on for the texts of his secular pieces include Boccaccio; his secular output includes 5 *ballate*, a lively *caccia* (*A poste messe*), and ten 2-part madrigals, of which *Da da a chi avareggia* is very florid with virtuoso ornamentation and much use of imitation. One Sanctus also survives.
CE: in *CMM* 8/iii, ed. N. Pirrotta; *PMFC* vii, ed. W. T. Marrocco

Lublina, Ján z (fl. 1537–48) Polish organist. A monk at Kraśnik, near Lublin, he compiled a very large and important organ tablature, which is the principal source for early C16 Polish music; it also contains an introduction giving rules for composition.
CE: *CEKM* 6, ed. J. White

Ludford, Nicholas (b. *c*1485; d. London, *c*1557) English composer. At its dissolution in 1547, he was a musician at St Stephen's, Westminster (he was described as a verger, a post with musical duties), and was in receipt of a pension till about 1556. His output includes 7 festal Masses and 7 'Lady Masses' (one for each weekday), together with a Magnificat and some votive antiphons. The short Lady Masses contain parts of the Proper of the Mass and are a rare example of 3-part writing in Tudor polyphony, while Ludford's more florid writing is nevertheless restrained by comparison with some earlier masters.
CE: *Collected works* (*CMM* 27), ed. J. Bergsagel (Rome, 1963–   )

Lupi (Leleu), Johannes (b. Cambrai, *c*1506; d. Cambrai, 20 Dec 1539) Franco-Flemish composer. He was a choirboy at Cambrai cathedral, a singer there from 1526, and choirmaster from the following year, though his tenure was beset by difficulties and illness. He issued a volume of motets *à 4–8* and further motets, 3 Masses and 26 chansons in anthologies. His chansons are often in a serious contrapuntal idiom, though with clear cadences and short phrase-lengths.

Lupi Second, Didier (d. ?Lyons, after 1559) French composer, not identical with any composer called Lupus. Lived in Lyons, and published sacred and secular chansons (Lassus' very popular *Susanne un jour* is based on his chanson of the same name) and French psalm settings.

Lupo, Thomas (fl. 1610) English composer. It is not certain which of 2 composers called Thomas Lupo, both in court service in the early C17 and dying respectively in 1628 and before 1660, is the composer of a corpus of some 80 viol consorts. These include fantasias and In nomines, some having virtuoso writing for bass viol; a number were published at Amsterdam. A Thomas Lupo also composed some anthems, motets and songs.

Lute Plucked string instrument with gut strings and frets, round back and pear-shaped body. Of great antiquity, the lute came to Europe from the East. In the earlier Middle Ages it had 4 or 5 strings and was used for solo lines in ensembles, played with a plectrum. By the later C15 a lute with 6 double courses of strings was in use, and an idiomatic style of playing with the fingers was developing; Tinctoris (1487) refers to some of the earlier virtuoso lutenists, such as PIETROBONO. In the Renaissance it was the most highly regarded instrument of all; played now only with the fingers, it developed a brilliant technique and was capable of great delicacy of expression. Famous virtuoso lutenists abounded throughout the C16, and the instrument acquired a huge repertory of solos, both original and transcribed from vocal pieces, accompaniments and parts in consorts–beginning with SPINACINO's tablature of 1507. The greatest composers of lute music were Francesco da Milano, Albert de Rippe and John Dowland. A typical C16 lute was very lightly constructed and had 6 courses of strings tuned upwards from G, but 7 or 8 courses gradually became common. Its functions were gradually usurped by the keyboard during the C17.

Related instruments included:

Angélique ARCHLUTE with long neck, 16 or 17 single gut strings, and 2 pegboxes. Its diatonic tuning supposedly made it easy for amateurs, but Praetorius did not regard it as a serious instrument.

Colascione European development of the longnecked lute; its very long neck had 24 movable frets, and

there were 3 courses of metal strings. Its body might be made partly of parchment.

Longnecked lute Medieval instrument with strong Moorish associations (it may be the instrument called 'guiterre moreche'). It had a long neck and small body with a movable bridge; according to Tinctoris its 3 strings produced an unsatisfactory sound.

Pandurina Small-sized MANDORA with 4 or 5 strings tuned upwards from g, played with fingers or plectrum and used especially in France.

Lute song C16/17 song for voice and lute, especially in England (see AYRE). The lute part was fully realized in tablature; English lute songs sometimes had 1 or 2 additional *obbligato* parts (e.g. for bass viol, treble viol).

Luyton, Charles (b. Antwerp, c1556; d. Prague, Aug 1620) Flemish composer and organist. Served the Imperial court from 1566 until his retirement in 1611 as chorister, organist and (from 1603, in succession to Monte) court composer. A pupil of Vaet and Monte, he published church music, including some very succinct Masses, and madrigals in a conservative style; his *Fuga suavissima* for organ is more adventurous in its approach to modulation. He is said to have owned an archicembalo, a keyboard instrument described by Praetorius with 77 keys in 4 octaves, giving separate keys, for example, for F sharp and G flat.

Luzzaschi, Luzzasco (b. Ferrara, c1545; d. Ferrara, 11 Sep 1607) Italian composer. A pupil of Rore in Ferrara, he served at the court chapel there from 1567, becoming organist by 1576 and also being employed at the Accademia della Morte and (possibly) the cathedral. He was Frescobaldi's teacher, and published 8 books of madrigals without accompaniment, one with accompaniment, and one book of motets. Even in quite early madrigals he expressed himself in an individual, chromatic idiom that anticipated Gesualdo, but his most important works were the *Madrigali per cantare et sonare* of 1601, brilliantly written for 3 voices and (written-out) keyboard accompaniment – the earliest example of this texture in madrigals though firmly in the tradition of virtuoso professional court music.

1601 madrigals in *MMI* 2nd ser., ii, ed. A. Cavicchi

Lwówczyk, Marcin (Leopolita, Martinus) (b. Lwów, ?c1530; d. Lwów, ?1589) Polish composer, possibly a pupil of S. z Felsztyna. Organist and composer at the Kraków court from c1560 until 1564; greatly esteemed in his own day, but little of his church music now survives. His 5-part *Missa Paschalis* is the earliest surviving complete setting of the Ordinary by a Polish composer; it is based on 4 traditional Polish Easter songs, and its style has much in common with Gombert's.

Lyra viol Method of playing solos on an ordinary bass viol, rather than an instrument in its own right, though a few specially small lyra viols, occasionally with extra sympathetic strings, did exist. The repertory, read from tablature, developed after 1600 and exploited all the viol's technical possibilities, such as double- and triple-stopping and pizzicato. Many different tunings were used to facilitate this.

Lyre Plucked string instrument inherited from classical antiquity and used by Anglo-Saxon minstrels and their Continental contemporaries. The early medieval lyre had 2 arms leading from the soundbox and joined by a yoke, and about 6 or 7 strings running from pegs on the yoke to a tailpiece at the base. In the later Middle Ages it was superseded by the more versatile harp and crowd.

Lyre, 73 cm

M

Machaut, Guillaume de (b. ?Machaut, Ardennes, c1300; d. Rheims, Apr 1377) French composer and poet. Born of a noble family in the Champagne region, he became a priest and in 1323 secretary to the King of Bohemia. From 1330 he had many benefices in France and from 1340 his principal residence was Rheims; by 1349 he was in the service of the King of Navarre, and his works show that he had many royal connections. He was briefly in the employ of the King of Cyprus after 1364 and also had connections with the court of Savoy. In the early 1360s he had a one-sided love affair with a young girl called Péronne, which he chronicled in the lyrical poetry of *Le livre du Voir Dit*.

Machaut was the supreme master of the French *ars nova* and among the great composers of any period. His few religious works include the celebrated Mass and 2 motets with liturgical connections; the remainder of his output is secular—21 motets and nearly 120 compositions based on the secular song forms (*lai, virelai, rondeau* and *ballade*). The *lais* are lengthy and mainly monophonic; the *virelais* are largely monophonic too (in this respect Machaut shows himself wedded to the trouvère tradition); the *rondeaux* and *ballades*, however, are almost all polyphonic, in 2, 3 or occasionally 4 parts, often best performed by one voice with instruments. Nearly all the motets are based on isorhythmic tenors drawn from plainsong melodies or secular songs, but Machaut's structural skill is matched by melodic sensitivity. The Mass, the earliest complete polyphonic setting of the Ordinary by one composer, is an important landmark in medieval music; entitled *La Messe de Nostre Dame*, it may have been intended for Rheims cathedral, which was dedicated to Our Lady, or simply as a votive Mass in her honour. It is not a unified work; the Gloria and Credo are in conductus style, whereas the other sections are built on isorhythmic tenors taken from plainsong Mass chants.

CE: *Musikalische Werke*, ed. F. Ludwig (Leipzig, 1926; repr. 1954); *PMFC* ii, iii, ed. L. Schrade

Macque, Jean de (b. Valenciennes, c1550; d. Naples, Sep 1614) French composer. A pupil of Monte at the Imperial court in Vienna, he spent much of his life in Italy, in Rome from 1568 and in Naples from 1586. There he served the Prince of Venosa (Gesualdo's father), was organist at SS. Annunziata in 1590, and from 1594 served the royal chapel as organist and later director of music. He wrote 14 volumes of madrigals and *madrigaletti*, one of motets, and a quantity of keyboard music; this last combined a boldness of modulation (as in *Consonanze stravaganti*) with contrapuntal resource from his northern training in ingenious toccata and canzona movements. He was the most outstanding of those Flemish madrigalists who worked in southern Italy.

Madrigal The term covers 2 separate types of Italian secular vocal music. In the C14 it refers to settings of poems with stanzas of 8–11 lines and a distinctive rhyme scheme. In the C16 the madrigal was a setting of any more or less serious non-strophic poem involving deliberate musical attention to individual words and to the overall rhetorical effect. The genre lasted from about 1520 well into the C17; the English madrigal, modelled on the Italian type, belongs to a much shorter period c1590–1620.

Madrigal comedy A madrigal cycle or complete *commedia* set to polyphonic vocal music in the later C16, in which characters are represented not by solo voices but by groups. It grew out of the madrigal-singing tradition of the ACCADEMIE and was for private rather than public entertainment. Orazio Vecchi and Banchieri are the chief exponents.

Madrigaletto Playful type of light madrigal of the middle and late C16, in up to 4 parts. Like the CANZONETTA, it stands between the madrigal and villanella.

Maestro Piero see **Piero da Firenze**

Magnificat The canticle of the Virgin Mary, sung in Catholic rites at the Office of Vespers to one of the 8 psalm tones. Polyphonic settings from the C15 onwards kept the association with plainsong modality and were usually for ALTERNATIM performance (though Lassus and others wrote parody Magnificats in the same way as parody Masses). In English translation, the Magnificat became part of Evening Prayer in the Anglican church.

Mahu, Stephan (b. ?1480–90; d. after 1541) Austrian composer. Served King Ferdinand I from 1528 as a sackbut player and from 1532 as vice-*Kapellmeister*. Some of his secular songs and church music appeared in anthologies from 1526 onwards; the fact that some of these were published by Rhaw suggests that though employed at a rigidly Catholic court he had Protestant sympathies. Other works survive in MS.

Maillard, Jean (fl. 1538–57) French composer, of whose life nothing certain is known. He may have lived in Paris. He published volumes of Masses and motets, and many motets and chansons appeared in anthologies. His Mass *Je suis desheritée* uses its model (a chanson by Cadéac) unchanged as the final Agnus Dei, with both original and liturgical texts underlaid. Palestrina based a Mass on his motet *Eripe me*.

Mainerio, Don Giorgio (b. Parma, ?c1545; d. Aquileia, nr. Monfalcone, 4 May 1582) Italian composer. A singer at Udine cathedral until 1570 and then at Aquileia cathedral, becoming *maestro di cappella* there in 1578. His *Primo libro di balli* of 1578 is one of the few Italian dance collections of the period; it contains embryonic suites consisting of pairs of *passamezzo antico* and *moderno*, with variations on each. He also published some church music.

Dances in *MD* v, ed. M. Schuler

Maio, Giovan Thomaso (di) (d. Naples, Jan 1563) Italian composer. He worked in Naples and was a leading exponent of the villanella style, publishing an important collection of very simple 3-part *canzone villanesche* in 1546.

Maistre Jhan (real name **Jean le Mi(s)tre**) (fl. 1512–41) French composer. Sang in Alfonso d'Este's chapel at Ferrara from 1512 and ultimately became director of music to Ercole II d'Este in 1541. (He is not to be confused with Jean le Cocq, another French singer, nor with Nasco or Gero.)

Malbeque, Guillaume (fl. 1431–60) Franco-Flemish composer. Sang in the

Papal choir in Rome from 1431 to 1438, and thereafter was a cleric at Soignies until at least 1460. He composed a small number of chansons.

CE: in *CMM* 11/ii, ed. G. Reaney

Malvezzi, Cristofano (b. Lucca, 28 June 1547; d. Florence, 22 Jan 1599) Italian composer. Canon at S. Lorenzo in Florence from 1571, and became *maestro di cappella* to the Medici choir there by 1577 (Peri was among his pupils). He published madrigals and ricercars, and contributed music to the *intermedi* performed at weddings in 1579, 1585 and 1589. In 1591 he published the music for the wedding of 1589, with a detailed description of the festivities.

Manchicourt, Pierre de (b. Béthune, c1510; d. Madrid, before end Jan 1562) Franco-Flemish composer. A singer at Arras cathedral in youth and canon there much later, he held church posts in Tournai (1539–45) and at Notre Dame, Antwerp (1557). In 1561 he took over the Flemish choir of Philip II in Madrid, bringing boy choristers from the Low Countries. Highly regarded in his day, he published 2 books of motets, one of chansons and a Mass, but further pieces were widely disseminated in anthologies. The chansons show both a melancholy vein and the light, witty French style, while the Netherlands idiom is more to the fore in his motets, with typical paired imitations and double counterpoints.

CE: *Collected works* (*CMM* 55), ed. J. Wicks and L. Wagner (Rome, 1971–)

Mandola see **Guitar**

Mandora Plucked string instrument. A more compact form of lute with rounded back, 4 or 5 strings, and 9 frets, it became fashionable in the later C16. A 6-stringed type was a miniature lute, and the 'archimandoire' was a miniature ARCHLUTE with extra bass strings. Recent research has suggested that the medieval instrument to which the name mandora has been applied – a plucked equivalent of the rebec with rounded back, 4 strings and a distinctive sickle-shaped pegbox – should in fact be called a GITTERN, and that the name mandora was not used in the medieval period.

Manelli, Francesco (b. Tivoli, c1595; d. Parma, before 27 Sept 1667) Italian composer and singer. Sang at Tivoli cathedral from 1605 to 1624, and was *maestro di cappella* there from 1627 to 1629, when he left to devote himself to opera. He lived for many years in Venice, composing and producing operas and (from 1638) singing at St Mark's. His *L'Andromeda* opened the S. Cassiano theatre (the first public opera house in Venice) in 1637. Other operas were performed in Bologna, Parma and Piacenza, and he published 2 volumes of arias and cantatas which show his liking for a *parlando* recitative style.

Mangolt, Burk Servant to the Minnesinger Hugo de Montfort (1357–1423) who admitted freely that Mangolt wrote the melodies for his song texts. These tunes combine elements of Minnesang and folk-song styles; the setting of a debate between a beautiful and sensuous lady, representing the World, and an ascetic knight, is particularly attractive.

Mannerism A term applied in the history of art and architecture to the stylistic features of the period c1530–1600, particularly in Italy. It signifies self-conscious preoccupation with style, with details emphasized at the expense of the whole, and with contrasts and distortions. Though it has been applied by some to the musical phenomenon of the Italian madrigal as a whole, it is perhaps more useful as a specific label for the generation of later madrigalists – Marenzio, Wert and Gesualdo – whose music conforms most closely to mannerist principles, particularly in its *fin de siècle* tendencies (melodic or harmonic waywardness, extreme chromaticism).

Manuscripts (before c1400)

Winchester Tropers English monophonic tropes etc. of the mid-C11; also the earliest English polyphony.

St Martial Aquitanian monophony and 2-part polyphony c1100–1170.

Compostela Codex Calixtinus, Santiago; music in 1, 2 and 3 parts for the liturgy of St James c1140.

Magnus Liber Organi 3 C13 MSS at Florence and Wolfenbüttel containing 2-part organa by Leonin for the entire church year (both Mass and Office), organa by Perotin, and also clausulae, conductus and motets.

Montpellier Late C13 motets; the largest source of *ars antiqua* music.

Bamberg Late C13 motets and pieces based on the tenor 'In saeculum'.

Las Huelgas Late C13 and early C14 organa and conductus; a late source of Notre Dame and *ars antiqua* music.

Robertsbridge The earliest known example of keyboard notation, c1325; the manuscript's origin is English, but the pieces intabulated in it are not.

Roman de Fauvel see separate entry.

Ivrea French motets, Mass sections and secular music, c1360.

Squarcialupi Florence; secular works by Landini and other composers of the Italian *trecento*.

Chantilly Late C14, mostly secular music from S. France, often of considerable notational complexity.

Faenza The early C15 layer is an important early source of keyboard music.

Marcabru (fl. 1129–48) Troubadour, from Gascony, who became one of the most famous of the older generation of troubadours. He was not of aristocratic descent and his patrons included William X of Aquitaine and Alfonso VII of Castile. Unusually for a troubadour he was a misogynist, and he initiated the 'trobar clos' style (a cryptic poetic idiom). More than 40 of his poems survive but only 4 of the melodies, including the famous Crusade song *Pax in nomine Domini* which probably dates from 1137.

Marenzio, Luca (b. Coccaglio, nr. Brescia, 1553x54; d. Rome, 22 Aug 1599) Italian composer. While a chorister at Brescia cathedral he studied with Giovanni Contino. For 9 years from 1578 he served Cardinal Luigi d'Este in Rome as musician and later choirmaster, making contacts at the Cardinal's brother's court in Ferrara. He was in Florence in 1588–9 and contributed to the music for the *intermedi* performed at a celebrated court wedding of 1589. In 1594 he came under Cardinal Aldobrandini's wing and met the poets Tasso and Guarini; the following year the Cardinal arranged his appointment to the King of Poland, at whose court in Warsaw he worked in 1596–8. By the time of his death a year later he was back in Rome as a Papal court musician.

Marenzio was the greatest of those Italian composers whose fame rests entirely on their madrigals; his output includes no less than 500 such pieces and 80 villanellas, not to mention a small quantity of sacred music. The Rome in which he spent so much of his life was a thriving centre of amateur madrigal singing, which provided a ready market for the steady flow of madrigal books which he published from 1580 onwards. From the outset he showed complete fluency and mastery in setting light pastoral verse to music which combines an intimate response to the words with deft counterpoint and pleasantly varied rhythms and textures. Later Marenzio came to favour more serious, even morbid, texts and to write in a style that was at once austere and intense, making full use of dissonant and chromatic harmonies and yet hardly departing from a chaste, even flow. The majority of his madrigals are for 5 voices, with many for 6 and rather fewer for 4; in the larger textures he increasingly uses the top 2 as equal high voices in an almost 'concerted' manner. Marenzio's madrigals made an immediate impact in England, and enormously influenced the English madrigalists; some were issued in Yonge's *Musica Transalpina* of 1588.

CE: *Opera omnia* (*CMM* 72), ed. B. Meier and R. Jackson (Rome, 1978–   )

Marini, Biagio (b. Brescia, c1597; d. Venice, 20 Mar (?) 1665) Italian composer and violinist. He became a musician at St Mark's, Venice, in 1615, returning to Brescia in 1618 and then joining the court orchestra at Parma. From 1623 he spent periods in Germany serving the Duke of Neuburg and later in Düsseldorf, but from time to time revisited Italy. He finally returned there to work in Venice, Vicenza and Padua. He published many volumes of secular and instrumental music, laments, monodies and psalms; the instrumental chamber music is most important for its development of the sonata and dance suite forms, often with ostinato elements and prefatory slow sections. His *Lagrime d'Erminia* (1618) is a fine and moving example of the monodic lament.

Marselh see **Folquet de Marselh**

Martini, Johannes (d. Ferrara 1498) Franco-Flemish composer, possibly from Armentières. He was in the Sforza court chapel at Milan in 1474 with Josquin and Compère, and later that year moved to Ferrara to serve Duke Ercole I. Apparently a friend of the Austrian court organist Hofhaimer, Martini was invited to persuade him to give his services to the Innsbruck court. He was friend and mentor to the young Isabella d'Este; their correspondence is preserved. His secular music was partly issued by Petrucci; other secular and sacred works survive in MSS. One of the latter is a *Missa Cucu* with the appropriate motive in the tenor, but there are other pieces showing a well-developed imitative style overlaying traditional cantus firmus treatment.

Secular music in *RRMM* i, ed. E. Evans; Sacred music in *AMMM* xii, ed. B. Disertori

Maschera, Florentio (b. Brescia, c1540; d. Brescia, c1584) Italian composer, violinist and organist. A pupil of Merulo at Venice; organist at Brescia cathedral from 1557. One of the earliest composers to write canzonas consisting of short contrasted sections, he published in 1584 a volume which was twice reprinted.

Mascherata A type of villanella sung in costume during a masked ball, procession, or staged entertainment.

Mason, John (fl. 1505–21) English composer. He took an Oxford B.Mus. degree, was a clerk at Eton 1505–8, *Informator Choristarum* at Magdalen College, Oxford, 1509–10, household chaplain to Cardinal Wolsey in 1520, and priest at Chichester cathedral in 1521. He is represented by 4 pieces in the Peterhouse partbooks, including the fine votive antiphon *Vae nobis miseris*.

Masque Stage production at the courts of James I and Charles I, combining poetry, vocal and instrumental music, dancing and acting. Originating in Italy and France, they were in vogue in C17 England. Many were written by Ben Jonson; Campion, Coprario and (especially) H. Lawes composed music for them.

Mass The principal service of the Catholic church. Its musical items belong either to the 'Ordinary' or to the 'Proper'. The Ordinary comprises what is normally regarded as the Mass in polyphonic settings, i.e. the parts which do not vary: Kyrie, Gloria, Credo, Sanctus, Benedictus, Agnus Dei. The Proper comprises the parts that do vary according to the church calendar, i.e. Introit, Gradual, Alleluia, Offertory and Communion, whose music is usually left in plainsong, though in the Middle Ages Graduals and Alleluias often received polyphonic settings. Apart from the musical items, a certain amount of the Mass text is chanted or spoken (aloud or quietly).

Massaino (Massaini), Tiburtio (b. Cremona, before 1550; d. Lodi or Piacenza, after 1609) Italian composer and Augustinian monk. Held church posts in Italy – at Salò in 1585–7, and at Cremona, Piacenza and Lodi from 1594 – and in the intervening years worked at Innsbruck, Salzburg and Prague. He published 8 volumes of madrigals, 9 of motets, 4 of Masses and 2 of psalms. In addition he contributed 2 unusual canzonas to a Venetian anthology of 1608, one for 8 trombones and the other for 4 viole and 4 archlutes.

Sacred works in *IM* 1st ser., vi, ed. R. Monterosso; also *DTO* cx

Massenzio, Domenico (b. Ronciglione; d. Rome, *c*1650) Italian com-

poser and priest. A pupil of G. F. Anerio and Agazzari, he held various musical and ecclesiastical posts in Rome, including those of singer in the Cappella Giulia (1610–14) and *maestro di cappella* to the Jesuit Congregazione dei Nobili from 1612. He published 5 volumes of tuneful small-scale motets, and 8 of psalms in up to 8 parts, in which he makes effective use of varied voice-groupings.

Matheus de Perusio (Matteo da Perugia) (b. Perugia; d. before 13 Jan 1418) Italian composer. A singer at Milan cathedral from 1402–7 and between 1414 and 1416; in the intervening period he was at the archbishop of Milan's court at Pavia. His output consists of 5 Gloria settings, an isorhythmic motet and 23 chansons in various forms. Though an Italian he set French texts and embraced the most extreme and artificial manifestations of the virtuosic, rhythmically complex late C14 French school. His extravagantly dissonant and syncopated *Le greygnour bien* is one of the most extreme, even bizarre, pieces in this style, and is written out in such a way as to use the maximum number of subtle notational and mensural devices.

Secular works in *CMM* 53/i, ed. W. Apel; in *PMFC* x, ed. W. T. Marrocco

Matheus de Sancto Johanne see **Mayshuet**

Matteo da Perugia see **Matheus de Perusio**

Mauduit, Jacques (b. Paris, 16 Sep 1557; d. Paris, 21 Aug 1627) French composer. He held various official posts at the French court, was a friend of the poet Baïf, after whose death he organized the Académie du Palais, and rescued some of Le Jeune's works from destruction after his death. His music includes a volume of chansons to texts by Baïf, psalms, and a Requiem for Ronsard, all in the MUSIQUE MESURÉE style. He introduced instruments into church music, and wrote music for *ballets de cour* in which large numbers of voices and instruments are combined.

Secular music in *MMRF* x

Mayone, Ascanio (d. Naples, 9 Mar 1627) Italian composer. A pupil of Macque in Naples, and worked at SS. Annunziata there as organist from 1593 and *maestro di cappella* from 1621; he was also organist at the royal chapel from 1602. He published madrigals, but his main work is his 2 volumes of keyboard music, *Capricci per sonar* (1603, 1609). These contain canzonas, toccatas, variations and arrangements of vocal pieces, many of which are distinctively Baroque rather than C16 in style.

Mayshuet (de Joan), (Matheus de Sancto Johanne) (fl. 1378–86) French composer. In 1378 he was a member of the chapel of Louis I of Anjou, and from 1382 until at least 1386 he was at the Papal court at Avignon. He may also be the Mathieu of the monastery of St Jean who was at the Naples court in 1363. He composed 3 *ballades* (one, with Latin text, for Pope Clement VII) and 2 *rondeaux*, which are found in the Chantilly MS, and a 5-part isorhythmic motet in the Old Hall MS; part of the text of this piece is a tirade against the vainglory prevalent among musicians.

Mazzocchi, Domenico (bp. Città Castellana, 8 Nov 1592; d. Rome, 21 Jan 1665) Italian composer and priest. Possibly a pupil of G. B. Nanino, he had by 1640 been 20 years in the service of the Aldobrandini family in Rome. He composed operas in which stretches of recitative are contrasted with tuneful songs and dance-like choruses, and oratorios, and published 5-part

madrigals and 2 volumes of arias and dialogues. These contain some of the earliest printed dynamic indications, including signs for 'crescendo', 'diminuendo', and 'messa di voce'.

Secular works in *CM* iii, ed. W. Witzenmann

Meane, mene In English C15–17 music, a vocal part in polyphony, usually lying in an alto range relative to the highest part (Latin *medius*). It can specifically refer to the male alto voice (Sheppard's 'Mass for a Mene', i.e. for adult voices with male alto on top). The term is also applied to a cantus firmus derived from plainsong. (See also FABURDEN.)

Medius see **Meane**

Meiland, Jacob (b. Senftenberg, nr. Cottbus, 1542; d. Hechingen, nr. Tübingen, 31 Dec 1577) German composer. A chorister at the Saxon court at Ansbach under Le Maistre and Walter, he returned there as *Kapellmeister* in 1564. In 1576 he was an organist in Celle and in 1577 became *Kapellmeister* to the Hohenzollern court at Hechingen. He was one of the first German composers to adopt the villanella style in secular songs; his motets, however, show the influence of Lassus and Clemens. He published 5 volumes of songs and motets; 3 Passions survive in MS.

Meistersinger C15–16 German literary and musical movement cultivated by the craftsmen's guilds; a middle-class continuation of the aristocratic MINNESINGER. Poems were sung to various standard melodies ('tones') with obscure names, notated in a quasi-plainsong manner with free rhythm, and often laid out in BARFORM.

Mel, René (Renatus) del (b. Ellemelle,

nr. Liège, c1555; d. after July 1597) Franco-Flemish composer. *Maestro de capilla* at the Lisbon court from 1572–80, and then worked in Rome (where he knew Palestrina) and various other Italian cities. He published 12 volumes of *madrigaletti* and spiritual madrigals, and 5 of motets in up to 12 parts.

Mene see **Meane**

Mensural notation The system of notation used for part music from c1250 until 1600. It is known as 'white mensural notation' from 1450 or so on account of the white (void) note shapes which superseded the earlier black ones. The main difference from present-day notation is that the relationship between note values of different lengths could vary according to the 'mensuration sign', i.e. a breve (*brevis*) could equal 2 or 3 semibreves, and a semibreve (*semibrevis*) 2 or 3 minims.

The following chart gives the principal note-shapes in use during the period for monophonic song and also polyphony. The first five were derived from the square shapes acquired by plainsong neumes by c1200: they are the *longa* (1), *brevis* (2), *semibrevis* (3) and descending and ascending ligatures (4 and 5). The precise rhythmic interpretation of ligatures was an important element in so-called modal notation just before 1200 (see RHYTHMIC MODES). By the C14 innovations had resulted in the addition of the *minima* (6) and *semiminima* (7). The remaining note-shapes (8 to 15) represent the hierarchy of rhythmic symbols in white mensural notation; *longa* to *semiminima* (8–12), the *fusa* (13: a later addition of c1450), and the ligatures (14–15).

1 2 3 4 5 6 7

8 9 10 11 12 13 14 15

Merbecke, John (b. ?Windsor, c1505; d. Windsor, c1585) English church musician and theologian. He worked at St George's, Windsor, from 1531 (he was organist there in 1541), and in 1544 was pardoned after being condemned to death for having Calvinistic sympathies. He composed a festal Mass and some motets (and also published a Bible concordance and several theological treatises) but is best known for his *Booke of Common Praier Noted* (1550); a syllabic setting of the new English liturgy, based to some extent on Sarum chants. Rendered obsolete by the 1552 prayerbook, it returned to use c1850.

Sacred works in *TCM* x

Mersenne, Marin (b. La Soultière, Maine, 8 Sep 1588; d. Paris, 1 Sep 1648) French theorist who concerned himself with the relation of philosophy, physics and music, and with the nature of sound. His major work, *Harmonie universelle* (2 vols., Paris, 1636–7), includes an important treatise on instruments.

Meruco, Johannes de Late C14 French composer, of whose life nothing is known. His music is of the rhythmically complex type cultivated by the Avignon composers of the period; his *De home vray* is an intricate and dissonant piece in 4 parts.

Merula, Tarquinio (b. ?Cremona, c1590; d. Cremona, 10 Dec 1665) Italian composer. He was employed at the Polish court in 1624, but had returned to Italy by 1628 to hold church posts in Cremona. In 1631–2 he directed music at S. Maria Maggiore, Bergamo, but was dismissed for indecent behaviour; he then worked at the nearby cathedral.

He spent his last years back in Cremona. He published 8 collections of church music, 4 of canzonas and sonatas and 5 of secular music (madrigals, dialogues and monodies). A notable instrumental composer, he was concerned with matters of musical structure; this preoccupation appears also in his church music, in which stock basses like the ROMANESCA or ostinato figures from plainsong are used to give unity to longish psalm or Mass settings.

CE: *IMM* Collected works ser., vii, ed. A. Sutkowski; Keyboard works in *MMI* 1st ser., i, ed. A. Curtis.

Merulo, Claudio (bp. Correggio, nr. Modena, 8 Apr 1533; d. Parma, 5 May 1604) Italian composer and organist. Organist at Brescia cathedral in 1556; the following year became second organist at St Mark's, Venice, and in 1564 succeeded Annibale Padovano as first organist. By 1586 he moved to Parma as court organist, and served as organist at the cathedral there in 1587 and at the ducal church of La Steccata in 1591. He was an organ builder as well as player, and during his time in Venice was active as a music publisher.

Merulo's output consists of 4 volumes of madrigals, 2 of Masses, 6 of motets, 6 of organ music and one of instrumental ricercars; some of these were issued posthumously by his nephew, who succeeded him at Parma. His madrigals were craftsmanlike rather than profound or experimental. It is in keyboard music that Merulo excels. He developed the ricercar and canzona forms, but made his most significant contribution to the toccata, imparting to it an impressive formal balance between brilliant, improvisatory writing and sterner contrapuntal passages whose ideas might be cleverly reworked as the piece proceeded. Of all the Italian organ composers, Merulo perhaps did most to further a self-sufficient keyboard idiom.

CE: Sacred works in *CMM* 51, ed. J. Bastian (Rome, 1970–   )

Michael, Rogier (b. Mons, *c*1554; d. Dresden, after 25 Jan 1619) Franco-Flemish composer. A chorister at the Imperial court; studied with Annibale Padovano at the archducal court in Graz and probably also with A. Gabrieli in Venice. In 1574, after a period at Ansbach, he went to the Saxon Electoral court at Dresden as a singer, becoming *Kapellmeister* there in 1587. He published 4-part hymns and 5-part introits, left a 'Christmas Story' in MS, and was the teacher of Schein.

Mielczewski, Marcin (b. 1590; d. Warsaw, Sep 1651) Polish composer. A singer in the Rorantist choir at Kraków in 1617, member of the royal chapel and later court composer from 1628, and *Kapellmeister* to the Bishop of Płock from 1645, he was one of Poland's most important early C17 composers. Though most of his many Masses and motets are polyphonic in style, some do use the concertato manner, with solo voices and *obbligato* instruments. His purely instrumental music has a distinctive Polish flavour.

Mikołaj z Krakowa (Nicholas of Kraków) (fl. 1488) Polish composer. His name appears in the archives of Kraków university for 1488, and he may have been organist at the court there. His dances, preludes and transcriptions of songs and sacred pieces are preserved in Polish organ tablatures, including the Lublin tablature, dating from the period 1526–48. His well-known song *Aleć nade mną Wenus* is sometimes referred to as a Polish madrigal.

Milán, Luis (b. ?Valencia, *c*1500; d. ?Valencia, after 1561) Spanish vihuela player, from a noble family, who worked at the court of the viceroy Don Fernando of Aragon at Valencia. His famous publication *El maestro* (1536) was the first of a series of Spanish vihuela books; it contains Spanish, Italian and Portuguese songs and fantasias, *tientos* and pavanes. Milán was one of the first to write tempo indications. In songs he uses a variation technique so that the music is embellished on its repeat; in fantasias he writes pseudo-polyphony, in his *tientos* there are more running passages; he requires the music always to be played with flexibility of tempo, alternating fast and slow movement.

CE: *El maestro*, ed. R. Chiesa (Milan, 1966); ed. C. Jacobs (Pennsylvania, 1971)

Milano, Francesco (Canova) da (b. Monza, ?18 Aug 1497; d. 15 Apr 1543) Italian lutenist; one of the great virtuoso performers of the C16. Served at the Gonzaga court in Mantua from about 1510, at the court of Cardinal Ippolito de' Medici from c1530, and lastly at the Papal court of Paul III. His 3 volumes of lute pieces were very popular and contained intabulations of Janequin's *La guerre* and other programmatic pieces. Called *Il divino*, he entertained prelates and princes, often with improvisations. His ricercars are free studies in lute style, while his fantasias are contrapuntal and closer to organ music. In arranging vocal music, he applied brilliant trills, turns and runs to the model to produce a thoroughly idiomatic lute piece.

CE: *The Lute Music*, ed. J. Ness (Cambridge, Mass., 1970); *Opere complete*, ed. R. Chiesa (Milan, 1971)

Milanuzzi, Carlo (b. S. Natoglia, nr. Rome; d. c1647) Italian composer and monk. His career as a church musician alternated between central Italy and the north, and 3 of his posts were in or near Venice. Despite his priestly vocation he composed 8 books of tuneful, secular arias, as well as several volumes of mostly small-scale church music, some of which uses ground basses and repeated sections to unify longer pieces such as psalms.

Minnesinger Aristocratic German poet-musicians of the C12–14, similar to the French troubadours. The poetry of *Minnesang* was sometimes narrative in type, often devotional (especially pieces addressed to the Virgin), and the modal melodies were often laid out in BARFORM. Their name was derived from 'minne'–courtly love.

Minstrels Wandering musicians casually employed by medieval feudal households. The allegedly dubious influence of some minstrels caused a reaction by church and state, but they nevertheless survived attempts at suppression. The term could also apply to respected household instrumentalists or town employees whose skills were handed down from father to son.

Missa pro defunctis see **Requiem**

Missal A liturgical book containing all the texts for the Catholic Mass.

Modal rhythm see **Rhythmic modes**

Moderne, Jacques (b. Pinguento [Buzet, N. Yugoslavia]; d. c1561) French music publisher of Slovene origin who was active in Lyons from 1523. He published works not only by the local circle of composers but also by Parisians and major figures like Gombert, Morales and other Papal musicians. His largest series was *Le parangon des chansons* (10 volumes, 1538–43); his *Musique de Joye* was a collection of ricercars and dance music.

Modes The theoretical basis of plainsong melody and, in the Renaissance, of harmony also; by the C17 the emergence of modern tonality was weakening their influence. The various modes were distinguished by the position of the semitones in relation to whichever diatonic note was the modal 'final', and by the position of the final within the overall compass. The basic modes commonly used in the Renaissance are shown below; the 'transposed' modes arose through the addition of a B flat signature. The Renaissance modes differed from the original plainsong ones in the addition of the Aeolian and Ionian; the latter in its transposed form (on F) superseded the Lydian, whose lack of a B flat caused a prominent tritone, often actually modified in plainsong by B flat accidentals. (See also RHYTHMIC MODES.)

Modes

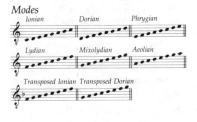

Molinaro, Simone (b. Genoa, c1565; d. Genoa, c1615) Italian composer. He was *maestro di cappella* at Genoa cathedral from c1602, and issued a 6-volume edition of GESUALDO's madrigals, in score, in 1613. His own canzonets, and church music for from one to 10 voices, show the influence of Gesualdo in their declamatory style and advanced chromatic harmonies; the latter are also to be found in his 1599 lute book. This includes fantasias, and important examples of the variation suite consisting of groups of dances whose separate sections are all based on the same chord progression.

Molinet, Jean (b. Desvres, Pas-de-Calais, ?c1435; d. Valenciennes, 23 Aug 1507) Franco-Flemish poet, chron-

icler and musician. In the service of the Burgundian court by 1463 and became its chronicler in 1474. He had considerable knowledge of music and his writings contain many references to important musical events; a friend of many leading composers, he wrote poems in their honour and they reciprocated by making many settings of his verse. He may also have composed.

Molins see **Pierre des Molins**

Moniot d'Arras (b. c1190; d. after 1239) Trouvère; a monk at Arras who had many noble patrons. He wrote a JEU-PARTI jointly with Guillaume le Vinier, and 23 of his poems, with 13 tunes, survive. His especially fine *Ce fut en Mai* was used by Hindemith in the suite *Nobilissima Visione*.

Monk (Monge) of Montaudan (b. ?Vic-sur-Cère, Dordogne; d. ?c1220) Troubadour; became prior of the monastery of Montaudan, and his activity as a poet seems to span the period from 1155 to 1220. 17 poems and 2 tunes survive.

Monochord String instrument whose strings are stopped by movable bridges. Said to have been invented by Pythagoras, it was much favoured by medieval scholars for theoretical demonstrations, but too unwieldy to be of much practical use until application of the keyboard principle to it produced the clavichord.

Monody A term from Greek antiquity meaning music for one singer; usually applied to the accompanied solo song developed in Italy around 1600 and often characterized by a recitative-like style of singing. The term ought not to be used of music for more than one singer (see CONCERTATO).

Monophony Music consisting of one

single notated melodic line without accompaniment. Most ancient and early medieval music, including plainsong and secular song, was monophonic.

Monte, Philippe de (b. Malines, 1521; d. Prague, 4 July 1603) Franco-Flemish composer. He was in Naples from 1541 to 1544, and knew Lassus there; he then came via Rome and Antwerp to England as a member of Queen Mary's chapel, but returned to Naples, for the predominance of Spaniards in this choir (Mary was married to Philip II of Spain) was not to his taste. In 1568 he became *Kapellmeister* to Emperor Maximilian II and remained at the Imperial court in Vienna and Prague until his death.

Monte was scarcely less prominent than Lassus or Palestrina among late Renaissance polyphonists and was one of the most prolific composers of the time – he wrote no less than 1,073 secular and 144 spiritual madrigals, 45 chansons, 319 motets and 38 Masses. In his madrigals, mainly written during his Italian years, he comes closer perhaps to Palestrina than to Lassus in the mixture of polyphony and homophony, in the fine contrapuntal technique he displayed and in his fondness for the spiritual madrigal. Later, with the Imperial court comparatively isolated from new trends, he declined to follow the fashion for dramatic writing or chromaticism, claiming that it 'did not suit him'. Most of his Masses and motets were written at the Imperial court, the former being mostly parody Masses, rich and impressive in style.

CE: *Opera omnia*, ed. J. van Nuffel and others (Düsseldorf, 1927–39); *Opera*, ed. R. Lenaerts (Louvain, 1975–   )

Monteverdi, Claudio bp. Cremona, 15 May 1567; d. Venice, 29 Nov 1643) Italian composer. He studied with Ingegneri at Cremona and published his earliest works at the age of 16. In 1589 he entered the service of the Gonzaga court at Mantua, first as a string player and from 1601 as director of the Duke's private music for both chapel and chamber; in 1599 he married one of the court singers. He left Mantua in 1612 and the following year was appointed *maestro di cappella* at St Mark's, Venice, the post in which he spent the remainder of his life. While in Venice he maintained connections at the Mantuan court which provided an outlet for his continuing activities as a dramatic composer until the opening of the Venetian opera houses.

Monteverdi dominated the Italian musical scene during the crucial years of the early Baroque. His surviving works include 3 operas and several ballets and other dramatic works; 9 volumes of madrigals and 2 of *Scherzi musicali;* and 3 large compilations of sacred music containing 3 Masses, the Marian Vespers and many other Vesper psalms and motets. In these 3 spheres of activity his works reflected, and often led, great changes of style. With *Orfeo* (1607) he brought the infant genre of opera to an amazing level of refinement, vocal expression and formal planning; his late Venetian operas show the beginnings of public opera for the merchant classes. The madrigal he transformed from conventional unaccompanied part-music to the brilliant baroque concerted idiom with virtuoso solo and instrumental writing and continuo accompaniment, though even before this change he was composing 5-part madrigals of remarkable harmonic daring and expressive profundity. In sacred music he ranged between the staid STILE ANTICO of the Masses, through the bold, experimental but transitional conglomeration of style in the Marian Vespers, to the assured manner of the Venetian psalms, with their craftsmanlike refrain and *ostinato* structures. As a musical thinker Monteverdi coined the terms PRIMA PRATTICA and SECONDA PRATTICA, and conceived the STILE CONCITATO found in certain late works.

CE: *Tutte le opere*, ed. G. Malipiero (Asolo, 1926–42; repr. Vienna, 1966–8); *Opera omnia*, ed. R. Monterosso and others (Cremona, 1970–   )

Morago, Estêvão Lopes (b. ?Vallescas, nr. Madrid; fl. 1597–1628) Portuguese composer. Studied at Evora, and from 1599 to 1628 was *maestro de capilla* at Viseu cathedral. Some of his church music survives, but most was lost in the Lisbon earthquake of 1755.

Morales, Cristóbal de (b. ?Seville, *c*1500; d. Málaga, 4 Sepx7 Oct 1553) Spanish composer. Choirmaster at Ávila cathedral from 1526 and at Plasencia cathedral from 1527/8–31. In 1535–45 he sang in the Papal chapel in Rome, probably as a tenor, and on his return to Spain resumed his career as a choirmaster, at Toledo cathedral till 1547 and at Málaga cathedral from 1551, in the meantime serving the Dukes of Arcos at Marchena (near Seville).

Apart from one or 2 secular pieces, Morales' output consists entirely of sacred music–21 Masses, 16 Magnificats, 91 motets, 11 hymns and a set of Lamentations. He was the most widely praised of the C16 Spanish polyphonists for many years after his death, and his Magnificats were especially popular. He himself regarded the Masses highly, supervising their publication personally and writing more of them than did any other polyphonist of his generation, or indeed any Spaniard of the period. They illustrate his superb contrapuntal technique–more refined than Josquin's and looking ahead to Palestrina (who in fact based a Mass on

his fine motet *O sacrum convivium*–and his own discerning parody technique, whereby he enriched and transformed his models. Morales wrote in a severely modal idiom; his motets are more intense and personal, often using a cantus firmus with a separate text that glosses or alludes to the principal one (*Emendemus in melius*, for example).

CE: *Opera omnia* (in *MME*, various vols.), ed. H. Anglés (Rome, 1952–1971)

Moresca C16 dance or vocal piece in Neapolitan dialect, performed by singers in costume with blackened faces. It was a ribald burlesque of African slave characters in the manner of a street ballad (*moresca*=Moorish).

Moritz, Landgrave of Hesse-Cassel (known as 'The Learned') (b. 25 May 1572; d. Eschwege, nr. Kassel, 15 Mar 1632) German ruler (1592–1627) and composer. Not only a patron of the arts (he sent Schütz to study in Venice) he was also a player of many instruments and a competent composer. A Protestant, he published congregational psalm tunes, motets which show the influence initially of Lassus but, after Schütz's return from Italy, of the Italian style. His dances and secular songs survive in MS; unfortunately his court's flourishing musical life was destroyed by the 30 Years' War.

Morlaye, Guillaume de (b. *c*1515; d. after 1560) French lutenist. Said to have engaged in the slave trade, he was a pupil of Albert de Rippe, whose music he published with his own in 6 volumes between 1553 and 1558. He also published dances and his own arrangements for voice and lute of Certon's psalm-settings; he wrote for guitar as well as lute.

Morley, Thomas (b. ?London, 1557;

d. London, Oct 1602) English composer. The most famous pupil of William Byrd, he took the Oxford Mus. Bac. in 1588 and soon afterwards became organist at St Paul's cathedral, London. In 1592 he was appointed a Gentleman of the Chapel Royal, and in 1598 took over the printing licence earlier held by Tallis and Byrd. His *Plaine and Easie Introduction to Practicall Musicke*, published in 1597, was the most notable English treatise of the period.

Morley was active in almost every contemporary genre of English music, publishing many volumes of secular pieces (canzonets, balletts and madrigals), a book of lute ayres and one of consort lessons, and also writing Anglican services, anthems and motets and some keyboard music. His consort lessons were arrangements rather than original works, but are among the first music written for a specified instrumental ensemble (a BROKEN CONSORT). Morley was the main arbiter of taste in the flowering of the English madrigal, and wrote in the most derivative Italian style, leaning towards the lighter canzonet and ballett rather than the true madrigal (a preference shown by English madrigalists as a whole). His balletts are nevertheless often full of musical invention lacking in their Italian prototypes.

Madrigals in *EM*. i–iv, rev. edn.; Lute ayres in *EL* 1st ser., xvi, rev. edn.; *The first book of Consort Lessons*, ed. S. Beck (New York, 1959)

Mornable, Antoine de (b. c1512x15) French composer. A choirboy at the Sainte Chapelle in Paris, he became *maître de chapelle* to Count Guy de Laval in 1546. Though not apparently himself a Protestant, he published 2 volumes of French psalm-settings; motets, Magnificats and chansons by him appeared in anthologies.

Mortaro, Antonio (b. Brescia; d. ?Verona, after 1620) Italian composer and organist. Probably a pupil of Antegnati; became a Franciscan in 1595 and except for a period as cathedral organist in Novara (1602–6) lived mainly in Brescia. His 4 volumes of 3-part madrigals were many times reprinted; he also published much church music in up to 12 parts, and polychoral instrumental music.

Morton, Robert (b. c1440; d. after Jan 1476) English composer who worked on the Continent. He was a singer and chaplain at the Burgundian court, where he knew Hayne van Ghizeghem and Busnois. The theorists Hothby and Tinctoris refer to Morton, and 12 chansons are attributed to him, of which 4 may however not be his; they are Franco-Flemish rather than English in style. Josquin based a Mass on his *N'auray je jamais*.

Motet The most important form of polyphonic vocal music in the Middle Ages and Renaissance. In medieval France motets were mainly secular with only the tenor cantus firmus having Latin words; such pieces tended to be occasional in function. From the Renaissance onwards motets have normally had Latin sacred texts and are designed to be sung during Catholic services. Ceremonial motets honouring an event or person, religious or otherwise, were also written in the Renaissance period. In the early C17 the motet quickly forsook the polyphonic in favour of the monodic or CONCERTATO style. (See also PSALM MOTET.)

Moulu, Pierre (b. c1480x90; d. c1550) Franco-Flemish composer. Possibly a pupil of Josquin, he contributed many Masses, motets and chansons to anthologies published between 1521 and 1560. His motet *Sicut malus* is found in many keyboard arrangements, and his *Missa duarum facierum* is a remarkable piece, composed in such a way that the long rests in all parts may be either observed or disregarded in performance.

Mouton, Jean (b. Holluigue, Pas-de-Calais, *c*1459; d. S. Quentin, 30 Oct 1522) Franco-Flemish composer. In 1477 he was a chorister at Nesles, later becoming priest and cantor there; around 1500 he served as master of the boys at Amiens cathedral and a year later as a teacher to the clerics at S. André, Grenoble. In 1502 he may have entered Queen Anne's service; by 1512 he was a singer in the chapel of her husband, Louis XII. He probably went with the next king, Francis I, to Bologna for a conference with the Pope in 1516 and to the Field of the Cloth of Gold in 1520 when Francis met Henry VIII of England. In his last years he held a benefice at S. Quentin.

Mouton's surviving works consist of 14 Masses and a Credo, 10 Magnificats, about 110 motets and some 25 chansons; many others are lost. Though one of Josquin's most distinguished pupils, his own style was distinctive; he preferred smooth, conjunct lines and beautifully polished, flowing polyphony. He liked to rework motives, bringing them back to achieve musical coherence, as in the attractive motet *Quaeramus cum pastoribus*; at other times his handling of canonic technique is impressive, as in the quadruple canon *Nesciens mater* in 8 parts. A number of Mouton's motets were written specifically for French court occasions.

CE: *Opera omnia* (*CMM* 43), ed. A. Minor (Rome, 1967–)

Mudarra, Alonso (b. *c*1508; d. Seville, 1 Apr 1580) Spanish player of the vihuela. Brought up in a noble household, he travelled in Italy before becoming a canon of Seville cathedral

in 1547. His *Tres libros* (1546) contains solo songs to Italian as well as Spanish texts, and examples of all types of music suitable for the solo vihuela: arrangements of vocal pieces (especially by Josquin), fantasias in a relatively non-contrapuntal style, and variations (*diferencias*) on ground basses. Some of the pieces are arranged in 'suites' consisting of a *tiento* or prelude, followed by a fantasia and an arrangement of a Mass movement.

Tres libros in *MME* vii, ed. E. Pujol

Mügeln, Müglin see **Heinrich von Mügeln**

Muelich von Prag Mid-C14 Bohemian Minnesinger. He was working during the reign of John of Luxembourg. He gave new life and freshness to the courtly *Minnesang* by introducing less stylized, bourgeois elements; 4 of his poems, and 2 melodies, survive.

Mulliner Book An important MS collection of mid-C16 English keyboard music (?1545–70). Its contents are a mixture of liturgical pieces based on chant (e.g. organ hymns), song arrangements, dance pieces and freer compositions.

CE: *MB* i, ed. D. Stevens (rev. edn.)

Mundy, John (b. *c*1550x54; bd. Eton, 30 June 1630) English organist and composer, son and pupil of W. Mundy. Organist at Eton, and in 1585 succeeded Merbecke at St George's, Windsor, receiving the degree of D.Mus. at Oxford in 1624. He published a volume of *Songs and Psalms* in 1594, contributed to the *Triumphs of Oriana*, composed English and Latin sacred music, and is represented in the Fitzwilliam Virginal Book. His *Goe from my window* variations are a particularly fine example of this type of virginal composition.

Songs and Psalms in *EM* xxxv (rev. edn.)

Mundy, William (b. *c*1529; d. ?1591) English composer. A singer at Westminster Abbey from 1543; later a singer at St Paul's cathedral and Gentleman of the Chapel Royal. His output includes fine examples of both the large-scale Latin votive antiphon and the short English anthem, as well as Masses and Latin psalm settings; his style is vigorous and eloquent. He is represented in the Mulliner Book.

Latin works in *EECM* ii, ed. F. Harrison

Muris see **Johannes de Muris**

Muset see **Colin Muset**

Musica ficta Medieval and Renaissance theory of chromatic notes – those not in the diatonic scale based on the HEXACHORD. It is applied more particularly to the conventions governing the addition of accidentals during the period *c*1350–1600 in such contexts as leading notes at cadences and the avoidance of melodic tritones.

Musica reservata A term widely known in C16 Europe, but first coined by Coclico in 1552 as a description of Josquin Desprez' music. Of the various interpretations, one logical usage refers to music 'reserved' for private use (e.g. by a patron or employer) – as with certain of Lassus' works which were at first for his patrons' ears only, and did not appear in print until many years later. Lassus' admirer at Munich, Samuel Quickelberg, outlined another usage of the term in 1560 when he referred to the power of Lassus' music to convey images so vividly that they can almost be seen as well as heard (this is the sense in which Coclico applied the term to his own compositions).

Musica Transalpina Two volumes of Italian madrigals with English singing translations published by Nicholas Yonge in 1588 and 1597. Though proof of an already well-developed taste for Italian madrigals in England, the 1588 volume did also act as a tremendous spur to the growth of a school of English madrigalists.

Musique mesurée à l'antique A late C16 type of music to French poetic texts which aimed to preserve the classical poetic metres. The strong and weak syllables of the texts are given respectively long and short rhythmic values (1 long=2 short), resulting in bars of irregular, fluid rhythm. The influence of *musique mesurée* was felt in the AIR DE COUR, in the BALLET DE COUR and, later, in French recitative. Chansons written in it had a clear-cut form, alternating a 'rechant' (refrain) with several 'chants' (strophes).

Mute cornett see **Cornett**

N

Naich, Hubert C16 Franco-Flemish composer, of whose life nothing is known. His publication (at Rome) of 4- and 5-part madrigals is undated; he also contributed to anthologies.

Nakers see **Drum**

Nanino, Giovanni Bernardino (b. Vallerano, c1560; d. Rome, 1618) Italian composer, brother and pupil of G. M. Nanino. *Maestro di cappella* at S. Luigi dei Francesi in Rome from 1591 to 1608 and later at S. Lorenzo in Damaso; taught at his brother's music school in Rome where his pupils included his son-in-law, P. Agostini, and Allegri. He published 5-part madrigals and church music, including small-scale motets; he was one of the first Roman composers to use the basso continuo, but though his music is of high quality, his reputation is overshadowed by that of his better-known brother.

Nanino, Giovanni Maria (b. Tivoli, c1544x45; d. Rome, 11 Mar 1607) Italian composer. A pupil of Palestrina whom he succeeded as *maestro di cappella* at S. Maria Maggiore in Rome, he later held similar posts at S. Luigi dei Francesi (from 1575) and the Sistine Chapel (from 1604) and was also a Papal singer. In 1580 he started a music school, where the composition teachers included Palestrina as well as himself and his brother G. B. Nanino. One of the best of the Roman composers who adopted the Palestrina style, he published madrigals, canzonets and church music; his remarkable set of 157 counterpoints and canons in up to 11 parts on a can-

tus firmus by C. Festa survives in MS. Motets in *RRMR*, ed. R. Schuler

Narváez, Luys de (b. Granada, c1500; d. ?after 1550) Spanish player of the vihuela. In 1538 he served Don Francisco de las Colvas, a friend of the Emperor Charles V, in Valladolid. From 1548 he served Prince Philip (later Philip II), taking charge of his choirboys and accompanying him on travels to Flanders, Italy and Germany. His collection of vihuela music *Los seys libros* (1538) contains the earliest surviving examples of variation writing, based on Gregorian melodies and Spanish romances, and includes arrangements of Franco-Flemish polyphony and smoothly contrapuntal fantasias modelled on the motet or organ ricercar.
Los seys libros in *MME* iii, ed. E. Pujol

Nasco, Giovanni (d. ?Treviso, before 1561) Italian composer. Became *maestro di cappella* to the Accademia Filarmonica in Verona in 1547; later worked in Vicenza, and was *maestro* at Treviso cathedral from 1559. A friend of Willaert, whose publications of 1542 and 1547 included pieces of his, he published villanellas and madrigals in up to 8 parts; a posthumous sacred collection including 2 Passions and a Lamentation setting became very popular, being reprinted several times.

Navarro, Juan 1 (b. Marchena, nr. Seville, c1530; d. Palencia, 25 Sep 1580) Spanish composer. Probably studied in Seville before holding posts as *maestro de capilla* successively at the cathedrals of Ávila, Salamanca, Ciudad Rodrigo and Palencia. He was greatly esteemed by his contemporaries as an exemplary polyphonist, whose work was on a level with that of Victoria, Morales and Palestrina; a volume of his sacred music was published posthumously, and more church music and sacred and secular songs survive in MS.

Navarro, Juan 2 (b. Cadiz, c1560; d. Mexico, after 1604) Spanish composer and Franciscan monk. He went to Mexico, and his 1604 volume of Passion and Lamentation settings was one of the first music publications to appear in the New World.

Neidhart von Reuental (b. c1180; d. 1237x46) Austrian Minnesinger, from an aristocratic but poor family. Went on a Crusade in 1217–19 before settling down in Austria. A younger contemporary of Walther von der Vogelweide, he is one of the earliest German poets some of whose poems survive complete with melodies–there are at least 17, and nearly 40 more of his poems were given tunes that are unascribed and thought to be by his imitators. His songs show a fusion of court and folk music traditions; many of them celebrate seasons of the year, or deal with the lives of peasants and farmers and their rustic jollifications. Their style is generally fresh, simple and popular; and they were so highly regarded as to survive into the era of music printing. In fact Neidhart was the only Minnesinger whose music was printed during the Renaissance.

CE: *DTO* lxxi

Nenna, Pomponio (b. Bari, c1550; d. Rome or Naples, c1615) Italian composer. His name first appears in an anthology of 1574, but all we know of his life is that he served Gesualdo, Prince of Venosa, at Naples in 1594–9, and that he had moved to Rome by 1608, having received the Order of the

Golden Spur from the Pope in 1603. He wrote 2 books of Responsories (for Christmas and Holy Week) and 9 books of madrigals, printed mostly in Naples, which mark him as the most brilliant of the 'southern' Italian madrigalists. It is possible that Gesualdo studied with him; certainly Nenna reveals a most individual and chromatic vein in his sacred music and his later madrigals.

Nesle see **Blondel de Nesle**

Newsidler, Hans (b. Pressburg [Bratislava], 1508; d. Nürnberg, 2 Feb 1563) German lutenist of Hungarian descent. Lived in Nürnberg from 1530, and published 4 volumes of lute music, including instructions on playing as well as pieces. These books contain arrangements of sacred and secular vocal pieces, preludes in a polyphonic rather than improvisatory style, and dances of various nationalities.

Lute pieces in *DTO* xxxvii

Newsidler, Melchior (b. Nürnberg, 1531; d. Augsburg, 1591x92) German lutenist, the son – not brother – of H. Newsidler. From 1552 he was in the service of the Fugger family at Augsburg; he visited Italy in 1565 and the archducal court at Innsbruck c1580. His lute tablatures of 1560 were frequently reprinted, and the *Teutsch Lautenbuch* of 1574 includes fantasias, dances and skilful arrangements of motets and secular pieces by the leading composers of the day. As late as 1584 he published lute arrangements of 6 Josquin motets.

Niccolò da Perugia (Ser Nicolaus, etc.) (fl. c1350–1400) Italian composer; probably an ecclesiastic from Perugia who worked in Florence. His large output of secular music included several *cacce* (see CACCIA)–an unusual feature since most composers appear to have written only one – and he was one of the first to write polyphonic rather than monophonic *ballate*, producing c20 of these, as well as 15 madrigals. Some of his pieces were used as *laude*, with sacred texts replacing the original secular ones.

CE: in *PMFC* viii, ed. W. T. Marrocco

Nicholas of Kraków see **Mikołaj z Krakowa**

Nicholson, Richard (d. 1639) English composer. Became master of the choristers at Magdalen College, Oxford, in 1595, and the first Professor of Music at Oxford in 1627. He composed English and Latin church music, and consort songs, in humorous rather then melancholy vein, and contributed to the *Triumphs of Oriana*.

Madrigals in *EM* xxxvii, ed. J. Morehen

Nola, Gian Domenico del Giovane da (b. Nola, nr. Naples, c1510; d. Naples, 5 May 1592) Italian composer. Organist and (from 1563 to 1588) also *maestro di cappella* at SS. Annunziata in Naples. One of the first important composers of *canzone villanesche*, he published several volumes of 3-part pieces in the deliberately primitive early villanella style, with consecutive 5ths, which became very popular. Some of these were reworked in a more refined style by Willaert and Lassus; Nola also published serious madrigals and church music.

Secular works, ed. L. Cammarota (Rome, 1973)

Norman, John (fl. 1509–22) English composer. Master of the choristers at St David's cathedral from 1509 until 1522, and may have been a clerk in London (from 1528) and Eton (1534–45). His 5-part Mass in the Forrest-Heather partbooks, on an Easter plainsong, is not especially florid for its time; his 3-part *Miserere mihi* in the Ritson MS is much more elaborate, in some ways resembling the style of Taverner's responds.

Mass in *EECM* xvi, ed. J. Bergsagel

Notation see **Mensural notation**

Note nere Italian for 'black notes'; the term was applied to madrigals written in C (modern 4/4) time as against ¢ time, with crotchets as the normal unit. Passages of quick *note nere* crotchet movement could also interrupt a generally slower-paced madrigal as a response to the words, so it could be regarded as an expressive device.

Notker Balbulus (b. c840; d. 912) Swiss monk and musician. He discovered the idea of the plainsong SEQUENCE from a book of chants in the possession of a monk who fled from Jumièges (Normandy) to S. Gallen (Notker's monastery), in which words had been added to the notes of elaborate Alleluia melismas. Notker took these melismas, broke them into short phrases, and added his own texts in syllabic settings. He also described the use of letters found in chant MSS from S. Gallen, which indicate variations of rhythm or pitch.

O

Obrecht, Jacob (b. ?Bergen-op-Zoom, 22 Nov 1450 or 1451; d. Ferrara, 1505) Franco-Flemish composer, perhaps the only Dutchman among the important contemporaries of Josquin Desprez. He was choirmaster at Cambrai cathedral 1484–5 and succentor at the church of S. Donatien, Bruges, 1485–91 and 1498–1500, working at Notre Dame, Antwerp, 1492–6 and 1501–4, and at his birthplace in 1496–8. In 1487 he was famous enough to be invited to visit Ferrara by Duke Ercole I d'Este, who attempted to persuade him to stay. He returned to Bruges; only in 1504 did he go back to Ferrara, where the following year he fell victim to the plague.

Obrecht's output consists of some 26 Masses–a considerable number for that period–32 motets and 30 secular pieces, some untexted. The Masses contain some of his finest music, and display the notable structural ingenuity once regarded as the chief characteristic of Netherlands music of this generation. In the *Missa Maria zart* he divides the melody on which the work is based into segments, only presenting it complete in the Agnus Dei as a structural climax; while in the *Missa Sub tuum praesidium* additional plainsong cantus firmi are added to the original one as the Mass proceeds, and the number of voices increases movement by movement from 3 to 7, with a resultant textural climax. It has been suggested that both works are laid out according to a secret, symbolic mathematical structure, an argument not widely accepted. Obrecht's motets can be more modern in style with the texts declaimed more clearly, though there

is little use of the fully developed manner of Josquin. His fondness for sequences is typical of his orderliness and facility, and a device often found in his secular music is the combination of playful rhythmic lines against a pre-existing melody in long notes. His secular output includes chansons, arrangements of Dutch popular tunes, and instrumental pieces, some canonic.

CE: *Werken*, ed. J. Wolf (Amsterdam and Leipzig, 1912–21, repr. 1968); *Opera omnia*, ed. A. Smijers (Amsterdam, 1953–   )

Ochsenkuhn, Sebastian (b. Nürnberg, 6 Feb 1521; d. Heidelberg, 20 Aug 1574) German lutenist. The son of a barber-cum-instrument maker, he served at the court of the Elector Palatine (1534–71), at Neuburg an der Donau and later at Heidelberg. His 1558 tablature contains some of the very few examples of German Lieder transcribed for voice and lute rather than lute solo.

Ockeghem, Johannes (b. ?Dendermonde, *c*1425; d. Tours, 6 Feb 1497) Franco-Flemish composer. He may have studied with Binchois, but is first heard of as singer at Notre Dame in Antwerp in 1443–4; by 1448 he was a member of the chapel choir of Charles I of Bourbon at Moulins. From 1452–3 at latest he was at the French court, where he spent the rest of his life as singer, composer and later choirmaster; in the late 1450s the king granted him the honorary post of Treasurer to the Abbey of St Martin at Tours. Among his travels were visits to

Spain in 1470 and Flanders in 1484. To judge from the musical elegies written for him after his death, he was a much admired and respected musical mentor of the day.

Ockeghem's output was comparatively modest in size–10 complete Masses, some partial Masses and single movements, and also the earliest extant polyphonic Requiem, a handful of motets and 22 chansons. His best music can be found in the Masses, many of which are preserved in the 'Chigi Codex', a lavishly ornate manuscript in the Vatican Library. In some he followed the cantus firmus technique of Dufay's late Masses, but others are written, sometimes ingeniously, without any pre-existent musical material; the *Missa Prolationum*, for instance, consists of a series of mensuration canons. But such structural ingenuity, far from being drily academic, is beautifully and artfully concealed in an almost timeless flow of counterpoint that is the hallmark of Ockeghem's style. The comparative paucity of cadences creates a floating effect, but the ends of sections are marked by intricate rhythmic climaxes. He wrote for a choir whose 4 parts were equal in importance and often rather low in range, but hardly developed the idea of imitation, soon to be so important. His chansons are more conventional in style, in 3 parts with the focus on a melodious top line.

CE: *Collected Works* (Masses only), ed. D. Plamenac (repr. New York, 1959–66)

Oda see Frottola

Odhecaton Short title of a printed collection of 96 songs published by Petrucci in 1501 (in full *Harmonice musices Odhecaton A*). The earliest-ever printed polyphonic music, the volume was very important for its representation of secular polyphony c1470–1500.

Similar collections called *Canti B* and *C* followed in 1502–3.

Office In Catholic liturgy, the service of the Hours as distinct from Mass. The 8 Hours are Matins, Lauds, Prime, Terce, Sext, None, Vespers and Compline, which from the C15–17 were often adorned with polyphony (in England this came to an end with the Reformation and before that was generally according to the SARUM USE). At Matins, the responsories or responds were the most notable form; at Vespers and Compline the psalms, canticle, hymns and concluding Marian antiphon were set by composers in various ways.

Old Hall MS A manuscript collection of Mass sections and motets by named English composers c1370–1420, usually regarded as belonging to the Chapel Royal during Henry V's reign, but possibly intended for the household chapel of the Duke of Clarence, brother of Henry V.

CE: *CMM* 46, ed. A. Hughes and M. Bent (Rome, 1969–73)

Oliphant see Horn

Oliver Late C14/early C15 English composer. One of the more senior composers represented in the older layer of the Old Hall MS, his 4 pieces there are in a sonorous, sometimes ornamented, treble-dominated style.

Opera A drama sung throughout with scenery and acting. Its musical predecessors in the C16 included the ballet and the INTERMEDIO. Opera, however, required for its creation a kind of drama that lent itself to continuous music: the pastorale, culminating in the late C16 in Tasso's *Aminta* and Guarini's *Il Pastor fido*, provided the model for the early opera librettos set by Peri and Caccini.

Opitiis, Benedictus de (fl. 1514–22) Franco-Flemish organist and composer (not identical with Benedictus Ducis). Organist at Notre Dame in Antwerp from c1514 and at Henry VIII's court from 1516 to 1518. He was one of the composers who helped to introduce the Continental style of sacred music into England; 2 occasional motets from his Antwerp period were published, and more of his music survives in MS.

Oratorio A composition with an extended religious libretto performed outside the context of the liturgy. Early examples took their name from the oratorio (= oratory, chapel) of the Oratorians, a religious order founded in mid-C16 Rome by St Philip Neri, whose services were aimed at ordinary people and included scripture readings and the singing of LAUDE. The sacred dialogue and Gospel narration (see HISTORIA) are related antecedents of the oratorio.

Ordinary of the Mass see **Mass**

Organ The history of the church organ unfolds continuously from the Middle Ages to the Baroque, while there are 2 related instruments developing in the late medieval period (see Portative and Positive organ, below). Until around 1400 the organ had a single keyboard with a range of 1 to 3 octaves, the 'keys' being large and cumbersome, or consisting of sliders to be moved in and out; since there were no drawstops to allow variety of tone-colour, the sound was a fixed, loud 'mixture' of several ranks of pipes. Pedals and a second manual ('positive') were added in Germany and the Netherlands in the late Middle Ages, the latter having its own pipework behind the player (hence the German *Rückpositiv*). Drawstops came into use towards c1500. National styles of organ building emerged during the Renais-sance, and in Germany further manuals and novel, imitative tone-colours were added; Italian and English organs remained simple in design, often with just one manual, a basic chorus of stops with only one or 2 individually distinctive colours.

Positive organ With the refinement of the keyboard and development of finger technique in the C13–14, a small movable instrument was devised, suitable for church or secular surroundings. By contrast with the church organ it required only one person to work the bellows. Its secular version later became the chamber organ found in English homes and used in consort music.

Portative organ Known as the *organetto* in Italy, this was the smallest type of medieval organ (post-1300), played with one hand while the other worked the bellows. As its name implies, the player could carry it as he played – for example, in processions.

Portative organ, 82 cm

Organ hymn ALTERNATIM setting of a Catholic Office hymn current in the C15–16, in which alternate verses

are sung in plainsong and played on the organ in polyphonically elaborated form. Some of the earliest examples were German (e.g. in the Buxheim Organ Book); Blitheman and Tallis were among English pre-Reformation composers who turned to the genre (examples in the Mulliner Book). It existed also in France, Italy and Spain (e.g. A. de Cabezón).

Organ Mass Settings of the Mass Ordinary consisting of short polyphonic organ versets alternating with choral plainsong. It developed in the C15 and became common in France and Italy.

Organi, Bartolomeo degli see **Bartolomeo degli Organi**

Organum The earliest type of polyphony (C9 to mid-C13) consisting of a liturgical plainsong tenor with one or more contrapuntal parts added. Notre Dame composers (Leonin, Perotin) restricted *organum* to the most ornate Mass Proper chants–the Gradual and Alleluia–and only treated the soloist's part, leaving the rest to be sung chorally in unadorned chant.

Orologio, Alessandro (b. *c*1555; d. ?Vienna, 1633) Italian composer and trumpeter. Before 1580 a musician at the Imperial court in Prague, and from 1603 to 1613 Imperial vice-*Kapellmeister*, he also worked at the courts of Hesse (where he met Dowland), Dresden and Wolfenbüttel, and finally became choirmaster at the Austrian monastery of Garsten. He published several volumes of madrigals and canzonets, but is most notable for his INTRADAS of 1597, one of the earliest publications of its kind to appear in Germany.

Orpharion Plucked string instrument; smaller than but similar in shape to the BANDORA, and essentially a metal-strung lute. Its 6 (7 by 1600) courses use the same tuning as the lute, whose solo repertory was therefore available to it; though possessing a very different tone-quality, it was sometimes specified as a possible alternative to the lute. It was most common in England.

Ortiz, Diego (b. Toledo, *c*1525; d. after 1570) Spanish composer. Worked from 1555 to 1570 at the vice-regal court of the Duke of Alba in Naples. His publications consist of a volume of sacred music (hymns, Magnificats and motets) and a treatise of outstanding importance on viol playing, the *Tratado de glosas* of 1553. This is a noteworthy source of Renaissance ornamentation and improvisational practice, containing variations on stock basses, arrangements of madrigals where the viol plays ornamental figures to a keyboard accompaniment, cadential embellishments and so on. His techniques led to the English 'divisions on a ground' and the improvisatory, viola bastarda style (see DIVISION VIOL).

Tratado, ed. M. Schneider (repr. Kassel, 1967)

Orto, Mabriano de (b. Ortho, nr. Laroche-en-Ardenne; d. Nivelles, nr. Brussels, Feb 1529) Franco-Flemish composer and singer. A Papal singer from 1484 to 1494, and singer to Philip the Handsome of Burgundy (whom he accompanied to Spain in 1506) from 1505, he also held ecclesiastical posts in Flanders and became chaplain to the future Emperor Charles V in 1515. Petrucci issued a volume of his Masses in 1505, and included his chansons, motets and Lamentations in anthologies; his style has technical similarities to that of Josquin.

Ostinato see **Ground**

Oswald von Wolkenstein (b. ?Schloss Schöneck, Pustertal, Tyrol, c1377; d. Merano, 2 Aug 1445) Austrian poet, composer and politician. From an early age he travelled widely in Europe and Asia, and was said to be fluent in 10 languages. From 1415 he was in the service of King Sigismund who took him to the Council of Constance and on various diplomatic missions. Between 1421 and 1427 he was involved in a series of bitter quarrels with other landowners (his wild and lawless behaviour led to his being twice arrested and imprisoned). From 1430 to 1432 he was again involved in politics, and attended the Council of Basel; he then retired to his estates and gave up writing music and poetry.

Some 120 of his songs survive, and they mark a new departure in the development of German song, being not courtly and stylised but the expression of genuine personal feeling. Many are love-songs, inspired by his various love-affairs and also his marriage (to Margarete von Schwangau in 1417), and these are especially heartfelt. Some are topical, containing references to current political events; others were inspired by his visit to Jerusalem (1409–11), and there are also a number of sacred texts. Oswald's style is individual, putting depth of expression before conventional rules; it is not shackled by the weighty traditions governing German courtly song which bound his predecessors, and contains elements borrowed from contemporary French and Italian song as well as from folksong. Most of his songs are monophonic, but some are in 2 or 3 parts and a few of these are *contrafacta* based on works by Machaut, Landini and others.

Songs in *DTO* xviii

Othmayr, Caspar (b. Amberg, 12 Mar 1515; d. Nürnberg, 4 Feb 1553) German composer. A student at Heidelberg from 1533 and pupil of Lemlin there, he was a schoolmaster at Heilsbronn, nr. Ansbach, from 1545 and briefly held ecclesiastical posts in Ansbach 1547–8 before going to Nürnberg. Along with Senfl and Hofhaimer, he raised the German polyphonic song to a new level of artistic achievement and sophistication; many of his songs were included in the anthologies of his fellow-student Forster, and his style was fresher and less conservative than that of some of his contemporaries. He also published church music.

Selected works in *EDM* xvi, xxvi

Ott, Johannes (b. Rain am Lech, nr. Donauwörth, c1500; d. Nürnberg, 1546) German book dealer and bibliophile. He lived at Nürnberg and edited the song collection *121 neue Lieder* published by Formschneider in 1534, an important impulse towards the dissemination of the Lieder repertory. He also edited motets, Masses and a second songbook of 115 pieces (1544).

P

Pacelli, Asprilio (b. Vasciano, Umbria, c1570; d. Warsaw, 4 May 1623) Italian composer. From c1589 he held various posts as *maestro di cappella*, including that at the German College in Rome (1592–1602); in 1603 he succeeded Marenzio as *Kapellmeister* to the brilliant Polish court in Warsaw. He published motets and psalms in up to 20 parts, many in the polychoral Venetian style.

Padoana, paduana see **Pavane**

Padova, da see under the first name of composers known thus

Padovano see **Annibale Padovano**

Paix, Jakob (b. Augsburg, 1556; d. after 1623) German organist and composer of Flemish descent. Worked as organist, schoolmaster and organ builder at Lauingen an der Donau 1576–1601, and from 1601, until obliged to leave on the return of Catholicism in 1617, was court organist at Neuburg an der Donau. His organ tablature of 1583 contains dances and fantasias, and transcriptions of motets and secular pieces by composers such as Josquin, Janequin and Lassus in which the models are obscured by quantities of stereotyped figuration. He also published church music, songs and a collection of canons.

Palestrina, Giovanni Pierluigi da (b. Palestrina, 9 May 1525; d. Rome, 2 Feb 1594) Italian composer. A choirboy at S. Maria Maggiore, Rome, in 1537, he was appointed organist and singer at Palestrina cathedral in 1544 under the Bishop who later became Pope Julius III. From 1551 onwards he was in Rome: in 1551–4 and from 1571 until his death as choirmaster to the Cappella Giulia (which sang in St Peter's); in about 1554 as singer in the Papal (Sistine) choir; as choirmaster at St John Lateran in 1555–60, at S. Maria Maggiore in 1561–6, and at the Roman Seminary in 1566–71. In the 1560s he also directed concerts at the Tivoli villa of Cardinal Ippolito d'Este, and had a Mass commissioned by the Duke of Mantua, who tried to persuade him to leave Rome for the Mantuan court.

Though he was hardly at all employed as a musician in the Papal choir, much of Palestrina's music was destined for performance by it. His output contains 105 Masses (a remarkable number even for that period), some 250 motets, several volumes of specific liturgical works (Offertories, Litanies, hymns, Magnificats and Lamentations), 2 books of madrigals and 2 of spiritual madrigals. His preference for writing Masses and for remaining in Rome within the orbit of the Papacy marks him as a man of conservative inclinations, though his style did develop away from the mainly contrapuntal towards more chordal and harmonically orientated writing – a fact often masked by the use of his music today as a model for the discipline of counterpoint. He shunned the pressures of his age towards the expression in music of moods or words, choosing to set even quite highly-charged texts in an abstract, perhaps impersonal idiom possessed of a beautiful equilibrium of melodic line and harmonic euphony. Though he wrote parody Masses on his own and others' pieces, much of his sacred music springs from plainsong, and many Masses are based on Gregorian melodies or on motets themselves so based. His madrigals were, as might be expected, conservative compared with progressive developments in that form.

CE: *Werke*, ed. F. Espagne and F. X. Haberl (Leipzig, 1862–1907); *Le opere complete*, ed. R. Casimiri and others (Rome, 1939–   )

Pallavicino, Benedetto (b. Cremona, ?1551; d. Mantua, 6 May 1601) Italian composer. A singer at the Gonzaga court in Mantua from 1582, and in 1596, on Wert's death, secured the post of court *maestro di cappella* which Monteverdi had coveted. His madrigals were extremely popular (though Burney thought them uninventive) and 10 volumes were published, some posthumously; he also composed church music, including motets in up to 16 parts. (The monk Benedetto Pallavicino who issued the composer's various posthumous publications was his son.)

Paminger, Leonhard (b. Aschach, nr. Linz, 29 Mar 1495; d. Passau, 3 May 1567) Austrian composer. After studying in Vienna, he settled in Passau in 1513 as teacher (later Rector) at St Nicholas school, but had to give up his post by, at latest, 1558 on account of his Protestant beliefs. A friend of Luther and Melancthon, he wrote controversial religious pamphlets as well as a collection of motets (posthumously published), designed to provide music for the whole Lutheran year. Their style ranges from the simple and chordal to the richly imitative; Paminger also contributed some secular songs to Ott's collection.

Pandora see **Bandora**

Pandurina see **Lute**

Panpipes Wind instrument in which a hollow sound is produced by blowing across the top of a row of vertical pipes. Usually made of wood or pottery and often semicircular in shape, it had a diatonic range of between 5 and 11 notes. It was popular at the time of the troubadours, but was made obsolete by the increasing use of chromatic inflections and gave place to the transverse flute.

Panpipes, 12.5 cm

Paolo (Tenorista) da Firenze (d. Arezzo, Sep 1419) Italian composer. Abbot of the Camaldolese monastery at Pozzoveri, near Lucca, in 1404; also spent some time in Rome in the entourage of a Florentine cardinal, and in 1406 composed the madrigal *Godi Firenze* to celebrate Florence's conquest of Pisa. His use of the madrigal form–a third of his 30 surviving secular pieces are madrigals – is unusual at this time when other forms had largely superseded it. Secular works in *PMFC* ix, ed. W. T. Marrocco

Parabosco, Girolamo (b. Piacenza, 1520 or 1524; d. Venice, 21 Apr 1557) Italian organist and composer. After studying with Willaert in Venice he visited Florence, Brescia, Padua and Verona, where he was popular as poet and courtier as well as musician, before becoming organist at St Mark's, Venice, in 1551. Here he joined Annibale Padovano in performing works for 2 organs; his principal gift was for improvisation, and only 3 of his organ pieces survive, but he also published madrigals which show him to be a disciple of Willaert.

Paraphrase Mass Renaissance Mass setting based on a single pre-existing melody, whether secular or from plainsong, which permeates the vocal texture equally rather than being confined to one voice (as in cantus firmus treatment). Josquin Desprez wrote some excellent early examples, e.g. the *Missa Pange lingua*.

Parody Mass C16 Mass setting using musical material from pre-existing polyphonic pieces, as distinct from single melodies. Sometimes the whole texture of the model was taken over with a change of text, but usually composers used more subtle methods of borrowing, e.g. breaking up the model into sections to be interspersed with free material, or taking individual lines or combinations of lines and adding fresh counterpoints.

Parsley, Osbert (b. 1511; d. Norwich, 1585) English composer. For 50 years a singer at Norwich cathedral, he composed Anglican church music, complete Latin psalm settings, a set of Lamentations in which the traditional plainsong reciting tone is used as cantus firmus, and consort music. The well-known *Persli's Clock* is based on ascending and descending scales derived from the hexachord.

Sacred works in *TCM* x

Parsons, Robert (b. Exeter; drowned Newark, 25 Jan 1570) English composer. A member of the Chapel Royal from 1563, he composed fine Latin votive antiphons and psalms, Anglican church music in up to 7 parts, viol consorts containing some curious harmonic experiments, and consort songs which may have been written for

plays. His *Pandolpho* is one of the greatest of all tragic consort songs.

Parthenia The first printed collection of English virginal music (1612) containing works by the foremost virginal composers–Byrd, Bull and Gibbons.

Passamezzo Italian dance of 1550–1600 in moderately quick duple time (perhaps twice as fast as the pavane). Early examples use various stock bass figures such as the *passamezzo antico* and *moderno*, and the ROMANESCA.

Passamezzo antico

Passamezzo moderno

Passereau, Pierre (fl. 1533–5) French composer. A singer at Bourges cathedral, he contributed 23 chansons to anthologies published between 1533 and 1547. Most of these are humorous and/or obscene; his style is lively, with descriptive passages reminiscent of Janequin. *Il est bel et bon* became popular in a keyboard arrangement by G. Cavazzoni.

CE: *Opera omnia* (*CMM* 45), ed. G. Dottin (Rome, 1967)

Passion Musical setting of the Passion narrative from one of the Gospels. In plainsong settings for Catholic use 3 individuals respectively sang the parts of (1) the Evangelist, (2) Christ, and (3) other characters and the crowd; this would take place during various Holy Week services. In most ritual polyphonic settings only (3) was taken by the choir (and then sometimes only the crowd, or *turba*, part). In the 'through-composed' Passion, however, the *whole* text was set to polyphony. For the Lutheran Passion, see HISTORIA.

Paumann, Conrad (b. Nürnberg, 1410x15; d. Munich, 24 Jan 1473) German organist, blind from birth. In 1440 he became an organist in his native city, and in 1451 entered the service of the Dukes of Bavaria. As a performer on many instruments he won great renown, which became international with a visit to the Mantua court in 1470; both the Duke of Milan and the King of Aragón desired his services but he declined, fearing reprisals by competing Italian organists. His compositions include a few songs and organ pieces, and a treatise of 1452 (*Fundamentum organisandi*) copied into the last pages of the LOCHAMER LIEDERBUCH. This elucidates the embellishment of chant in keyboard style, and contains sensitive arrangements of chants and secular melodies.

Fundamentum in *CEKM* 1, ed. W. Apel

Pavane, pavan Early C16 court dance with slow solemn movements and dignified gestures, which originated in Italy but rapidly spread all over Europe. It was in slow duple time (some early Spanish examples however are in triple time) and was often followed by a galliard. Though this pairing yielded in popularity to the passamezzo/saltarello around 1550, it was retained in England, where the virginalists developed it into stylised keyboard music of great distinction. The German 'paduana' was used as an introductory movement to C17 instrumental suites.

Pedersøn, Mogens (b. *c*1585; d. Copenhagen, ?*c*1623) Danish composer. Studied in Venice with G. Gabrieli in 1605–9 and was in England in 1611–14; became vice-*maestro* at the Royal Chapel in Copenhagen in 1618. He wrote a book of Masses and motets, and while under Gabrieli issued a volume of madrigals which showed how thoroughly he had mastered an up-to-date, expressive madrigal idiom.

Peerson, Martin (b. March, nr. Cambridge, *c*1572; d. London, end Dec 1650) English composer. Studied at Oxford until 1613 and then became organist and choirmaster at St Paul's cathedral. His *Private Musick* of 1620 contains secular songs for 1 or 2 voices and viols or virginals; the *Motets or Grave Chamber Music* (1630), which includes 2 very fine songs of mourning, requires various combinations of voices and instruments with continuo, and is more forward-looking in style. He contributed to Leighton's *Teares* and Ravenscroft's psalter, and composed consort music in a relatively simple style and descriptive keyboard pieces.

Peguilhan see **Aimeric de Peguilhan**

Peire Cardenal (b. Veillac, nr. Le Puy, late C12; d. 1275) One of the most celebrated troubadours of his time; his 70 poems (for which only 3 tunes survive) contain much satirical criticism of the contemporary moral and political climate, sometimes verging on heresy.

Peire Vidal (b. ?Toulouse, *c*1160; d. ?Salonika [Thessaloniki], ?1205) Troubadour; active from 1175 onwards not only in Provence, Spain and northern Italy but also at the Hungarian court. Apparently an eccentric character, he exploited the esoteric style known as the 'trobar clos'; 13 of his 40 poems have surviving melodies. *Bim pac d'Iveru* covers a remarkable range of almost 2 octaves.

Pellegrini, Vincenzo (b. Pesaro, late C16; d. Milan, 23 Aug 1630) Italian composer and priest. A canon at Pesaro cathedral from 1594, he became *maestro di cappella* at Milan cathedral in 1611. He published church music in both old and new styles and a volume of organ canzonas, many of which are balanced formal structures in which material from one section returns (often varied) in a later one, or which develop one motif throughout in various manners.

Peñalosa, Francisco de (b. ?Talavera de la Reina, c1470; d. Seville, 1 Apr 1528) Spanish composer. From before 1497 until 1516 he held posts as singer at the court of Aragon and *maestro de capilla* to various members of the royal family; in 1517 he became a Papal singer in Rome. Probably the teacher of Morales, he was highly regarded by his contemporaries and contributed 10 songs, including a remarkable 6-part quodlibet, to the *Cancionero de Palacio*. His church music, much of it of high quality, survives in MS.

CE: Masses and *villancicos* in *MME*, i, v, x, ed. H. Anglés

Penorcon see **Cittern**

Peraza, Francisco (b. Salamanca, 1564; d. Seville, 24 June 1598) Spanish organist and composer. Organist at Seville, he had an exceptionally high reputation; it was said that 'an angel lived in each of his fingers'. Only one of his many organ works survives – a *Medio registro alto* which for its period contains a remarkable variety of figurations and freedom of modulation.

Percussion The fact that most of the following instruments are often pictured in the hands of angels does not necessarily mean that they were habitually used in church.

Castanets Pair of wooden clappers originating in medieval Spain; used especially to accompany the sarabande, but sometimes heard in church.

Cymbals Like modern cymbals in appearance, but thicker, and more domed in the centre. Of Eastern origin,

they were 6–10 inches/15–25 cm in diameter and played horizontally, not vertically.

Rommelpot The name means 'rumble pot', and the sound was produced by rubbing a stick which had been poked through a membrane stretched across a hollow receptacle. Entirely a popular instrument.

Tambourin Medieval string drum, with 2 or 3 gut strings, tuned to a keynote and its 5th, stretched over an oblong soundbox. All the strings were struck together, with a drone effect, and the tambourin, slung on the right wrist and played with the right hand, often accompanied a pipe held by the left hand.

Tambourine, timbrel Single-headed frame drum with jingles or small bells attached, often played by women.

Tambourine, 30 cm

Triangle Triangle (or other shape) of metal with rings hanging on lower bar, sometimes open at one corner to improve the resonance. Another instrument of Oriental origin, it was often used with the 3-holed pipe.

Peréz, Juan Ginés (bp. Orihuela, nr. Murcia, 7 Oct 1548; d. c1612) Spanish composer. Initially *maestro de capilla* at the cathedral in Orihuela, he took up a similar post in Valencia in 1581, returning to Oriheula in 1595. He composed much church music, some of which mixes the new expressive style with polyphonic sections; in one motet monodic solo passages are accompanied by a bassoon. He is believed to have composed some of the music for the *Misterio de Elche*, a religious drama traditionally performed on the feast of the Assumption (Aug 15).

Peri, Jacopo (b. Rome, 20 Aug 1561; d. Florence, 12 Aug 1633) Italian composer. He was a pupil of Malvezzi, and from about 1588 was active as singer, keyboard player and composer at the Medici court in Florence, and from 1579 to *c*1605 was also organist at the church of the Badia there. In 1595 he started work on *Dafne*, the earliest opera, which was performed at a carnival in 1597–8.

Peri was one of the principal composers to establish the new recitative style and the concept of opera. The music for *Dafne* is lost, but his *Euridice*, performed at the wedding of Maria de' Medici to Henry IV of France in October 1600, was one of the first published operas. He wrote music for later court entertainments, sometimes jointly with other composers, including operas, *intermedi* and *balli*; his first piece of this kind was one of the *intermedi* for the famous 1589 wedding entertainment. In *Euridice* there is no overture; Peri used just 4 accompanying harmony instruments and an occasional chorus. His 1609 songbook *à 1–3* contains sonnets, madrigals and arias. Where his colleague Caccini preferred tuneful, gracefully ornamented vocal writing, Peri excelled in dramatic and expressive declamation, allowing considerable flexibility in his operatic recitative.

Perissone Cambio see **Cambio, Perissone**

Perotin (b. *c*1160; d. 1200x1205 or 1220) French composer, one of 2 having that name whose lifespans are slightly different. Along with Leonin, he was associated with Notre Dame, Paris, possibly as a *magister cantus*, and was perhaps the greatest composer of

his time. His major achievement was the revision of Leonin's *organa* and the introduction of new elements of style and scoring. He used all the rhythmic modes, gave rhythmic interest to both voices in 2-part writing, and added 1 or 2 more voices to produce music in 3 or 4 parts. The celebrated *organa* on the Christmas and St Stephen's day Graduals (*Viderunt* and *Sederunt*) date from 1198 and 1199 respectively. These 4-part settings are conceived on a monumental time-scale fitting the building for which they were written, and are rich in eloquent, imaginative, yet delicate vocal writing; they are justly hailed as masterpieces of Gothic music. Perotin's *organa* were discussed and admired by later theorists; he was also noted as a composer of *clausulae* (which may have been used to shorten Leonin's *organa*) and conductus in up to 3 parts.

CE: *The Works of Perotin*, ed. E. Thurston (New York, 1970)

Perrin d'Angicourt (b. *c*1220; d. 1300) Trouvère. Worked at the court of Brabant, and in the entourage of Charles of Anjou. His 30 poems were sufficiently popular to be copied into many MSS; 21 melodies survive.

Perugia, Niccolò da see **Niccolò da Perugia**

Perusio, Matheus de see **Matheus de Perusio**

Pesenti, Martino (b. Venice, *c*1600; d. Venice, May 1647xMar 1648) Italian composer, blind from birth. A pupil and skilful imitator of Monteverdi, he published 8 volumes of concertato madrigals and arias; he was especially successful at matching melancholy texts with attractive and appropriate music. He also published 4 volumes of dances for keyboard, and one of church music for 1 to 3 voices.

Pesenti, Michele (b. Verona, c1475; d. after 1521) Italian composer and priest. Petrucci's anthologies (1505–14) contain 33 of his frottolas, some to his own texts, which helped to set the pattern of development for C16 Italian secular music.

Frottolas in *IM* 1st ser., i, ed. G. Cesari and R. Monterosso

Pestain see **Chaillou de Pestain**

Peterhouse partbooks A set of MS partbooks dating from Henry VIII's reign (c1540) and providing an invaluable source of Latin polyphony in England during the last years of the medieval choral tradition, especially of music by Fayrfax, Taverner, Ludford and Aston. Its repertory covers some 40 years, and includes Masses, Magnificats, votive antiphons and ritual pieces. The tenor partbook is lacking.

Petrucci, Ottaviano (b. Fossombrone, nr. Urbino, 15 June 1466; d. Venice, 7 May 1539) The first music printer and publisher, active in Venice and Fossombrone in 1500–20. He used a multiple-impression method – first the words, then the staves, then the notes – a difficult process whose problems he overcame brilliantly to produce very elegant results. His earliest prints, the ODHECATON and 2 succeeding collections of secular music, were followed by luxurious volumes of Masses and motets, some devoted to individual composers (Josquin, Obrecht, etc.), and books of frottolas, *laude*, lute music and keyboard pieces.

Petrus de Cruce (Pierre de la Croix) (b. ?Amiens, c1250; d. after 1300) French composer and theorist who lived in Paris, though it has also been suggested that he was an Italian who brought his ideas about notation to Paris, since they foreshadowed notational developments in C14 Italy. Although only 2 motets are securely to be attributed to him, they show the real innovation of dividing the breve into a variable number of semibreves (3 or more) in the top part or triplum, increasing its domination of the other 2 voices and lending it a *parlando* style of rapid declamation. His ideas rapidly became fashionable in late C13 France.

Peuerl, Paul (b. 1570x80; d. after 1625) Austrian composer and organ builder. Initially organist at Horn, near Krems, from 1602, he became Protestant organist in Steyr in 1609 but lost this post on his return to Catholicism. His 4-part *Newen Padovanen . . .* (1611) was the first German ensemble publication to group dances into 4-movement variation suites, each movement being based on the same material. He also published 2 further volumes of dances, and one of songs.

CE: *DTO* lxx

Pevernage, André (Andries) (b. Harelbeke, nr. Courtrai, 1543; d. Antwerp, 30 July 1591) Franco-Flemish composer. He was choirmaster at Notre Dame, Courtrai, in 1565–85 (apart from a period when Calvinists controlled the city), and then at Notre Dame in Antwerp. He published 5 volumes of chansons in a serious style more akin to the madrigal or motet; though never visiting Italy he both wrote madrigals and edited an anthology of them in 1583. His church music in up to 8 parts shows the influence of the double-choir style; 4 of his sacred pieces are legibly portrayed in contemporary paintings.

Phalèse, Pierre (b. c1510; d. Louvain, c1573) Flemish music publisher. He set up in business at Louvain in 1545, and entered into partnership with Bellère at Antwerp in 1572. In 1581 his son Pierre transferred the firm completely to Antwerp, where it flourished into the C17.

Philippe de Vitry (b. Vitry, Champagne, 31 Oct 1291; d. Meaux or Paris, 9 June 1361) French theorist, poet and composer. A canon at Clermont en Beauvais in 1323, and bishop of Meaux from 1351. Two letters to him from Petrarch survive which praise his poetry, music and enquiring mind. Unlike most medieval theorists he was a composer of international and lasting reputation and outstanding ability. The ROMAN DE FAUVEL contains 6 motets attributed to him, which he discusses in his treatise *Ars nova* of c1320. This treatise (along with the contemporaneous writings of Johannes de Muris) is the fundamental source of information on the development of the mensural system of notation, and treats especially of the relationship between the different levels of rhythmic time values (breve to long, semibreve to breve, and so on). De Vitry's music shows a new lyricism, and an effective use of the hocket device. Further motets of his are found in the later Ivrea MS; these illustrate the early use of isorhythm as a constructive principle.

CE: in *PMFC* i, ed. L. Schrade

Philippot see **Filippo da Caserta**

Philips, Peter (b. ?London, 1560x61; d. Brussels, 1628) English composer. A choirboy at St Paul's in 1574, but as a Catholic had to emigrate, travelling to Rome via Douai in 1582. In 1589–90 he served Lord Paget, travelling with him to Spain, France and the Netherlands. He then settled in Antwerp, though following a visit to Sweelinck in Amsterdam in 1593 he was arrested for allegedly planning to murder the Queen of England. Freed for lack of proof, he became organist at the Brussels court chapel in 1597, and in later life held various clerical posts in Flanders.

An important carrier of English musical style to the Continent, Philips was probably the most famous English composer of his day in northern Europe, his collections of vocal music being reprinted many times at Antwerp. They include 3 books of madrigals, 2 of choral motets and 3 of concertato motets *à* 1–3 with continuo, one of Litanies and one of *bicinia* to French texts; he also wrote keyboard music, preserved in the Fitzwilliam Virginal Book. His madrigals belong to a conservative Italian tradition, thanks to his Roman training; in these he revels in colourful textures and sonorities, though his concertato motets are evidence that he kept abreast of newer trends. The keyboard music includes transcriptions and reworkings of well-known Italian madrigals, one of which is Caccini's monody *Amarilli*.

Madrigals in *MB* xxix, ed. J. Steele

Phinot, Dominique (d. 1557x60) French (or Italian) composer. He is known to have been in Lyons at least in 1547–8, and later to have lived in Pesaro. He was apparently executed for grossly indecent behaviour. One of the most important and highly esteemed polyphonists of his day, he published chansons and church music, most of which is in the richly imitative style of Gombert. However, some of his motets, and a fine set of Lamentations, are important early examples of the double-choir style developed by Willaert.

CE: *Opera omnia* (*CMM* 59), ed. J. Höfler and R. Jacob (Rome, 1972–4)

Picchi, Giovanni (b. 1572; d. Venice, 19 May 1643) Italian composer. Organist of the Frari church, Venice, from 1607, and at the Scuola di S. Rocco from 1623, he published a volume of dances for harpsichord which contains examples of brilliant virtuoso keyboard writing, adventurous keyboard sonorities, and inventive variation techniques. He also published a volume of ensemble music, with frequent concertino passages for 1 or 2 of the instruments.

CE: *Collected Keyboard Works* (*CEKM* 38), ed. J. Kreider (Rome, 1977)

Piccinini, Alessandro (b. Bologna, 30 Dec 1566; d. Bologna, before 1639) Italian lutenist. Worked at the courts of Modena and Ferrara before entering the service of Cardinal Aldobrandini at Bologna in 1597. He published 2 volumes of lute music; the preface to that of 1623 praises the virtues of the chitarrone.

Piero da Firenze (Maestro Piero) C14 Italian composer, who may have been associated with the courts of Milan and Verona where he took part in musical contests. His surviving output of 9 works consists of 3 *cacce* (an unusually large number; most composers wrote only one *caccia*) including *Con dolce brama* which has a lively portrayal of the art of sailing, and 6 madrigals several of which are canonic.

CE: in *CMM* 8/ii, ed. N. Pirrotta.

Pierre de la Croix see **Petrus de Cruce**

Pierre des Molins C14 composer known by only 2 pieces. *De ce foul pense*, from the Chantilly MS, was exceptionally popular and one of the most frequently copied pieces of the period, surviving in keyboard as well as vocal versions. *Amis tout dous vis*, his other surviving piece, is also known in instrumental versions as *Die molen van Paris*.

Piéton, Loyset (fl. ?1519–45) French composer. He may have lived in Lyons and Italy, as his motets, psalms and chansons appeared in anthologies

published in both Lyons and Venice. His motets are distinguished examples of the imitative polyphony of the post-Josquin generation; *O beata infantia, à 6*, is in the unusual mode of C minor Dorian, and was included in a volume of motets by Willaert.

Pietrobono (Pietro Bono) (b. 1417; d. Ferrara, 20 Sep 1497) Italian lutenist. Lived mainly in Ferrara, where he was court doctor as well as musician from 1441. Though none of his works is extant he was one of the most revered musicians of his time; the theorist Tinctoris thought especially highly of his improvisations.

Pilkington, Francis (b. ?Lancashire, *c*1565; d. Chester, 1638) English composer and clergyman. Studied at Oxford until 1595, and from 1602 was a singer at Chester cathedral. Ordained in 1612, he was a curate at various local churches, became cathedral precentor in 1623, and was appointed rector of Aldford, near Chester, in 1631. He published 3 volumes of ayres and madrigals, including balletts in the style of Morley and lute songs, some of which are impressive and imaginative, though others are marred by excessively intricate accompaniments. He also wrote music for viol and for lute, and is represented in Leighton's *Teares*.

Madrigals in *EM* xxv–vi, rev. edn.; Lute songs in *EL* 1st ser., vii, xv, rev. edn.

Pipe Wind instrument with whistle mouthpiece. Many have survived from the Middle Ages, usually with 6 fingerholes. Double pipes with one melody and one drone pipe, or 2 melody pipes which could be played in 4ths or 5ths were also common. Despite the Old French name 'flajolet' there is no connection with the later flageolet, a C17 invention.

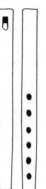

Six-holed pipe (front and rear views), 21.5 cm

Pipe and Tabor A 'one-man-band' much used for dance music. The long thin pipe had only 3 holes, producing its 1½-octave range from harmonics, and could be held in one hand, leaving the other free to beat a small drum slung from waist or wrist. Widely used from at least c1200 to the Renaissance, it has survived as a folk instrument.

Pipelare, Matthaeus (fl. c1500) Franco-Flemish composer. In 1498–1500 he taught singing at the brotherhood of Our Lady at 's-Hertogenbosch. His few Masses, motets and Magnificats survive in MS and in printed anthologies. His chanson *Fors seulement* is based on that of Ockeghem; it appeared in Kotter's keyboard tablature and provided the model for a Mass by Gombert. His Masses show ingenious craftsmanship, while his motet *Memorare mater Christi* is for 7 voices, symbolising the 7 sorrows of the Virgin and appropriately built on the tenor of a Spanish *villancico Nunca fué pena mayor.*
CE: *Opera omnia* (CMM 34), ed. R. Cross (Rome, 1966–7)

Pisador, Diego (b. Salamanca, c1509; d. after 1557) Spanish player of the vihuela. His father was in the service of the Archbishop of Santiago, and he took minor orders in 1526. His *Libro de Música* (1552) contains Spanish, French and Italian secular songs and motets arranged for voice and lute, fantasias in both polyphonic and improvisatory styles, and lute arrangements of 8 Josquin Masses.

Pisano, Bernardo (b. Florence, 12 Oct 1490; d. Rome, 23 Jan 1548) Italian composer. In 1511 he became choirmaster at Florence cathedral and baptistery, and a few years later was made a member of the Papal choir by the Medici Pope Leo X. In 1520 he settled in Rome as a Papal diplomat and informer. He is noted for his volume of Petrarch settings of 1520, the first that Petrucci published of a single Italian composer's works and an important document of the emerging madrigal style in its experimentation with freer poetic forms and imitative writing. Other secular works and Lamentations of his survive in Florentine MSS.
CE: in *CMM* 32/i, ed. F. d'Accone

Piva A quick triple-time dance, joined to the pavane and saltarello in Dalza's lute dance collection of 1508.

Plainsong (Gregorian chant) The liturgical chant of the Catholic church, named after Pope Gregory I (c600). The term is usually applied to Roman chant, one of the 4 'dialects' of the music of the Western Church, the others being Ambrosian, Mozarabic and Gallican chant. The word plainsong comes from the C13 term 'cantus planus'.

Planson, Jean (b. Paris, c1558; d. Paris, after 1612) French composer and organist. Worked in Paris, and won motet and chanson prizes at the 1578 Évreux composition contest; he may have met Dowland, who knew his work. He published 2 collections of chansons by himself and others, some in MUSIQUE MESURÉE style, and others in which a treble melody is given a very simple chordal accompaniment, anticipating the AIR DE COUR. Along with other composers, including Lassus, he set some of the poet Pibrac's psalm translations.

Plummer, John (b. c1410; d. Windsor, after 1484) English composer. Master of the Children of the Chapel Royal 1444–62, and a member of the choir of St George's, Windsor, probably 1458–84. What little of his music survives is of high quality; he was praised by the theorist Hothby and highly esteemed both in England and on the Continent, and is one of the most important English composers of the period. Three of his surviving motets are to Song of Songs texts; they are strongly English in style, especially in their triadic melodies and rhythmic simplicity. *Anna mater* is exceptionally forward-looking for its date, making much use of imitation in all 4 parts – an important innovation.

Poliphant see **Cittern**

Pommer Standard German name for SHAWM

Porta, Costanzo (b. Cremona, c1529; d. Padua, 19 May 1601) Italian composer, a pupil of Willaert; became a Franciscan monk and held posts in many Italian centres – at S. Antonio, Padua, in 1565–7 and 1595–1601, Ravenna cathedral in 1567–74 and 1580–9, and Loreto in 1574–80. He was an excellent teacher, numbering Viadana among his pupils. His output includes 3 extant books of madrigals, one of Masses, 4 of motets, and a further 4 of other liturgical music – Introits, hymns and psalms. In his Masses he

aimed to make the text intelligible according to the wishes of the Council of Trent. His motets show great contrapuntal skill, while his double-choir psalms are fine products of the fashion for CORI SPEZZATI. He also published keyboard music.

CE: *Opera omnia*, ed. S. Cisilino and J. Luiseto (Padua, 1964–   ); Keyboard music in *CEKM* 41, ed. B. Billeter

Porta, Ercole (b. Bologna, 10 Sep 1585; d. Carpi, nr. Modena, 30 Apr 1630) Italian composer. Held church posts in various small north Italian towns including Carpi; wrote a book of secular monodies and duets but was mainly a church composer, adopting the up-to-date concertato style. His *Sacro convito* (1620) contains an early 'orchestral' Mass for 5-part choir and church orchestra of 2 violins and 3 trombones; trombones are also used to sonorous effect in a duet motet.

Porter, Walter (b. c1588; bd. London, 30 Nov 1659) English composer. May have studied with Monteverdi in 1613–16; became a tenor singer in the Chapel Royal in 1618 and in 1639 was made choirmaster at Westminster Abbey, but lost the post in 1644. His Italianate leanings are apparent in his *Madrigals and Ayres* (1632) and duet motets of 1657. He introduced the figured bass (though this did not catch on in English church music) and wrote in recitative style with Italian types of ornamentation – a true baroque manner which stood quite apart from the English madrigal tradition. The 1632 collection includes instrumental toccatas, sinfonias and ritornellos as well as vocal pieces.

Madrigals and Ayres in *EM* xxxv, ed. D. Greer

Posch, Isaac (d. Carniola [Slovenia, N. Yugoslavia], beginning 1623) Austrian composer and organist. From 1614 an organist and organ builder in Carniola, he was in Oberberg [?Gornji Grad] in 1617–18 and Laibach [Ljubljana] in 1621. He published 2 volumes of instrumental suites in 4 and 5 parts, and one of concertos in up to 4 parts, some of which show the melodic influence of Slav folk music.

Power, Leonel (b. c1375; d. 5 June 1445) English composer. From about 1413 until 1421 he belonged to the chapel of the Duke of Clarence, brother of Henry V. In 1423 and from 1439–45 he was connected with Canterbury cathedral, and may have been master of the boys there. Power is the best-represented composer in the Old Hall MS, and, with Dunstable, one of the most influential English composers on the continent, to judge from the number of sources which preserve his music. His surviving works include at least one complete Mass, 22 Mass sections and 14 votive antiphons, all this showing considerable diversity of style as well as being of high quality. The earlier Mass sections (as in Old Hall) combine the French isorhythmic technique with a high level of dissonant writing, though Power experiments with various ways of unifying pairs of Mass movements. This culminated in his *Missa Alma redemptoris*, one of the earliest complete Masses to be unified by its cantus firmus, which is treated isorhythmically throughout. Many of his antiphons are chant-based, in various current styles including the 'treble-dominated', where the melody is freely decorated in the top part. Some late motets are, however, entirely free and remarkably consonant. Typically these are settings of texts addressed to the Virgin; they and similar pieces by Dunstable are in a 'new' style which was to be much favoured on the Continent. Power also wrote a treatise on DESCANT.

CE: *Complete Works* (*CMM* 50), ed. C. Hamm (Rome, 1969–)

Praeambulum C15/16 German term for prelude, found in keyboard and (later) lute sources, and written in either a free improvisatory or a contrapuntal style.

Praetorius, Hieronymus (b. Hamburg, 10 Aug 1560; d. Hamburg, 27 Jan 1629) German organist and composer, not related to Michael Praetorius. In 1582 he succeeded his father Jakob (also his teacher) as organist at the Jakobskirche in Hamburg. His *Opus Musicum* (collected church music; 1616–22) includes over 100 motets in up to 20 parts, many of which make skilful use of the Venetian polychoral style. His music is however old-fashioned for its time in that the basso continuo is still optional, and no use is made of the new monodic style or of *obbligato* instruments. He also published a collection of Latin and German sacred songs as used in his Hamburg church.

Selected works in *DDT* xxiii

Praetorius, Michael (b. Creuzburg, nr. Eisenach, 15 Feb 1571; d. Wolfenbüttel, 15 Feb 1621) German composer. The son of a pastor who had been a pupil of Luther, he became organist at the Marienkirche, Frankfurt an der Oder, in 1585. From 1595 he served the Bishop of Halberstadt as organist, demonstrating a new instrument there to many famous organists the following year. When his patron became Duke of Braunschweig-Lüneburg, he went with him to Wolfenbüttel and became his *Kapellmeister* in 1603. This post necessitated much travelling in Germany, which enabled him to earn widespread renown as a conductor of musical performances, an organ consultant, and a knowledgeable expert on practical music and on musical instruments.

Praetorius was a Lutheran church composer of amazing industry. Dominating his output is the 9-volume *Musae Sioniae* containing 1,244 chorale settings, but he published many others too, altogether including pieces on every conceivable scale from little *bicinia* to massive polychoral variations with instrumental support. He also wrote much other liturgical music and a set of 312 dances (*Terpsichore*). His 3-volume treatise *Syntagma Musicum* (1619) is an invaluable compendium of information on German music, musical instruments and performance, based on what he heard and saw in his travels.

CE: *Werke*, ed. F. Blume (Wolfenbüttel, 1928–40)

Precentor The title of the choirmaster in a cathedral or monastic church.

Pres, Josquin des see **Josquin**

Preston, Thomas (d. *c*1563) English organist and composer. Choirmaster of Magdalen College, Oxford, in 1543 and organist at Trinity College, Cambridge (1548–59), and St George's, Windsor (1559–63). He composed 12 Offertory settings for keyboard, including the popular *Felix namque*, and an *alternatim* organ Mass for Easter, containing the only known sequence setting of the time. His keyboard writing is uniquely virtuosic for the period, anticipating that of Farnaby, and genuinely instrumental in style. He exploits the instrument's full compass, and makes much use of complex syncopated rhythms and of canon.

Organ works in *EECM* x, ed. D. Stevens

Prima prattica Italian for 'first practice'; a term first used by Monteverdi's brother Giulio Cesare in the preface to Monteverdi's own *Scherzi musicali* of 1607, to describe music which 'commands the words' rather than the reverse (see SECONDA PRATTICA). He applied it to the sacred polyphony of the Franco-Flemings up to the mid-C16; in some respects it has affinities with the STILE ANTICO.

Prioli see **Priuli**

Prioris, Johannes (fl. 1490–1512) ?Franco-Flemish composer. Organist at St Peter's in Rome in 1490, and *maître de chapelle* to Louis XII of France in 1507. He published a fine Requiem which skilfully paraphrases the traditional plainsongs, and also composed attractive chansons and motets.

Priuli, Giovanni (b. Venice, *c*1575; d. ?Vienna, 1629) Italian composer. Served at Urbino, St Mark's, Venice, the court of Archduke Ferdinand at Graz and later Vienna, where he directed music from 1614 or 1615. His sacred music reveals a debt to G. Gabrieli, with whom he studied, in his handling of rich sonorities; this is true also of his instrumental canzonas, one of which has notated echo effects. He also published madrigals.

Motets and instrumental music in *CM* ii, ed. A. Biales

Processionale A Catholic liturgical book containing chants (mainly antiphons and responsories) for ritual processions before Mass.

Proper of the Mass see **Mass**

Proportion In mensural notation (1400–1600), the diminution or augmentation of normal note values. The most common were the 'proportio dupla', 'tripla', and 'sesquialtera', respectively requiring diminution in the ratios 1:2, 1:3 and 2:3. Renaissance singers were quite familiar with the system, whose more tricky applications offered a certain intellectual challenge.

Prosdocimus de Beldemandis (b. *c*1380; d. Padua, 1428) Italian theorist. A member of the arts faculty at Padua university, he wrote 8 treatises on musical matters, including 2 on notation which described the Italian notational practice of the C14 and pleaded (unsuccessfully) for its wider use.

Provins see **Guiot de Provins**

Psalm A number of complete psalms, each ending with the doxology ('Gloria Patri') constitute the major part of the OFFICE in the Roman rite; they were originally sung to one of 8 plainsong tones, according to the mode of the relevant antiphon. Polyphonic settings developed from simple FALSOBORDONE to fully-fledged composed pieces, often for double choir (derived from ancient antiphonal singing and especially common in the Venice region from 1520). Whole or partial psalm texts became frequently used for Latin or German motets and for English anthems for use outside the strict provisions of the liturgy; in Lutheran Germany the term 'psalm motet' describes such a piece. Protestant psalm tunes or settings were often collected together in psalters (e.g. those of East and Ravenscroft).

Psaltery Plucked string instrument with open metal strings stretched over a flat soundbox and played with a quill or the fingers. The shape varied, but the snout-like trapezoid with incurved sides was most common. (A triangular psaltery was sometimes called 'rote' or 'rotta'.) Its tuning was diatonic but the compass varied widely. Imported to Europe during the Crusades, the psaltery was very popular during the Middle Ages as both solo and ensemble instrument and there are many literary references to it; but during the C15 it gradually gave place to the chromatic harpsichord and virginals.

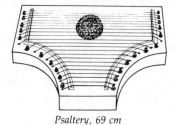

Psaltery, 69 cm

Pujol, Juan (Pablo) (b. Barcelona, 1573; d. Barcelona, May 1626) Spanish composer and priest. Held the post of *maestro de capilla* at the cathedrals of Tarragona (from 1593), Saragossa (Pilar) (from 1596), and Barcelona (from 1613). One of the most important Spanish composers of the early C17, he wrote much church music, some of which uses basso continuo. His 8-part Masses contain effective double-choir writing, and his psalm-settings make ingenious use of the Gregorian tones. His style is severe yet dramatic; his Holy Week music continued to be sung in Barcelona cathedral until at least the recent past.

CE: *Opera omnia*, ed. H. Anglés (Barcelona, 1926–32)

Pullois (Pyllois), Jean (d. 1478) Franco-Flemish composer. Choirmaster at Notre Dame in Antwerp from at least 1443 to 1447 (Ockeghem sang under him in 1443–4) and a member of the Papal choir from 1447 onwards. His compositions survive alongside those of his greater contemporaries in important sources such as the Trent Codices (which contain a cyclic Mass of his), but he was not considered good enough to win a post at the Burgundian court.

CE: *Opera omnia* (*CMM* 41), ed. P. Gülke (Rome, 1967–   )

Puy d'Arras One of several French societies that organized literary and musical festivals with competitions in the TROUVÈRE period.

Puy d'Évreux Composition competition (with classes for different types of vocal piece) founded by COSTELEY and held in Évreux on St Cecilia's day between 1575 and 1614. Lassus won prizes on two occasions; other winners included Titelouze and du Caurroy.

Pyamour, John (d. 1431) English composer. A member of the Chapel Royal in 1419–when a benefice at Lufford (Northants) was conferred on him –and from at least 1420 Master of the Children; in 1427 he was in France with the Duke of Bedford. His one surviving motet, *Quam pulchra es*, is in a mellifluous embellished conductus style, with few strong dissonances, which seems relatively advanced in comparison with the music of the Old Hall MS.

Pycard Late C14/early C15 French composer, who served in John of Gaunt's household in the 1390s. He is one of the most prolific and also most advanced composers represented in the Old Hall MS, and his music reveals a technical virtuosity unique in this period. Three of his Gloria settings are canonic, one being a double canon with a free 5th part; one of his Credos is a complex 3-part canon with 2 free voices, and an (incomplete) troped Sanctus sets the chant on which it is based as a canon 2 in 1. His style is often very dissonant in the *ars nova* manner.

Pygott, Richard (fl. 1516–33) English composer. A member of Cardinal Wolsey's household chapel from c1516 until 1529, and a Gentleman of the Chapel Royal in 1533. He has 2 pieces in the Peterhouse partbooks, and also wrote an imitative carol.

Pykini Late C14 French composer. His name may be a corruption of Picquigny, a town near Amiens; if so he may be Robert de Picquigny, chamberlain to Charles II of Navarre. His attractive *Plasanche or tost* is a spring song which makes much use of imitation.

Pyllois see **Pullois**

Q

Quagliati, Paolo (b. Chioggia, *c*1555; d. Rome, 16 Nov 1628) Italian composer and organist. He worked as an organist in Rome from 1574 (from 1601 at S. Maria Maggiore), and in 1621 was made an Apostolic Notary by Pope Gregory XV whose family he served. In 1611 he composed a dramatic cantata which includes both monodies and 5-part ensembles, and his monodies of 1623, some of which have *obbligato* violin parts, mark an important stage in the development of the chamber cantata. He also published motets for up to 8 voices; canzonets, concertato madrigals, and instrumental ricercars and canzonas.

Cantatas in *SCMA* xiii, ed. V. Gotwals and P. Keppler

Quodlibet The combination in a polyphonic composition of many different melodies or snatches therefrom. Folk or popular tunes were treated in this way; the form reached a high artistic level in the German polyphonic songs of Senfl.

R

Rackett Double-reed wind instrument with narrow cylindrical bore folded into 9 parallel tubes, and therefore of very low pitch relative to its size–the great bass, descending to C', is only 12 inches/30 cm high. The characteristic buzzing sound is produced by a wide reed set on a pirouette, and emerges from a small hole near the bottom of the instrument. The rackett first appeared in the later C16, and Praetorius lists 5 sizes, from great bass up to tenor, which play in consort at 16' pitch. A single instrument was useful for reinforcing bass lines at the octave; it was a considerable rarity even in the C16/17.

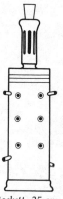

Rackett, 25 cm

Radino, Giovanni Maria (fl. 1592–1607) Italian lutenist and composer. May have visited Germany in youth, and was an organist in Padua from 1592 until 1598. His dances of 1592, which are unusual in the freedom of their modulations, appeared in 2 versions, one for lute and one for harpsichord (this latter is the earliest known published harpsichord music). He also published madrigals and a volume of instrumental ensemble music (some of this is by his son Giulio who died young) including polychoral canzonas.

Harpsichord dances in *CEKM* 33, ed. S. Ellingworth

Radomia, Mikołaj z Early C15 composer; may have been an instrumentalist at the Kraków court in 1422, and is the first important Polish composer. His surviving Mass movements, Magnificat, and motet show familiarity with the most modern Franco-Flemish styles (e.g. that of Ciconia), though they also contain features more reminiscent of the C14, showing the extent to which Machaut's influence spread into central Europe.

Raimbaud de Vacqueiras (b. 1155; d. 1207) Troubadour. Spent most of his life in Italy at the court of Boniface II of Montferrat, whom he accompanied on the Crusade of 1202. The author of the first known Italian poetry, he was also fluent in other languages–one of his poems has a verse in each of Provençal, Italian, French, Gascon and Galician-Portuguese. His *Kalenda maya*, now perhaps the best-known piece in the whole troubadour repertory, owes its dance-like character to its origins as an *estampie* played, according to the C14 descriptions, by 2 minstrels. Thirty-two of his poems and 8 melodies survive.

Rampollini, Matteo (bp. Florence, 2 June 1497; d. Florence, 23 Dec ?1553)

Italian composer; possibly a pupil of Isaac. He was teacher of music (1515) and later chaplain (1530–4) at the Medici chapel of S. Lorenzo in Florence, and 1520–8 was *maestro di cappella* at Florence cathedral in alternation with Verdelot. He contributed music to the festivities for the wedding of Duke Cosimo and Eleanor of Toledo in 1539, and published one of the earliest collections (c1550) of madrigal cycles to canzonas by Petrarch.

CE: *CMM* 32/vii, ed. F. d'Accone

Ramsey, Robert (fl. 1616–44) English composer. Took the Cambridge B.Mus. degree in 1616, and was organist at Trinity College, Cambridge, 1628–44. His output includes English and Latin church music, a dialogue between Saul and the Witch of Endor on the text later used by Purcell, and madrigals among which is a lament in dialogue form on the death of Prince Henry. The influence of the new Italian style can be seen in his work, especially in his settings of Latin texts.

Sacred music in *EECM* vii, ed. E. Thompson

Rasar (Rasor), William (fl. 1499–1514x15) English composer. A chorister at St George's, Windsor, in 1499; clerk and instructor of the choristers at King's College, Cambridge, from 1510 to about 1514 or 1515. His 5-part *Christe Jesu* Mass in the Forrest-Heather partbooks is not especially florid for the period but is unusual in having duple metre throughout. Thematic connections between the movements suggest that it may be based on a lost motet.

Mass in *EECM* xvi, ed. J. Bergsagel

Raselius, Andreas (b. Hahnbach bei Amberg, c1563; d. Heidelberg, 6 Jan 1602) German composer and theorist. A schoolmaster in Heidelberg, but having left the city as the result of Protestant intrigues returned later as *Kapellmeister* to the Elector Frederick IV. His Gospel motets of 1594 contain vivid descriptive passages; he suggests an accompaniment of horns, trombones and organ. In his chorale settings the congregation sing the melody accompanied by 4-part choral polyphony. He also wrote a history of Regensburg, where he went after leaving Heidelberg.

Sacred works in *DTB* xxix–xxx

Rasi, Francesco (b. Arezzo, c1575) Italian singer and composer, probably a pupil of Caccini. At the Florentine court in 1593–5; served at the Gonzaga court in Mantua in 1598–1620 (he may have sung the title role in Monteverdi's *Orfeo*) and composed an opera (*Ati e Cefale*) for a Mantuan wedding in 1617. In 1612 he journeyed to Vienna and Salzburg, dedicating a volume to the Archbishop of Salzburg. This is one of several publications of monodies in which Rasi followed the fashion for solo madrigals; his *Dialoghi* of 1620 are among the earliest Italian cantatas. His voice was singled out for praise in the preface to Gagliano's *Dafne*.

Rasor see **Rasar**

Rauschpfeife Double-reed wind instrument with expanding conical bore

Rauschpfeife, 47 cm

giving a compass of just over an octave. Essentially a reedcap SHAWM with loud incisive tone suitable for outdoor use, it was made in 5 or 6 sizes from soprano to great bass.

Ravenscroft, Thomas (b. *c*1590; d. *c*1633) English composer and theorist. Taught music at Christ's Hospital in 1618–22, and published a collection of psalms containing his own and others by the best composers of the day. He also issued several books of canons, catches and rounds which became the longest surviving collections of English popular song. Aimed at a lay public probably different from that which cultivated madrigal singing, they were a mixture of sacred and secular, the latter comprising ballads and settings of ribald verses. Some of the melodies may go back almost a century to the time of Henry VIII.

Reading Rota see **Sumer is icumen in**

Rebec Bowed string instrument, distinct from the fiddle, and descended from the Arab *rabab* and Byzantine *lūrā*. It was pearshaped, with round body

and flat soundboard, and, though larger sizes did exist, was most commonly a small soprano instrument with a piercing, nasal tone, played on the shoulder or across the chest. The number of strings varied between 1 and 5; some of these could be drones. It was especially associated with song and dance.

Recercare see **Ricercare**

Recitative A style of solo singing in imitation of natural speech inflections; it was one of the principal inventions of the Italian monodists (*c*1600), and was used particularly in the setting of narrative passages, such as prose texts in early opera. Accompanied by continuo, early recitative was impressive for its melodic design and emotive declamation, and less plain than the later *parlando* type.

Recorder Wind instrument with beak mouthpiece and 7 finger-holes

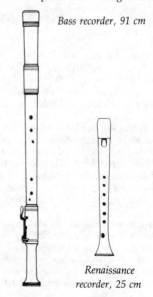

Bass recorder, 91 cm

Renaissance recorder, 25 cm

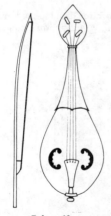

Rebec, 63 cm

at the front and a thumb-hole at the back. It was known in the Middle Ages and had developed several sizes by the late C14, when the name (meaning 'keepsake') was first used, but did not achieve its pre-eminent position among wind instruments until the Renaissance. It was the only wind instrument for which a tutor was published in the C16, by Ganassi in 1535, and this work shows that great technical brilliance was possible over a range of nearly 3 octaves. Virdung's *Musica getuscht* (1511) lists alto, tenor and bass sizes, but Praetorius gives 8, from great bass (lowest note F) to sopranino, and recommends a consort of the larger sizes as sounding best. Recorders, especially the lower ones, had a soft, expressive tone suitable for all sorts of music.

Recoupe see **Basse dance**

Redford, John (d. London, Nov 1547) English organist and composer. Organist at St Paul's cathedral from *c*1525 and choirmaster there from 1534; one of the main contributors to the Mulliner Book. All his organ music is liturgical; some is relatively vocal in style, but other pieces make full use of a 4½-octave keyboard, contain much imitation and idiomatic ornamentation, and require great technical skill. He also wrote songs for and produced dramatic entertainments at court, including the celebrated *Wyt and Science,* which does not survive.

Organ pieces in *EECM* vi, ed. J. Caldwell; x, ed. D. Stevens

Reed instruments Almost all medieval and Renaissance reed wind instruments would seem to have had a double reed (as on the modern oboe or bassoon). The only wind instruments with single reeds were the HORNPIPE (developed from the primitive one-piece reed pipe) and certain bagpipe

chanters with cylindrical bore. On some double-reed instruments, such as the SHAWM, the reed was attached directly to the instrument; on the medieval shawm it fitted into a flat metal disc against which the player's lips were pressed, but on the Renaissance model the reed was inserted into a funnel-shaped cup called a pirouette, so that only part of it projected to be taken into the player's mouth. This latter principle applied also to the RACKETT. On other instruments, such as the CURTAL and SORDUN (and also the largest shawms) the reed was mounted on a crook, or narrow tube emerging from the instrument. In the case of reedcap instruments, such as the CRUMHORN, the reed was entirely enclosed by a cap fitting over the top of the instrument, so that the player's lips had no direct contact with it.

Regal Small portable reed organ, with snarling tone reminiscent of a crumhorn consort. It usually had one rank of 8-foot pipes, and suffered from very unstable tuning. Henry VIII had 22 regals, and Monteverdi uses one to symbolize the underworld in *Orfeo.* The 'Bible regal' was an instrument which folded up into the semblance of a large book. The name 'regal' was also used for a Renaissance organ stop.

Regis, Johannes (b. Antwerp or Cambrai, *c*1430; d. ?Soignies, *c*1485) Franco-Flemish composer. Choirmaster at Antwerp cathedral *c*1463; thereafter Dufay's secretary until the latter's death in 1474, and then became a canon at Soignies. His surviving compositions include 2 Masses, 8 motets and 2 chansons; his music was heard in Cambrai towards the end of Dufay's life, and is close to Ockeghem in style, often with sonorous textures. Tinctoris praised him alongside Ockeghem and Busnois. His Masses contain an example of a secular tune used as cantus firmus retaining its profane words in the liturgical setting.

CE: *Opera omnia* (CMM 9), ed. C. Lindenburg (Rome, 1956)

Regnart, Jakob (b. Douai, c1540; d. Prague, 16 Oct 1599) Franco-Flemish composer. An Imperial chorister under Vaet; as an adult was variously a singer at the Prague court, vice-*Kapellmeister* in 1582–4 and from 1598, and *Kapellmeister* to the archducal court at Innsbruck from 1585 to 1596. He published 37 Masses, 195 motets, and a Passion, but is most important for his application to German secular song of the Italian styles of serious madrigal and simple villanella. Despite a Germanic tunefulness in the top line, his songs are more Italianate even than those of Lassus, and were the most popular of those appearing at that time.

CE: *Opera omnia* (CMM 62), ed. W. Pass (Rome, 1975–)

Rener (Reiner), Adam (b. Liège; d. Altenburg, Thuringia, c1520) Franco-Flemish composer. A chorister at the Imperial court under Isaac, from 1498–1500, he was from 1507 composer and historiographer to the Saxon court at Torgau; his last years were spent in poor health as a result of serious injuries received in a brawl. He wrote Catholic church music which shows the influence of Isaac, but some of it, including 5 Masses, was published in Rhaw's Lutheran collections, and by the time of his death he had probably become a Protestant.

CE: *IMM* collected works ser., ii, ed. R. Parker (Brooklyn, 1954–)

Reproaches see **Improperia**

Requiem A setting of the Mass for the Dead ('Missa pro defunctis'). Unlike the normal polyphonic Mass it included both Ordinary and Proper sections; there was no Gloria or Credo,

and a Tract and Sequence replaced the Alleluia verse. Ockeghem and Pierre de la Rue wrote the earliest extant settings. C16 Requiems were usually based on plainsong, sometimes with ALTERNATIM performance in the sequence *Dies irae*.

Resinarius (Harzer), Balthasar (b. Tetschen [Děčín], c1486; d. Böhmisch Leipa [Česka Lípa], 12 Apr 1544) German composer. A chorister under Isaac in Maximilian I's court chapel; became a Catholic priest in the service of Hans von Salhausen, but was an early convert to Lutheranism and an important member of the first generation of Protestant composers. His 80 responsories, issued by Rhaw in 1543, were Latin pieces aimed at the Lutheran schools, and he was generously represented in Rhaw's chorale collection of 1544 by some 30 settings, on the whole conservative in their cantus firmus style, imitative writing, and old-fashioned (under-third) cadences. One of these works is a Te Deum for 2 choirs in alternation.

Responsories in Rhaw, *Musikdrucke* i–ii (Kassel, 1955–7)

Reson (Rezon), Johannes Early C15 ?Franco-Flemish composer, of whose life nothing whatever is known. He employed the early C15 syllabic manner of word setting, and wrote a chanson, *Ce rondelet je vous envoye*, which is unusual in having 2 equally melodic voice parts of equal range. His Mass seems to be one of the earliest true cyclic Masses.

CE: in *CMM* 11/ii, ed. G. Reaney

Responsory, respond A type of plainsong piece growing out of ancient forms of psalmody, having a solo voice alternating with a choral refrain. It was a particular feature of the Office of Matins (in the SARUM USE, also of Vespers and Compline, and frequently set polyphonically by Tudor composers). The musical schemes *a B c B* or *a B c B c' B* or *A B c B A B* were found, *B* representing the textual refrain. Victoria's 18 Tenebrae Responsories are perhaps the best-known polyphonic examples.

Reuental see **Neidhart von Reuental**

Reyneau see **Gacien Reyneau**

Rezon see **Reson**

Rhaw, Georg (b. Eisfeld, nr. Coburg, 1488; d. Wittenberg, 6 Aug 1548) German printer and composer. In 1518 he became cantor at the Thomasschule in Leipzig, but as one of Luther's first followers he abandoned this post in 1520, and in 1523 became a schoolmaster in Wittenberg. He started a printing business there in 1525, and published many important collections of early Lutheran music including works by all the leading composers of the day who had Protestant sympathies. These publications contained simple congregational psalm settings and sacred songs, and also the more elaborate Masses and motets still used in Lutheran worship.

Hymns in *EDM* xxi, xxv; Chorale settings in *DDT* xxxiv

Rhys (Ryce), Philip ap Mid-C16 ?Welsh composer. Succeeded Redford as organist at St Paul's cathedral in 1547; along with Redford and Preston he was an important keyboard composer of the time. His music includes an *alternatim* organ Mass for Trinity Sunday and a setting of the Offertory chant *Felix namque*; his style is notable for its strongly contrasted rhythms.

Rhythmic modes A set of basic rhythmic patterns in ternary metre used in music by Perotin and possibly Leonin in the C12-13. The six patterns,

consisting of various permutations of long and short note values corresponding to poetic metres, are indicated by the notation and applied to the melody by the singer.

Rhythmic modes

Ricercar, ricercare C16–17 instrumental piece. The imitative ricercar for organ or ensemble was the most common type, being the instrumental counterpart of the motet in its distinct sections and contrapuntal development of each musical idea. An earlier type, sometimes spelt 'recercare' or in Spanish 'recercada', was designed to exploit the idiomatic resources of various instruments (e.g. lute, viol).

Richafort, Jean (b. Hainault, *c*1480; d. ?Bruges, *c*1547) Franco-Flemish composer. According to the poet Ronsard he studied with Josquin. In 1507–9 he was singing-master at S. Rombault, Malines; in 1531 he was serving Maria of Hungary, Regent of the Netherlands, and from 1543 directed music at S. Gilles, Bruges. He wrote Masses, a Requiem, motets and chansons widely disseminated in printed anthologies; Glareanus included his motet *Christus resurgens* in the *Dodecachordon*, while his attractive 4-part *Quem dicunt homines* was one of the most popular motets of its day, with its bright Ionian mode and rhythmic ebullience; Palestrina was among many who wrote parody Masses upon it.

Richard de Fournival (b. *c*1190; d. ?Amiens, 1260) Trouvère; son of a doctor and half-brother of Bishop Arnoul of Amiens; chancellor of Amiens cathedral from 1246. Twenty of his poems survive and 6 melodies;

he also wrote an allegorical tract on Love and an erotic poem in Latin.

Richard I (b. 1157; d. 1199) King of England 1189–99, known as 'Coeur de Lion' or 'Lionheart'. The son of Eleanor of Aquitaine, a leading patron of troubadours (Bernart de Ventadour for example), he was himself a trouvère. The picturesque tale of his rescue from prison by Blondel de Nesle is sadly apocryphal; 2 of his poems survive, one with music, and his death was mourned by Gaucelm Faidit in a moving *planh* or lament.

Richardson, Ferdinando see **Heyborne**

Rigatti, Giovanni Antonio (b. Venice, 1615; d. Venice, 25 Oct 1649) Italian composer. Choirmaster at Udine cathedral in 1635–7, and later a priest in Venice, singing at St Mark's and teaching singing at one of the Venetian conservatories; in 1646 he directed music for the Patriarch of Venice. Highly esteemed by the age of only 20, Rigatti was an outstanding church composer in the Venice of Monteverdi's last years. He published 9 volumes of sacred music (5 of solo and concertato motets, 4 of psalms also including 3 Masses) and 2 books of secular music (monodies and concertato madrigals). His music is distinguished by charming yet forceful melodies, imaginative structures and dramatic word painting.

Rimini, Vincenzo da see **Vincenzo da Rimini**

Rippe, Albert de (Alberto da Ripa) (b. Mantua, c1480; d. Paris, 1551) Italian lutenist. A renowned virtuoso whose death provoked tributes from such well-known poets as Baïf and Ronsard; from 1528 in the service of the kings of France. Six volumes of his music were published posthumously by his pupil

Morlaye; the surviving order to the printer to produce 1500 copies of one of them is testimony to the popularity of the lute in C16 France.

CE: in *CLF* xiii, xiv, xvii, ed. J. M. Vaccaro

Riquier see **Guiraut Riquier**

Ritornello 1. A section of music, usually in contrasted metre, setting the final couplet of a C14 Italian madrigal.

2. In early baroque Italian music, an instrumental interlude which recurs and thereby lends structural coherence to an extended piece. It may be related to the vocal sections it links. Monteverdi's *Scherzi musicali* of 1607 contain the earliest examples. It appears to be a development of the *ritornello* ('small return') in Italian dance music, whereby part of the 'main music' is inserted between sections of the whole piece.

Rivaflecha, Martín de (d. 1528) Spanish composer. Spent much of his life as *maestro de capilla* at Palencia cathedral, though financial problems connected with the post forced him to engage in litigation with the authorities. He was highly esteemed by his contemporaries, and his style is distinguished by its appropriate treatment of evocative texts and inventive melodies.

Robinson, Thomas (fl. 1603–9) English lutenist. In the service of the Earl of Exeter, and may have visited Denmark. Though the musical quality of his 2 publications is not high, the *School of Musick* (1603) is however valuable as a tutor for lute, orpharion, bandora and bass viol.

Robledo, Melchor (d. Saragossa, Apr 1587) Spanish composer. *Maestro de capilla* at Tarragona cathedral in 1549, and then spent a period as a Papal singer in Rome before becoming *maestro* at the Seo cathedral in Saragossa in 1569. His contemporary reputation was such that his was the only music allowed to be performed alongside that of Josquin, Victoria, Morales and Palestrina in the Pilar cathedral at Saragossa. His Masses, motets, Lamentations and other sacred works survive in MS.

Rogier, Philippe (b. Namur, *c*1560x61; d. Madrid, 29 Feb 1596) Franco-Flemish composer. Spent his life in the service of Philip II of Spain, as chorister (from 1572), vice-*maestro de capilla* under de la Hèle (from 1582) and *maestro* (from 1588), the last north European composer to hold such a position at the Spanish court. He wrote church music, some published, chansons and *villancicos*.

CE: *Opera omnia* (*CMM* 61), ed. L. Wagner (Rome, 1974–   ); Motets in *RRMR* ii, ed. L. Wagner

Rognoni Taeggio, Giovanni Domenico (d. before 1626) Italian composer. Organist in Milan *c*1605, and ducal *maestro di cappella* there from 1619. His publications include instrumental canzonas, some polychoral, madrigals in up to 8 parts and a setting of the Ambrosian-rite Requiem.

Roman de Fauvel A French MS of *c*1316 consisting of a continuous poetic narrative (in which a violent satirical attack is launched against the failings of the medieval church and contemporary political life) with over 150 monophonic songs and polyphonic motets interpolated. The latter include early examples of the isorhythmic motet by Philippe de Vitry. (See also CHAILLOU DE PESTAIN.)

Polyphonic music in *PMFC* i, ed. L. Schrade

Romance A form of Spanish vocal music current from the Middle Ages onwards, consisting of traditional melodies set to epic ballads on historical, lyrical or Biblical subjects. C16 polyphonic settings of these melodies reached a high degree of artistic perfection in the gravely beautiful romances of Luis Milán, and other vihuela composers.

Romanesca A famous C16 melody first known in Spanish lutebooks as *Guardáme las vacas*. Its harmonic scheme or bass line was used by many composers, especially Italians, as a basis for variations in both vocal and instrumental music.

Romanesca

Romanus, Antonius see **Antonius Romanus**

Rommelpot see **Percussion**

Rondeau An important medieval French poetic and musical form found in many polyphonic chansons of the C14 and C15. Apart from the earliest examples, the musical structure is *A B a A a b A B* (capitals indicate textual refrain, lower-case fresh sections of text).

Rondellus A technique of the pre-1300 period, equivalent to the round/canon, whereby two or three voices exchange musical phrases at regular intervals. It was practised especially, though not exclusively, in England.

Rore, Cipriano de (b. Malines, 1516; d. Parma, 11x20 Sep 1565) Franco-Flemish composer. Nothing certain is known of his early life or his arrival in Venice, but he sang in the choir of St Mark's in 1542–6 and studied with

Willaert. In 1547 he became director of music to Duke Ercole II of Ferrara. While he was away visiting Antwerp in 1559 his patron died and since the next duke did not retain his services, Rore took up a similar court post at Parma in 1560. In 1563 he succeeded Willaert as *maestro di cappella* at St Mark's, but finding the duties too onerous he returned to his previous post at Parma in 1564.

Rore's output consists of 5 Masses, 65 motets, one Passion, 8 psalms and Magnificats, 125 madrigals and a few chansons. His sacred music is on the whole conservative though at times most impressive (the motet *O altitudo divitiarum*, for example); but his madrigals are historically far more important. He was always concerned to capture the mood of his texts through musical devices, timing and contrasts. His preference was for serious, high-flown poetry. To some particularly intense texts he responded with daring chromaticism and modulations.

CE: *Opera omnia* (*CMM* 14), ed. B. Meier (Rome, 1959–); Madrigals *á 3, 4* in *SCMA* vi, ed. G. Smith.

Rosselli see **Roussel**

Rosseter, Philip (b. ?1568; d. London, 5 May 1623) English composer. A member of the Chapel Royal in 1604; with Robert Jones he acquired in 1610 a licence to present plays at the Whitefriars theatre. All his fine lute songs appeared in a joint publication with Campion, whose close friend he was; they belong to the light and lively rather than serious and profound type of song. He is represented in Morley's *Consort Lessons* of 1599.

Lute songs in *EL* 1st ser., viii–ix (rev. edn.)

Rossetti, Stefano (b. Nice; fl. 1559–80) Italian composer. From 1559 he held the posts of *maestro di cappella* at the cathedrals of Scio, Novara and Florence, where he served Cardinal de' Medici; he was court organist at Munich around 1580. He published many madrigals, a madrigal cycle, and motets.

Motets, madrigals respectively in *RRMR* xv, xvi, ed. A. Skei

Rossi, Luigi (b. Torremaggiore, nr. Foggia, 1598; d. Rome, 18 Feb 1653) Italian composer, singer and organist. Studied with Macque at Naples. After serving various dukes he became organist at S. Luigi dei Francesi in Rome in 1633, but moved to the Florentine court in 1635. In 1641 he returned to Rome as a musician to Cardinal A. Barberini, in whose service he composed the opera *Il Palazzo incantato*, 2 oratorios and many cantatas. In the late 1640s he made 2 trips to Paris; on the first of these (1647) his opera *Orfeo* was performed with great success.

Apart from the 2 operas and 2 oratorios just mentioned, Rossi's most important contribution was to the development of the cantata. He wrote some 384 cantatas, monodic songs, serenades, duets, and vocal quartets, though little of this music was published. The cantata on the death of Gustavus Adolphus of Sweden in the Battle of Lützen made his name widely known. His *Orfeo*, though greatly admired in France, is disappointing dramatically, with its main emphasis on lyrical expression and grace (it is the first opera in which arias outnumber recitatives).

Rossi, Salamone (b. Mantua, c1570; d. Mantua, c1630) Italian composer and violinist of Jewish descent. Served at the Mantuan court from 1587 to 1628 and was much respected by the Gonzagas, who exempted him from wearing the yellow badge Jews had to carry on their hats. His output includes 4

books of sonatas and dances for string ensemble, madrigals, *canzonette*, music for dramatic productions at Mantua and Jewish psalms. He was among the earliest composers to cultivate the trio sonata texture in his collections of 1607–8; he uses binary forms and movements featuring dance rhythms as well as ostinato basses.

1607–8 collections (*Sinfonie . . .*), ed. F. Rikko and J. Newman (New York, 1965–71); *Songs of Solomon*, ed. F. Rikko (New York, 1967)

Rote, rotta see **Psaltery**

Roussel (Rosselli), François (fl. 1546–77) French composer. His musical career was spent largely in Rome, as choirmaster to the Cappella Giulia at St Peter's (1548–50) and then, after a period in Lyons, at S. Lorenzo in Damaso (c1563–6), S. Luigi dei Francesi (1566–71) and St John Lateran (1572–5). His sacred music was examined along with that of Palestrina and Lassus by the Council of Trent. He also published 3 volumes of madrigals and one of chansons.

Rovetta, Giovanni (b. Venice, c1595; d. Venice, 23 Oct 1668) Italian composer. Spent his whole career at St Mark's, Venice – as chorister, instrumentalist, bass singer, assistant *maestro* to Monteverdi from 1627, and his successor as full *maestro* from 1644 until his death. His output includes 2 operas for the early public opera houses, several volumes of concertato madrigals, and a large amount of sacred music – Masses, psalms and motets. His style seems often that of one labouring in Monteverdi's shadow, though in some small-scale pieces he writes with distinctive melodic charm for voices and *obbligato* violins. One ceremonial Mass (1639) is an impressive example of this Venetian genre, the longer movements being

tightly knit yet varied, with sections for soloists contrasted with dramatic tuttis.

Rudel see **Jaufre Rudel**

Rue, Pierre de la (b. ?Tournai, c1460; d. Courtrai, 20 Apr 1518) Franco-Flemish composer. In the early 1480s he travelled to Italy and was a singer at Siena cathedral in 1482 and 1483–5. He belonged to a confraternity at 's-Hertogenbosch in 1489–92 and then became a singer in the Burgundian court chapel of Philip the Handsome and later Marguerite of Austria, briefly visiting Spain on 2 occasions. In 1501 he was a canon at the church of Notre Dame in Courtrai; he retired there from his court position in 1516.

One of Josquin Desprez' leading contemporaries, Pierre de la Rue wrote some 31 Masses, 7 Mass sections, 37 motets and 37 chansons. He was not so much affected by his visits to Italy as were other northerners of his generation, preferring a rigorously contrapuntal style with individuality of melodic line to the chordal, declamatory manner, and making quite frequent use of canon and ostinato. His Requiem is a work of sombre gravity, exploiting low vocal registers, and his chansons are sober and frequently sad – especially those written under the patronage of the ill-fated Marguerite – with continuous textures and imitative writing.

Rügen see **Wizlaw III von Rügen**

Ruffo, Vincenzo (b. Verona, c1510; d. Sacile, nr. Udine, 9 Feb 1587) Italian composer. Became a priest at Verona in 1531 and remained there, apart from a period (1542–6) in the service of Alfonso d'Avalos in Milan, until 1563; directed music at the Accademia Filarmonica in 1551–2 and at the cathedral from 1554, later becoming *maestro* at

Milan cathedral, Pistoia and finally Sacile. He was a prolific writer of Masses, motets and madrigals, whose works circulated widely. The madrigals show his contrapuntal skill, but more interesting historically are the Masses written while he was at Milan under S. Carlo Borromeo, a powerful advocate of the Tridentine reforms affecting verbal intelligibility in church music; these works show straightforward chordal writing and avoid any taint of secular inspiration.

Ruggiero A melody used as a ground bass for arias, instrumental dance pieces or variations in the C16/17. The name probably refers to a popular song that fitted this bass, which was first used by Ortiz.

Ruggiero

Rumelant, Meister (fl. *c*1275) Minnesinger. His *Daz Gedeones wollenvluis* is a *Minnelied* on the subject of the mystic love (*Minne*) of God for the Virgin Mary. He was the first to mention the 12 'tones' (standard melodies) of the legendary Meistersinger.

S

Sachs, Hans (b. Nürnberg, 5 Nov 1494; d. Nürnberg, 19 Jan 1576) German Meistersinger. By trade a shoemaker, he was the chief exponent of Nürnberg *Meistergesang*. He provided tunes for stage productions in the 1550s, and was master of a song-school in 1555–61. By 1567 he had devised several thousand songs from 301 'tones' (standard melodies), some of which he had invented himself; these fell into sacred, secular and dramatic categories. A fertile poet, he wrote an allegorical work in support of Luther. His melodies, though perhaps somewhat stilted, are unusual for their melismas at the beginnings and ends of lines.

CE: *Gesamtausgabe*, ed. A. v. Keller and E. Goetze (repr. Hildesheim, 1964)

Sackbut Wind instrument with cup mouthpiece, working on the telescopic slide principle (c.f. the trombone, whose appearance it closely resembles); a development of the slide TRUMPET. Praetorius lists 4 sizes from alto to great bass of which the tenor in B flat was the most useful (the proper treble to a sackbut consort was CORNETT or SHAWM). It was an enormously versatile instrument with a wide, fully chromatic compass, secure intonation and an expressive tone, and was capable of producing dynamic contrasts and adapting to different standards of pitch. Virtuoso players could negotiate brilliant coloratura passages, and a C17 church orchestra frequently consisted of sackbuts with violins and cornetts.

Salinas, Francisco (b. Burgos, 1 Mar 1513; d. Salamanca, 13 Jan 1590) Spanish organist and theorist, blind from birth. Vice-regal organist in Naples from 1553 to 1558, organist at the cathedrals of Henares (from 1559) and León (from 1563) and later professor of music at Salamanca university. Renowned as an organist, he also published a treatise, *De musica libri septem* (1579), which carries further many of Zarlino's ideas, and contains among its musical examples unique specimens of Spanish folksongs as known in the C16.

Saltarello Italian jumping dance of C14–16. The medieval saltarello had a variety of rhythms; in the Renaissance it was in quick triple time, and often coupled with the PASSAMEZZO, whose melody it might vary.

Sandrin (real name **Regnault**), **Pierre** (fl. 1538–60) French composer, who may have been a comic actor in early life. Became court composer to Francis I of France around 1543, and in 1554 served in the entourage of Cardinal Ippolito d'Este of Ferrara. Many of his chansons became famous; Lassus

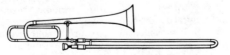

Bass sackbut, 130 cm

based the most dignified of his chanson Masses on Sandrin's beautiful and dignified *Doulce memoire*.

CE: *Opera omnia (CMM 47)*, ed. A. Seay (Rome, 1968)

Santa Croce, Francesco (b. S. Croce, nr. Padua, *c*1478; d. Loreto, 1556) Italian composer and priest. From 1519 held the post of cathedral *maestro di cappella* at Treviso, Chioggia, Udine, Verona and Treviso again; from 1551 he was a canon at the basilica in Loreto. His church music, surviving in MS, includes a double-choir Compline setting.

Santa Maria, Tomás de (b. Madrid, 1510x20; d. Valladolid, 1570) Spanish composer, theorist and Dominican monk. Organist at the monastery of S. Pablo in Valladolid, and published in 1565 a valuable 2-volume treatise on playing and composing for the organ which demonstrates the advanced state of Spanish organ technique in the mid-C16.

Saracini, Claudio (b. Siena, 1 July 1586; d. ?Siena, after 1649) Italian composer and nobleman. Travelled widely in Italy and abroad and was known to Monteverdi, to whom he dedicated his *Seconde Musiche*. This was one of 6 books of monodies which he published, which mark him out as one of the most notable masters of solo song, despite his amateur status. His music sometimes has oddly wayward harmonies which add to its expressive effect.

Sarto see **Johannes de Sarto**

Sarum Use The liturgical use of Salisbury in England, which prevailed in much of England throughout the later Middle Ages and until abolished at the Reformation. It differed from the Roman rite in many details, especially of ceremony and ritual.

Sayve, Lambert de (b. ?Liège, 1549; d. 1614) Franco-Flemish composer. Entered Imperial service in 1569 as choirmaster at the monastery of Melk, belonged to the archducal court at Graz in 1582, and his final post was as court *Kapellmeister* in Prague. His German songs published in 1602 show the influence of Regnart (2 of whose works he includes) and are in *canzonetta* style.

Scandello, Antonio (b. Bergamo, 17 ?Jan 1517; d. Dresden, 18 Jan 1580) Italian composer. In the 1540s he worked at Bergamo and Trent, but in 1549 was called to the Electoral court of Saxony at Dresden, where he became vice-*Kapellmeister* in 1566 and full *Kapellmeister* in 1568. He revisited Italy on many occasions, including during Dresden's plague year of 1567. His publications comprise German songs, both sacred and secular, and 2 books of *Canzone Napoletane* which were the first music to exclusively Italian texts to appear in Germany. His St John Passion (1561) exemplifies the mixed style of HISTORIA in which only the Evangelist's part is set in chant, while his *Österliche Freude* (1568) is an important prototype for Schütz's Easter *Historia*.

Scheidemann, Heinrich (b. Wöhrden, ?nr. Hamburg, *c*1596; d. Hamburg, beginning 1663) German organist and composer; a most important and prolific member of the north German school of Sweelinck, whose pupil he was. Organist at the Katharinenkirche in Hamburg from at least 1629. His organ music, surviving in MS tablatures, includes free preludes in a variety of styles, many plainsong-based pieces, colourful and virtuosic fantasias, and examples of many different types of chorale setting. He also published songs.

CE: *Orgelwerke*, ed. G. Fock and W. Breig (Kassel, 1967–71)

Scheidt, Samuel (bp. Halle, 3 Nov 1587; d. Halle, 24 Mar 1654) German composer and organist. He spent most of his life in his birthplace, becoming organist at the Moritzkirche in 1603. In 1608–9 he took time off to study with Sweelinck in Amsterdam, then returned to Halle to be court organist to the Margrave of Brandenburg, which also involved playing at the Moritzkirche once more. In 1619 he opened a new organ at Bayreuth in the presence of many princes and musicians, including Praetorius and Schütz. His career progressed through *Kapellmeister* (1620) to town director of music in Halle (1628), a post he held for only 2 years; in later life he devoted himself to composition and teaching.

Scheidt was one of Germany's most distinguished composers at that time, especially in the field of keyboard music. His 3 volumes of *Tabulatura nova* (1624) are a monumental compendium of song and dance arrangements, sets of variations, fantasias, toccatas, fugues and liturgical pieces (often plainsong-based) for the Lutheran Mass and Office. Likewise his 4 books of *Geistliche Konzerte* illustrate the ways of elaborating a chorale, fusing declamatory ideas with contrapuntal writing. He also published motets and instrumental dance music.

CE: *Werke*, ed. G. Harms and C. Mahrenholz (Hamburg, 1923–   ); *Tabulatura nova* in *DDT* i

Schein, Johann Hermann (b. Grünhain, nr. Zwickau, 20 Jan 1586; d. Leipzig, 19 Nov 1630) German composer. A choirboy at the Dresden court chapel in 1599, he was studying law in Leipzig in 1607. In 1613 he was in the service of Gottfried von Wolffersdorf as tutor and music director at Schloss Weissenfels, and in 1615 he was court *Kapellmeister* at Weimar. The following year he became cantor at the Thomaskirche in Leipzig. He is known to have been a close friend of Schütz.

Schein was one of the major figures in the evolution of the baroque *geistliches Konzert* and the spiritual madrigal. His varied output includes German songs, large-scale Latin and German motets, many spiritual madrigals or *Konzerte* with continuo, secular concertato pieces, dance suites and chorale harmonizations. At first an adherent of the traditional Lassus-inspired *prima prattica*, he quickly came to favour up-to-date Italian styles of emotional declamation, combining these with the setting of Lutheran chorale melodies in a most original way in the *Opella nova* (1618, 1626). In his sacred madrigals he adopted the Italianate idiom of Marenzio and early Monteverdi, making use of dramatic contrasts of texture and harmony and handling contrapuntal ideas in masterly fashion.

CE: *Neue Ausgabe sämtlicher Werke*, ed. A. Adrio (Kassel, 1963–   )

Schlick, Arnolt (b. ?Heidelberg, *c*1455; d. Heidelberg, *c*1525) German organist and composer. Blind, possibly from birth, he played at the installation of Archduke Maximilian (later Emperor) at Frankfurt, and thereafter travelled widely as organist and organ expert, collaborating with organ builders. From 1485 his basic employment was in his native city as Electoral court organist. In 1516 he was at the Saxon Elector's court at Torgau with Hofhaimer, another celebrated organist, and at Charles V's coronation at Aachen in 1520 he is said to have improvised 10-part canons upon the plainsong tune of the Christmas Sequence.

Schlick's *Spiegel der Orgelmacher und Organisten* (1511) is the earliest printed treatise on organ building and playing, while his *Tabulaturen etlicher lobgesang und lidlein* (1512) is the earliest printed keyboard tablature, and contains 14 organ pieces, 12 lute songs and 3 lute solos. The organ pieces are mostly based on plainsong, but have an astonishingly idiomatic and sophisticated style of keyboard counterpoint, as the fine *Salve Regina* setting demonstrates.

CE: *Orgelkompositionen*, ed. R. Walter (Mainz, 1970)

Schmid, Bernhard 1 (b. Strasbourg, 1535; d. Strasbourg, 1592) German organist and composer. Spent his working life in Strasbourg, as organist first at the Thomaskirche and then (from 1564) at the Minster. His volumes of organ tablatures, published in 1577, contain dances and transcriptions of motets. These latter are mainly by Netherlands composers, especially Lassus, and are in the 'colourist' style which encrusts its models with stereotyped figurations. His son, Bernhard Schmid 2, succeeded him in his posts, and published in 1607 a tablature containing mainly transcriptions of Italian music.

Schröter, Leonhard (b. Torgau, c1532; d. Magdeburg, c1601) German cantor and composer. From 1561 he was cantor at Latin schools, first in Saalfeld and later in Magdeburg. One of the best German composers of his time, he published motets, German sacred songs, and collections of Christmas music and of hymns; his 8-part Te Deum of 1571 shows familiarity with the most modern Venetian styles.

Schryari, Schreierpfeife Reedcap wind instrument; a reedcap shawm. No specimens survive, but Praetorius lists alto, tenor and bass sizes, each with the compass of a 9th, and describes the tone as 'strong and fresh'.

Schütz, Heinrich (b. [Bad] Köstritz bei Gera, 14 Oct 1585; d. Dresden, 6 Nov 1672) German composer. A choirboy at the Landgrave of Hesse-Cassel's court at Kassel, and studied law at Marburg university. The Landgrave paid for him to study with Giovanni Gabrieli in Venice from 1609–12, after which he was court organist at Kassel. In 1617 he became *Kapellmeister* to the Elector of Saxony at Dresden. He was given leave of absence to return to Venice in 1628 to familiarize himself with the latest Italian music by Monteverdi and Grandi. In 1633–5 and 1642 he visited the Copenhagen court as director of music. The 30 Years' War had such a disastrous effect on Dresden court music that Schütz travelled around to work at other, less badly-off German courts. By 1651 he was ageing and out of sympathy with the newest music, and asked to be released from regular duties so as to return to his boyhood home of Weissenfels.

Schütz's very long life-span covers the establishment and early development of baroque style in Germany, and his 2 visits to Italy had a most significant effect on the direction taken by German music; his early works reflect what he observed in Italy, whether in the vividly expressive madrigals, the splendid polychoral *Psalmen Davids* (1619), or the delicate vocal and instrumental textures of the *Symphoniae Sacrae I* (1629). Apart from the early madrigals and the lost opera *Dafne* all his output was of sacred music and works of the oratorio type. While the sacred music came to effect a synthesis of Italian elements and a German contrapuntal seriousness, the oratorio pieces belong more firmly in a German tradition of *historia*, based on Gospel narration by an Evangelist alternating with polyphonic movements for other characters or crowd scenes. The 3 late Passions are in an archaic style without accompaniment, the narration being quasi-plainsong; the *Christmas Story* (1664) has Italian-style recitative for the narration and opulent *intermedia* for voices and instruments depicting successive scenes from the narrative.

CE: *Sämmtliche Werke*, ed. P. Spitta (Leipzig, 1885–94, repr. Wiesbaden, 1968–74); *Neue Ausgabe Sämtlicher Werke*, ed. K. Ameln and others (Kassel, 1955–)

Scotto Venetian publishing house. Founded in 1480 by Ottaviano Scotto (d. 1498) who was one of the first to publish liturgical books with music, and used a type-face a little less elegant than that of PETRUCCI. The business descended to his cousin, Ottaviano 2, and remained in the family until at least 1607.

Scotto, Gerolamo (d. Venice, 3 Sep 1572) Italian publisher and composer. He entered the family business in 1539, and among the music he published were 6 volumes of his own madrigals and 3-part *canzone Napoletane*.

Seconda prattica Italian for 'second practice'; a term first used by Monteverdi's brother Giulio Cesare, in the preface to Monteverdi's own *Scherzi musicali* of 1607, to describe music which is 'commanded by the words' rather than the reverse (see PRIMA PRATTICA). Monteverdi applied it to the Italian madrigal repertory of Willaert, Rore and others in which the words determine much of the musical detail. It has, perhaps loosely, been equated with the *stile moderno* or modern style which Monteverdi came to cultivate.

Segni, Giulio (b. Modena, 1498; d. Rome, 24 July 1561) Italian organist and composer. A pupil of G. Fogliano in Modena; became second organist at St Mark's, Venice, in 1530 and entered the service of Cardinal Santa Fiore in Rome in 1533. He published a volume of ricercars in 1550, and is represented with Willaert and G. Cavazzoni in the *Musica Nova* anthology of 1540.

Selesses see **Senleches**

Selle, Thomas (b. Zörbig, nr. Halle, 23 Mar 1599; d. Hamburg, 2 July 1663) German composer. Possibly a pupil of Calvisius and Schein at Leipzig; held various teaching posts before becoming cantor at the Johanneum and organist at the Hauptkirche in Hamburg in 1641. He composed nearly 300 motets, some old-fashioned and polyphonic, some making effective use of polychoral techniques, and some tending towards the concertato style. His St John Passion of 1643 is the earliest 'oratorio Passion', and contains imaginative instrumental writing; his secular songs show the transition from polyphonic to monodic style.

Senfl, Ludwig (b. Basel, *c*1486; d. Munich, 2 Dec 1542x10 Aug 1543) Swiss-German composer. Possibly a choirboy in Maximilian I's court chapel in 1496; a singer in the Imperial chapel by 1507, and in 1517 succeeded Isaac as court composer, though the chapel was dissolved when Maximilian died in 1519. Thereafter he worked in Passau, and 1523 became 'first musician' at the Munich court. Though remaining Catholic, he admired Luther and sympathized with the Reformation, and had a lively correspondence with the Protestant Duke Albrecht of Prussia.

Senfl may well have studied with Isaac; certainly he was thoroughly well-versed in the Franco-Flemish style of the day. His output contains 7 Masses, and many motets and Magnificats for the Latin liturgy, some notable early Lutheran chorale elaborations, and about 250 German songs, on which his reputation chiefly rests. These latter illustrate every imaginable approach to the traditional German song melodies, from simple chordal harmonizations to masterly canonic pieces with sharply contrasted counterpoints in the non-canonic parts. A type Senfl made especially his own was the quodlibet in which 2 or 3 different song tunes would be combined in a dazzling contrapuntal display yet would remain recognizable.

CE: *Sämtliche Werke*, ed. O. Ursprung and others (Wolfenbüttel, 1937–74)

Senleches, Jacques de (Selesses, Jacomi) (fl. 1378–95) French composer. Probably worked before 1378 at the court of John I of Aragon at Barcelona (where he was known as 'Lo Begue' and is not to be confused with Jacomi the bagpiper who was there 1372–1404). In 1378 he accompanied the Duke of Gerona to Flanders; in 1379 he was at the court of Castile and in 1383 was harpist to Cardinal Pedro de Luna. He was again at the Aragon court between 1391 and 1395. His surviving music consists of 2 *virelais* and 4 very complex *ballades*.

Secular music in *CMM* 53/i, ed. W. Apel

Sequence In Gregorian chant, a syllabic setting to a poetic text largely in double-line stanzas. Discovered in the C9 probably by NOTKER BALBULUS, it came to use rhymed verses by the C12; it thus became rather like a long HYMN except that the melody was not constant for every strophe. All but 4 of the sequences that proliferated in the late Middle Ages were abolished by the Council of Trent; these 4 remained part of the Proper of the Mass for Easter, Pentecost, Corpus Christi and the Requiem.

Sermisy, Claudin de (b. *c*1490; d.

Paris, 13 Sep 1562) French composer. Possibly a choirboy at the Sainte Chapelle in Paris; a singer there in 1508, the year in which he joined Louis XII's private chapel choir. Under Francis I he travelled to Italy in 1515 and to the Field of the Cloth of Gold in 1520, becoming *sous-maître* of the Sainte Chapelle in 1530, a canon there in 1533, and finally attaining the rank of choirmaster in 1547.

Claudin (as he is usually known) published 3 books of motets, 11 Masses and a Passion, but is best known for the 160 or so chansons which came out in many printed anthologies, including Attaingnant's first collection of 1528 where he is represented by 17 pieces. These constitute the quintessential French chansons – lyrical miniatures with attractive melodies carefully declaiming the words in mainly syllabic fashion, and a chordal idiom without much contrapuntal elaboration in a basic 4-part texture. So popular were some of his chansons that they appeared in numerous arrangements for all manner of vocal and instrumental combinations. In sacred music Claudin often adopted a chanson-like style with simple textures and passages for alternate pairs of voices. His Masses are thus distinct from those of his northern contemporaries (Gombert, Clemens).

CE: *Opera omnia* (*CMM* 52), ed. G. Allaire and I. Cazeaux (Rome, 1970–   )

Serpent Bass wind instrument with finger-holes and cup mouthpiece; bass of the CORNETT family, with very widely expanding bore. Possibly invented in France in the late C16, it was initially keyless, with 6 finger-holes, and was especially useful for doubling male voices in a choir. Despite its formidable technical problems the serpent had a useful life of over 200 years in churches and bands.

Serpent, 80 cm

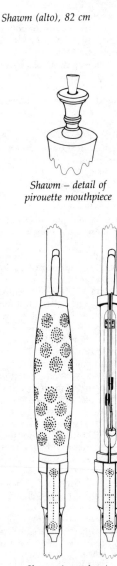

Shawm (alto), 82 cm

*Shawm – detail of
pirouette mouthpiece*

*Shawm (great bass) –
detail showing fontanelle
in position and removed*

Shawm Double-reed wind instrument with expanding conical bore and a brilliant penetrating tone, suitable for outdoor use. The leading double-reed instrument until the C17, it came to Europe from the Saracen armies during the Crusades; originally keyless, with its reed set on a metal disc, it had by the C14 acquired a funnel-shaped pirouette mouthpiece. It was used for military, ceremonial and dance music.

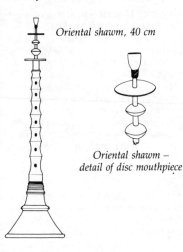

Oriental shawm, 40 cm

*Oriental shawm –
detail of disc mouthpiece*

During the Renaissance 6 sizes from sopranino to great bass were available, each with the basic compass of an 11th. The larger sizes had keys to extend their range downwards, whose mechanism was protected by a movable key cover called a *fontanelle*. A shawm with a reedcap was called SCHRYARI. The standard German name for shawm was *Pommer*.

Sheppard (Shepherd), John (b. *c*1515; d. *c*1560) English composer. *Informator Choristarum* at Magdalen College, Oxford, 1543–8; became a Gentleman of the Chapel Royal by (at latest) 1552, and in 1554 supplicated for the degree of D.Mus. at Oxford; he was last listed in Chapel Royal documents in 1559.

Sheppard is one of the major figures in English church music during the period of change between 1530 and 1560. His output of Latin music was second in quantity only to that of Byrd among C16 English composers, and contains 5 Masses, 21 Office responds, 18 hymns and a quantity of votive antiphons, psalms, canticles, etc. He also wrote a few English anthems. Though his techniques are often conservative— traditional cantus firmus structures, little organized imitative writing— Sheppard's music is surprisingly rich. The vocal textures are uniform, without much light and shade, but combine virtuoso scoring (reminiscent of the Eton Choirbook period) with lushness of sonority and masterly control of the interplay between harmony and rhythm. The comparatively large number of hymns and Office responds in his output reflects changes of taste in music for the Office; the larger settings, which manifest the last English flowering of music simply as ornament to the liturgy, may have been written for Mary Tudor's chapel.

CE: Responds in *EECM* xvii, ed. D. Chadd; Masses in *EECM* xviii, ed. N. Sandon

Sicher, Fridolin (b. Bischofszell, nr. S. Gallen, 6 Mar 1490; d. S. Gallen, 13 June 1546) Swiss organist and priest. A pupil of Buchner; organist at S. Gallen both before and after the temporary expulsion of the monks, and also held ecclesiastical posts at Bischofszell and in Alsace. He copied the S. Gallen organ tablature, the most important organ MS of its time, which shows the progress of German organ music in its transcriptions of pieces by such leading composers as Josquin Desprez and de la Rue. One piece only is by Sicher himself.

Side drum see **Drum**

Silva, Andreas de (b. 1475x80) Composer, probably of Spanish origin. A Papal singer in 1519, he was working at the Mantuan court in 1522. Composed early madrigals, Masses (one is quoted as an example by Glareanus) and motets, 2 of which were used as the basis for Masses by Arcadelt and Palestrina respectively.

CE: *Opera omnia* (*CMM* 49), ed. W. Kirsch (Rome, 1970–   )

Simpson, Thomas (bp. Milton, Kent, 1 Apr 1582; d. after 1625) English composer. An instrumentalist at various German courts and (1622–5) at the Danish court in Copenhagen. One of the most important English instrumental composers working on the Continent, he published 2 volumes of dances (one also contains items by Dowland, Farmer and Tomkins) which helped to influence the development of the German suite; his style is more tuneful and Italianate than that of Brade.

Sinfonia Italian for 'symphony'; one of several terms (sonata and toccata were others) used for introductory instrumental sections in an early baroque operatic scene or concertato madrigal or sacred work.

Slide trumpet see **Trumpet**

Smert, Richard (b. *c*1400; d. *c*1479) English musician. A vicar choral at Exeter cathedral from 1428 until *c*1474, and vicar of Plymtree, near Exeter, in 1435–77. He collaborated with John Trouluffe in the compilation of the collection of carols which forms the oldest part of the Ritson MS; he may be jointly responsible, again with Trouluffe, for composing one of the antiphons in the MS.

Solage Late C14 French composer. In the service of Jean, Duke of Berry, for whom one of his pieces was written (2 more were for a royal wedding). He is the most heavily represented composer in the Chantilly MS, with 10 pieces. Some retain the clarity and simplicity of Machaut's style, but others embrace the most extreme characteristics of the late C14 Avignon school, with complex rhythms, virtuoso melismas and involved syncopations. His extraordinarily chromatic *Fumeux fume*, with its unusually low tessitura, is one of the most extravagant, even bizarre, manifestations of this style, and was probably written for the Fumeurs, an eccentric literary clique which flourished in the 1360s and 1370s.

Secular music in *CMM* 53/i, ed. W. Apel

Solmization A system invented by GUIDO D'AREZZO to designate the degrees of the scale (in his scheme, the HEXACHORD), and used for learning singing until 1600, when it was rendered obsolete by the more extensive use of chromatic notes. In the 'Guidonian' system each note of the whole musical compass had its own peculiar designation, according to the hexachord(s) in which it lay, beginning with 'gamma-ut', i.e. the Greek for G and 'ut' in the hexachord beginning on G.

Sordello (d. after 1269) Italian troubadour, some of whose poetry survives, but without music. (He is the hero of Browning's eponymous long poem.)

Sordun Double-reed wind instrument with cylindrical double bore, therefore very low-pitched for its length. It has 12 finger-holes requiring the use of the middle joints of both index fingers as well as the tips of all fingers and thumbs. Its tone is quiet and muffled, emerging from a small hole in the side. Praetorius lists 5 sizes from great bass (lowest note F) to tenor, each with the compass of a 13th. The COURTAUT is a form of sordun.

Sordun (tenor), 26 cm

Soriano (Suriano), Francesco (b. Soriano, nr. Viterbo, 1549; d. Rome, 19 July 1621) Italian composer. A pupil of Palestrina and G. M. Nanino; apart from a period as *maestro di cappella* at the Mantuan court (1583–6), worked as *maestro* at a succession of Roman churches, ending at St Peter's (from 1603). He worked with F. Anerio on the 1614 revision of the *Graduale* and published canzonets with spiritual texts, a dramatic Passion, and church music. This includes an 8-part arrangement of Palestrina's *Papae Marcelli* Mass, Masses and Magnificats in an old-fashioned style, and polychoral psalms and motets.

Souterliedeken see under **Clemens non Papa**

Spataro, Giovanni (b. Bologna, *c*1458; d. Bologna, 17 Nov 1541) Italian theorist and composer. *Maestro di cappella* at S. Petronio in Bologna from 1512, was a disciple of the theorist Ramos de Pareja, whom he defended in his quarrel with GAFORI. He carried on much correspondence dealing with theoretical matters, and composed a great deal of church music.

Spinacino, Francesco (b. Fossombrone, nr. Urbino, late C15; d. Venice, after 1507) Italian lutenist and composer, who probably worked in Venice. His 2 books of *Intavolatura* for lute, issued by Petrucci in 1507, were the first publication of their kind; it contains possibly the earliest use of the term 'ricercar', applied to the non-polyphonic preludes Spinacino provides for his transcriptions of chansons and motets. These arrangements contain many features that were to become characteristic of lute music throughout the C16.

Spinet Plucked string keyboard instrument, normally with one set of strings and a 4-octave compass. The most common shape was an uneven hexagon, with the strings running either parallel to the keyboard along the longest side or diagonally. Praetorius suggests that it may have been a small instrument tuned an octave or 5th above normal pitch.

Spiritual madrigal Type of C16 Italian madrigal with a devotional text. Especially popular in Rome as an alternative to the amorous secular madrigal, it was a product of a resurgence of fervour inspired by the Counter-Reformation and the Jesuit movement. Palestrina, Marenzio and Monte were among those who contributed to the genre.

Squarcialupi, Antonio (b. Florence, 27 Mar 1416; bd. Florence, 6 July 1480) Italian organist and composer. A licensed butcher, he was however cathedral organist in Florence from 1432 until his death and visited Naples and Siena. He was highly esteemed by his contemporaries, including Dufay, with whom he corresponded. None of his compositions, regarding which he was excessively self-critical, survive, but he possessed, and may have copied, the important MS known as the Squarcialupi Codex (see MANUSCRIPTS).

Stabile, Annibale (b. Naples, *c*1535; d. Rome, April 1595) Italian composer; a pupil of Palestrina. Between 1575 and 1595 *maestro di cappella* successively at St John Lateran, the German College and S. Maria Maggiore in Rome; at some time in the late 1570s he was Polish court *Kapellmeister* in Kraków. He published 3 volumes of motets in the Roman style and 3 of madrigals, including a joint publication with G. M. Nanino.

Staden, Johann (bp. Nürnberg, 2 July

1581; bd. Nürnberg, 15 Nov 1634) German organist and composer. Court organist at Bayreuth from 1604, and from 1616 onwards held various posts as organist in Nürnberg. He published attractive German dance songs, and motets in various styles: polyphonic and old-fashioned, Venetian polychoral, and modern concertato. These last use *obbligato* instruments and ritornellos, as well as basso continuo.

Selected works in *DTB* vii/l, viii/l

Stadlmayr, Johann (b. Freising, *c*1560; d. Innsbruck, 12 July 1648) German composer. In 1603 he entered the service of the Prince-Bishop of Salzburg, and from 1607 was court *Kapellmeister* at Innsbruck. He was a prolific church composer, writing 6 books of Masses in up to 16 parts and many other volumes of liturgical music, in which he showed a sure grasp of both the old-fashioned polyphonic and new concertato styles.

Hymns in *DTO* v

Stile antico The conscious cultivation in the C17 of a strict C16 contrapuntal style, in distinction to the *stile moderno* with its soloistic vocal lines, instrumental writing and dramatic expression. It was often used by church composers in setting the fixed parts of the liturgy (Masses and psalms), whereas the new idiom was more favoured for motets.

Stile concitato Italian for 'agitated style'. Devised by Monteverdi for the purpose of conveying warlike feelings in his *Combattimento di Tancredi e Clorinda* (1624), it involved rapid repeated notes on stringed instruments (like a measured *tremolando*), rapid vocal declamation and fanfare-like figures.

Stile moderno see **Stile antico**

Stile rappresentativo The term used *c*1600 for the new monodic recitative

style, with its capacity to depict emotions.

Stobäus, Johann (b. Graudenz [Grudziadz, N. Poland], 6 July 1580; d. Königsberg [Kaliningrad], 11 Sep 1646) German composer; a pupil of Eccard. Spent his working life in Königsberg, as cantor at the cathedral from 1603 and court *Kapellmeister* from 1626. He issued Eccard's last publication, and also published his own motets, including chorale motets in which the imitative and rhythmically free lower parts do not obscure the chorale melody on top.

Stockem, Johannes (b. nr. Liège, *c*1440; d. 1500) Franco-Flemish composer. A Papal singer in 1487–8; later worked as choirmaster at the brilliant Hungarian court at Buda. His chansons appeared in Petrucci's anthologies; no other works of his survive, but he was respected by his contemporaries as a composer, and was a friend and correspondent of Tinctoris.

Stoltzer, Thomas (b. Schweidnitz [Swidnica, nr Wrocław], 1480x85; d. Znaim [Znojmo], nr. Brno, ?Mar 1526) German composer. Held an ecclesiastical post in Breslau [Wrocław] from 1519; though sympathetic to Luther's reforms, remained a Catholic and in 1522 was called to direct music at the court of Queen Maria of Hungary at Buda. He was an outstanding German composer of his day, his surviving works including about 150 compositions – Masses, Latin hymns and psalms, Introits, responsories, antiphons and German songs, psalms and chorales. His liturgical music recalls Isaac and Heinrich Finck, but his German psalms show a humanistic declamation and monumental conception of form that suggest Josquin. His German psalm *Erzürne dich nicht* was sent with a letter from Queen Maria to the Duke of Prussia in 1526; Stoltzer may have been seeking a change of employment.

Selected works in *EDM* xxii, lxvi; Hymns and psalms in *DDT* lxv

Strambotto see **Frottola**

Strauss, Christoph (b. ?*c*1575; d. Vienna, 1x20 June 1631) Austrian composer and organist, whose family had been for generations in Hapsburg service. He himself served the Imperial court from 1594 as organist, administrator, and from 1617 vice-*Kapellmeister*; he was dismissed in 1619 and by 1626 had become *Kapellmeister* at St Stephen's cathedral in Vienna. His church music includes polyphonic pieces and brilliant polychoral Masses with instruments, including a fine Requiem for high and low choirs. His use of word painting proves his acquaintance with the newest Italian music, though his textures are more old-fashioned.

Requiem in *DTO* lix

Striggio, Alessandro 1 (b. Mantua, *c*1535; d. Mantua, 1589x95) Italian lutenist and composer of noble birth. Worked at the Medici court in Florence from 1560 to 1574, when he moved to the ducal court in Mantua. He contributed music to many of the *intermedi* supplied for Florentine festivities, such as that of 1565 in which he collaborated with Corteccia. His madrigal publications include lively descriptive pieces such as the *Cicalamento delle donne al bucato* ('The chattering of the women at the washtub'); he also wrote some church music.

Madrigal comedies in *CP* iv, xi

Striggio, Alessandro 2 (b. Mantua, *c*1573; d. Venice, 6 June 1630) Son of A. Striggio 1; a poet and string player at the Mantuan court in the first decades of the C17 (till 1628). He saw some of

his father's madrigal books through the press, and wrote the libretti for Monteverdi's *Orfeo* and *Tirsi e Clori*; he was a lifelong friend and correspondent of Monteverdi's, collaborating with the latter after he had moved from Mantua to Venice.

Strozzi, Piero (b. Florence, mid-C16) Italian composer and aristocrat. A member of the Florentine CAMERATA, he collaborated with Striggio 1 and Merulo on music for the 1579 wedding celebrations; one of his songs is the earliest surviving example of the type of expression aimed at by the early monodists. In 1595 he set Rinuccini's *La mascherata degli acetate* and later collaborated with Caccini.

Stump see **Cittern**

Sturgeon, Nicholas (d. 31 May 1454) English composer. May have been among the musicians who accompanied Henry V to France in 1416; Prebendary of Reculver in 1440 and in 1442 became Precentor of St Paul's cathedral and a canon of Windsor. In 1443 he became also steward at Windsor, where he remained until given the prebend of Kentish Town at St Paul's in 1452. Only 5 of his 7 known compositions survive complete. He wrote an isorhythmic Benedictus jointly with Damett, possibly for the King's visit to France in 1416.

Sumer is icumen in A famous English composition of *c*1270. A canon in 4 parts on the main melody proceeds simultaneously with a 2-part RONDEL-LUS (called *pes*) which provides a foundation. Sometimes known as the 'Reading Rota', it is the oldest existing canon.

Suriano see **Soriano**

Susato, Tilman (b. ?Soest; d. Antwerp,

1561x4) German printer, publisher and composer. Worked in Antwerp from 1529 as a copyist, cathedral musician and later town instrumentalist; founded his publishing business in 1543 with a volume of 4- and 5-part chansons; the venture was so successful that he was able to build his own premises ('At the Sign of the Crumhorn') in 1547. He issued chansons, Dutch songs, and motets by the most illustrious composers–Janequin, Josquin, Lassus, Rore, Willaert–and his chanson anthologies include a wide cross-section of the genre's development in the Low Countries and France. His dance arrangements showed taste and discernment, using popular songs, dance tunes and chanson adaptations, and preserving a modicum of independent part-writing.

Sweelinck, Jan Pieterszoon (b. Deventer, May 1562; d. Amsterdam, 16 Oct 1621) Dutch composer and organist. Learnt music from his father, whom he succeeded as organist of the Oude Kerk, Amsterdam, in about 1580 (his own son in his turn succeeded him). He was active outside the church, belonging to a circle of musicians both professional and amateur in the city, and numbered the Germans Scheidt and Scheidemann among his pupils.

Sweelinck holds a key position as the founder of baroque organ music. Strongly influenced by English virginalists like Bull and Venetian organists like Merulo and G. Gabrieli, with whose music he was closely acquainted, he in turn looked forward to the C17, and passed his art on to his German pupils. Though he published chansons, psalms for Calvinist use and Latin motets, keyboard music dominates his output, and his repute as an organist was immense. From the Venetians he developed the ricercar and toccata; the fantasia he modelled on the contrapuntal motet (some are chromatic, and others written 'in the manner of an echo'); the English virginalists gave him the starting point for the variation technique which he applied to songs, dance tunes and chorale melodies–the last ushering in the evolution of the chorale prelude which culminated in Bach. Sweelinck's chansons stand in the French Renaissance tradition, and his motets have been called a 'noble sunset' to the art of Franco-Flemish polyphony.

CE: *Werken*, ed. M. Seiffert (Leipzig, 1894–1901, repr. 1968); *Opera omnia*, ed. G. Leonhardt and others (Amsterdam, 1957–); Organ chorales in *MD* iii, ed. G. Gerdes

Symphony or **hurdy-gurdy** The earliest mechanized string instrument to which the keyboard principle was applied. The bow is replaced by a wheel, cranked by hand, which produces a continuous sound from all the strings, and the fingering is also mechanized, each string being stopped at different points to produce different notes. Before the C13 this popular medieval instrument was very large and required 2 players–one turning the handle and the other operating the unwieldly keyboard; it was called the 'organistrum' and had a waisted shape. The later instrument was more compact, requiring only one player and capable of moving faster; it had a single melody string and several fixed-pitch drones. This version was called the 'symphony', and was sometimes box-like in shape. By the C16 the in-

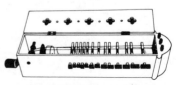

Symphony (hurdy-gurdy) with lid open showing interior, 46 cm

strument had acquired more strings and a chromatic keyboard, but was chiefly associated with beggars and wandering minstrels; it has survived largely as a folk instrument.

Szadek, Tomasz (b. Szadek or Kraków, c1550; d. ?Kraków, c1611) Polish composer. A singer at the court chapel in Kraków from 1569 until 1574, and then a vicar at the cathedral there and singer in the Rorantist choir. For all their technical limitations, his 2 surviving Masses (one on a chanson probably by Crecquillon) are important as the first Polish works to show the influence of the Roman school.

Szamotułczyk, Wacław (b. Szamotuły [nr. Poznań], prob. c1520; d. ? Pińczow, c1560) Polish composer. Court composer at Kraków in 1547–54, and in 1555 became *Kapellmeister* to 'The Black' Prince Michael Radziwiłł, leader of the Polish Calvinists. The most important Polish composer of his day and highly esteemed by Catholics and Protestants alike, he published both Polish sacred songs–some motet-like and others simple harmonizations of folk-like tunes–and Latin church music. His 8-part Mass, the earliest Polish double-choir music, does not survive, but his motets (some published in German anthologies) and Lamentations are fine pieces in a fully-developed Franco-Flemish style akin to that of Gombert and Clemens.

T

Tablature A system of notation usually for keyboard or plucked string instruments in which tones are indicated by letters or figures rather than notes on a stave. The most important types were German and Spanish keyboard tablatures and Italian, French and German lute tablatures. The lute tablatures are 'finger notation', in which horizontal lines represent the strings and numbers or letters the finger position (fret), while rhythms are indicated by separate signs above the staff. In the Italian system (used in Spain), numbers are used and the lowest line represents the highest string and vice-versa; in the French (used in England), letters are used and the highest line represents the highest string; the German was hard to read but simple in practice, not always using lines but having a mixture of numbers and letters to indicate each intersection on the fingerboard. The keyboard tablatures are more complex; the Spanish uses numbers and the German (which continued in use until the C18) letters and other symbols. The term tablature is also applied to a volume of music entirely written in this form of notation.

Tactus C15–16 term for a beat, both a conductor's beat and measured musical time. Normally represented by the semibreve, it had a relatively fixed duration of Mm. 50–72, and was defined by GAFORI as equivalent to the human pulse rate.

Taglia, Pietro (fl. 1555–64) Italian composer. Worked in Milan and was one of the composers who, under the influence of Rore, wrote madrigals containing advanced harmonic and rhythmic experiments. His music is sometimes harsh, and even chaotic in its approach to rhythm and chromatic harmony; some of it appeared in Rore's publications, but he also published 4 volumes of his own, of which only 2 survive.

Talea see **Isorhythm**

Tallis, Thomas (b. c1505; d. Greenwich, 23 Nov 1585) English composer. Organist at Dover Priory in 1532, clerk at St Mary-at-Hill, London, in 1537, and master of the Lady Chapel choir at Waltham Abbey at its dissolution in 1540. In 1541–2 he was clerk at Canterbury cathedral and between 1542 and 1544 he became a Gentleman of the Chapel Royal, remaining there until his death. In 1575 he and Byrd were granted a licence to print music for 21 years, and immediately issued the joint *Cantiones Sacrae*.

Tallis was the most important of the English church composers whose careers spanned the years of change and upheaval around the Reformation. His output falls into several categories: pre-Reformation liturgical works – 2 Masses, one incomplete Mass, 8 hymns, 9 responds and 8 other items; Elizabethan Latin music – the 2 sets of Lamentations and 16 motets mostly in the *Cantiones Sacrae*; Anglican service music and anthems; keyboard music, including organ hymns; and a few secular and consort pieces. The Latin music in particular shows the gradual change from the brilliant, florid and texturally varied manner typical of earlier Tudor composers, through a 'Continental' phase of rich imitative writing, to a sombre, sometimes declamatory and harmonically coloured style, as in the Lamentations. Not surprisingly, a more chordal approach is seen in the Anglican music.

CE: Latin church music in *TCM* vi; English church music in *EECM* xii–xiii, ed. L. Ellinwood, rev. P. Doe; *Complete Keyboard Works*, ed. D. Stevens (New York, 1953)

Tambourin, tambourine see **Percussion**

Tannhäuser (b. ?Oberpfalz region, c1200; d. 1266) Minnesinger. Possibly of noble birth (the name Tannhäuser may be an alias), he was for a long period at the Vienna court, and participated in the Crusade of 1228–9; after the death of his patron, King Frederick, he spent some time as a wandering musician before settling at the court of Otto II of Bavaria. One of his melodies survives.

Tapissier (alias **Noyon**), **Jean** (d. 1408x10) Franco-Flemish composer. *Valet de chambre* at the Burgundian court from 1391 and travelled twice to Avignon. One of the 3 composers (the others being Carmen and Césaris) described by Le Franc in *Le Champion des Dames* (c1440) as having 'astonished all Paris' with their music before that of Dunstable and Dufay was heard there, he is now known only for his sacred music. There survive one isorhythmic motet and 2 Mass movements, with chanson-like textures.

CE: in *CMM* 11/i, ed. G. Reaney

Tarditi, Orazio (b. Rome, 1602; d. Forlì, 18 Jan 1677) Italian composer. Travelled much of northern Italy in his career as a church musician, ending up as choirmaster at Faenza (1647–70). His output was large, including concertato motets, Masses and psalms, and continuo madrigals, canzonets and solo arias.

Tassin Probably a French minstrel at the court of Philippe le Bel in 1228. His name survives in the title of the *Chose Tassin*, an instrumental dance tune often used as a tenor for other compositions.

Taverner, John (b. Tattershall, Lincolnshire, c1490; d. Boston, 1545x46) English composer. In 1524–5 he was a lay clerk at the collegiate church of Tattershall, and in 1526–30 master of the choristers at Cardinal (now Christ Church) College, Oxford, by invitation of Cardinal Wolsey. In 1528 he was briefly involved with Lutheran heretics active in the College. He left in 1530, probably returning to Lincolnshire. In the early 1530s he was a lay clerk in the Guild of St Mary at Boston parish church, though the choir there was disbanded in the late 1530s, a period when Taverner knew Thomas Cromwell, agent of the approaching Reformation. By 1537 he was known to be a member of the Guild of Corpus Christi in Boston (he was its treasurer in 1541–3).

Taverner was the greatest English composer of the early C16; his output consists of 8 Masses, 28 motets and 3 secular pieces. The magnificent festal Masses written for great feasts at Cardinal College stand at the zenith of the development of the early Tudor Mass. They are sonorously written for 6 voices, use cantus firmi, and show a resourceful use of contrasted voice-groupings and full choir passages to create large-scale balance, while in detail Taverner often resorts to imitations, sequence, ostinato, canon and delicate melodic ornament. The smaller Masses include the first English Mass based on a secular tune, the 'Western Wind', which is heard 9 times in each movement in various voices, surrounded by imitative and most imaginative counterpoint. His motets include a number of votive antiphons, which also divide into festal and simpler categories, and *alternatim* pieces including Magnificats and responds. The responds have the appropriate plainsong running through the polyphonic sections in equal note-values: a particularly fine example is the 5-part *Dum transisset I*, with its points of imitation and smoothly curving vocal lines.

CE: *TCM* i, iii; *EECM* xx and further vols, ed. H. Benham (London, 1978–)

Teramo see **Zacharia**

Terzi, Giovanni Antonio (fl. 1593–9) Italian lutenist, of whose life nothing is known. His 2-volume *Intavolatura* (1593, 1599) is chiefly notable for its miniature variation suites, consisting of passamezzo and gagliarda, each in several sections with each section based on the same chord progressions; there is a gradual diminution of note values. The volumes also contain fantasias and transcriptions of vocal pieces.

Tessier, Charles (b. Pézeras, nr. Montpellier, *c*1550) French lutenist and composer. A chamber musician to Henry IV of France; travelled in Germany and visited London, where his 4- and 5-part chansons and *airs de cour* were published in 1597. A further volume of 3-part airs appeared in Paris in 1604. In both publications tuneful treble parts are highlighted by the very simple chordal accompaniments.

Theorbo Plucked string instrument in lower register; like the chitarrone it was developed as an accompanying instrument with a more resonant lower register than the lute, and was less well-adapted for the rapid finger-work of solo lute music. It had 14–16 courses of gut strings, 8 of which were unstopped bass strings (tuned upwards from F) with a separate pegbox. Developed in Italy in the mid-C16, it became a useful continuo instrument, regarded as interchangeable with the chitarrone, and acquired a small solo repertory. A smaller version was called the tiorbino.

Theorbo, 113 cm

Thibaut IV (b. Troyes, 30 May 1201; d. Pamplona, 7 July 1253) Count of Champagne, King of Navarre (1234–53) and trouvère. One of the most important of his generation of trouvères and especially distinguished as a writer of love songs showing a genuine depth of feeling. Sixty-three of his songs were published in 1742, but with the melodies inaccurately transcribed.

Tiburtino, Giuliano (b. Tivoli, c1510; d. Tivoli, 16 Dec 1569) Italian viol da gamba player, described by Ganassi in 1543 as a famous virtuoso. A Papal court musician 1545–64; in 1549 he published a volume of 3-part Masses, motets and madrigals, and also *Fantasie e recerchari*, a collection of 3-part instrumental pieces (including works by Willaert, Donato and others) of individual character; he treats themes from Josquin Desprez's Masses in an obsessively motivic fashion.

Tiento C16 Spanish organ or lute composition in strict imitative counterpoint, with the loose structure of the fantasia. A. de Cabezón wrote a number for organ.

Tigrini, Orazio (b. ?Arezzo, c1535; d. Arezzo, 15 Oct 1591) Italian composer and theorist. Except for the years 1571 to 1587, when he was *maestro di cappella* at Orvieto cathedral, he worked from 1560 until his death in Arezzo, ultimately becoming *maestro* at the cathedral. He published madrigals, psalms and a treatise on counterpoint and composition.

Tinctoris, Johannes (b. Nivelles [Brabant], c1436; d. Nivelles, before 12 Oct 1511) Franco-Flemish theorist and composer. Singer at Cambrai in 1460, where he met Dufay. By 1475 he was in Italy, serving at the court of Ferdinand of Sicily and Aragon; though he is known to have returned to France and his homeland in 1487, he probably remained in his Italian post till his patron died in 1494. Later he was a canon of Nivelles. He was the most important theorist of his time, writing 12 treatises of which 2 were printed. His surviving musical output consists of 4 Masses, 2 motets, a La-

mentation setting, 7 chansons and one Italian song.

CE: *Opera Omnia*, ed. F. Feldmann (Rome, 1960–   )

Titelouze, Jehan (b. S. Omer, 1563x4; d. Rouen, 24 Oct 1633) French composer of Netherlandish descent. Spent most of his career in Rouen, becoming organist at S. Jean in 1585 and at the cathedral from 1588; acquired French citizenship in 1604, and was knowledgeable on instrument-making and musical theory, corresponding with Mersenne and supervising the building of organs. He was an important, if conservative, composer of organ music, issuing volumes of organ hymns and fugues (1623) and organ Magnificats on the 8 plainsong tones (1626). Though the hymns use a variation technique, and Titelouze's subtle dissonance treatment looks forward to the era of tonality, his art belongs in the realm of traditional polyphony, with its continuous part-writing and artful contrapuntal device.

Toccata Literally, Italian for 'touched': a keyboard composition in a free idiomatic style, contrasting full chords, running passages and perhaps imitative sections. The Venetian organists A. Gabrieli and Merulo developed the form, which Frescobaldi subsequently organized into an alternation of free and fugal sections. The term is also used of certain fanfare-like instrumental ensemble pieces, such as the overture to Monteverdi's *Orfeo*.

Tomkins, Thomas (b. St David's, 1572; bd. Martin Hussingtree, nr. Worcester, 9 June 1656) English composer. Born into a musical family; probably became a choirboy at St David's in 1578, and later studied with Byrd. Appointed organist of Worcester cathedral in 1597, and graduated in music at Oxford in 1607; became a

Gentleman of the Chapel Royal between 1617 and 1620, and was its organist in 1621. During the Civil War he retired from the Worcester post to live on his son's estate and devote himself to writing virginal music.

Tomkins was the last and longest-lived of the English masters of virginal music, Anglican church music and madrigals. His output covers all these genres and includes keyboard and consort works, one book of *Songs* (à 3–6), and a large quantity of church music (5 services, preces and psalms and 94 anthems) collected and issued posthumously by his sons as *Musica Deo Sacra* (1668). The anthems in this collection divide into 'full' and 'verse' types, of which the latter display considerable virtuosity in vocal writing and have organ parts of some independence and imagination, which do not however in any way diminish the importance of the choral element. The *Songs* of 1622 contain genuine madrigals and also some exquisite sacred songs such as the famous *When David heard*, with its intensely expressive dissonant harmony. Tomkins' keyboard music, though harking back to Byrd and Bull at a time when tastes were changing, covers a wide range of forms with great distinction.

CE: *Musica Deo Sacra* in *EECM* v, ix, xiv, ed. B. Rose; Anthems in *RRMR* iv, ed. R. Cavanagh; Songs in *EM* xviii, rev. edn.; Keyboard music in *MB* v, ed. S. Tuttle

Tordion A dance added to a BASSE DANCE, e.g. in Attaingnant's collection of 1529.

Trabaci, Giovanni Maria (b. Montepeloso [Irsina, nr. Potenza], c1575; d. Naples, 31 Dec 1647) Italian composer. Organist at the Naples court from 1603 and in 1614 succeeded his teacher Macque as *maestro di cappella* there. During a popular rising in 1647 he took refuge in a local monastery where he died. He published church music, including settings of all 4 Passions, madrigals, villanellas and 2 volumes of organ music. These include examples of almost all contemporary types of keyboard music, including polyphonic ricercars on several themes, toccatas which anticipate Frescobaldi, and Venetian-style canzonas, some using variation forms.

Keyboard music in *MMI*, 1st ser., iii–iv, ed. O. Mischiati

Tregian, Francis (b. Cornwall, 1574; d. London, 1619) English musician. As a Catholic, he was imprisoned for his religious (and political) views from 1609 until his death, during which time he copied out the enormous FITZWILLIAM VIRGINAL BOOK, which includes 4 of his own pieces.

Treibenreif see **Tritonius**

Trent Codices 7 MS volumes of C15 polyphony in the libraries of Trent in the Italian Tyrol; a large and important source of works from 1420–80 by some 75 composers of many nationalities, including Dunstable, Power, Dufay, Binchois, Ockeghem and Busnois.

Triangle see **Percussion**

Trio sonata A type of baroque chamber music à 3, for 2 upper parts of similar range (usually violins) together with a supporting basso continuo for keyboard and (possibly) a melody instrument. The form first appeared in Italy c1610 with examples by G. P. Cima, S. Rossi and Buonamente.

Trionfo di Dori, Il An anthology of madrigals published in 1592, each of the poems set ending with the words 'viva la bella Dori'.

Trisagion see **Improperia**

Tritonius, Petrus (real name Peter Treibenreif) (b. Bozen [Bolzano], c1465; d. Hall am Inn, ?1525) Austrian composer and humanist. Spent much of his life as a schoolmaster in the Tyrol, mainly at Bozen and Hall am Inn; but early in the C16, as a member of a literary and humanistic circle in Vienna, he Latinized his name and published a volume of settings of Horace's Odes in which the unmeasured rhythms attempt to follow the scansion of Latin verse. Though extremely plain and homophonic in style, these were reprinted many times and imitated by Polish and Hungarian composers.

Triumphs of Oriana, The A collection of English madrigals issued by Morley in imitation of the Italian TRIONFO DI DORI. Posthumously dedicated to Queen Elizabeth I in 1603, nearly all the 29 pieces in the collection end with the words 'Long live fair Oriana'. The volume includes works by the leading English madrigal composers of the day, and also by some of their less well-known contemporaries.

Trobadors see **Troubadours**

Troiano, Massimo (b. Corduba, nr. Naples, early C16) Italian composer and poet. Probably a pupil of Nola at Naples; worked from 1560 in Augsburg, Treviso and Venice, and by 1568 was at the Bavarian court in Munich. He wrote the poems for Lassus' madrigal comedy *La cortegiana inamorata*, performed at Duke Wilhelm's wedding in 1568, and also designed the scenery and acted in the production, but in 1570 he became involved in a murder case and fled from Munich, after which all trace of him disappears. He published 4 volumes of Neapolitan songs, edited an anthology of music by Munich composers and wrote an

account of the 1568 wedding festivities.

Tromba marina Bowed MONOCHORD, with a long, tapering triangular body. It played only harmonics, produced by touching the string lightly. By the C15 it had 2 strings of different lengths; because one foot of the bridge was not fastened down it had a rattling sound. Little is known of its use and the origin of the name is a mystery.

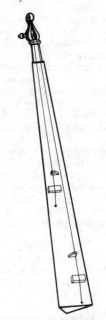

Tromba marina, 120 cm

Trombetti, Ascanio (bp. Bologna, 27 Nov 1544; d. Bologna, 20x21 Sep 1590) Italian composer. From being a member of the Bologna town band, became *maestro di cappella* at the church of S. Giovanni in Monte in 1583. He published motets in up to 10 parts which show Venetian influence, Neapolitan songs, and madrigals.

Tromboncino, Bartolomeo (b. Verona, *c*1470; d. ?Venice, after 1535) Italian composer. Spent long periods in the service of the Mantuan court from 1487 to 1512, though in 1499 he was in Vicenza; that year he murdered his wife and her lover, though even this was forgiven on account of his talent. He was in Ferrara in 1513 and later seems to have served at the Florentine court. With Cara, he was a prolific master of the frottola, having many published by Petrucci and Antico and arranged for voice and lute by Bossinensis. He also wrote Lamentations, 22 *laude*, and music for dramatic productions at court (including Plautus' *Asinaria*, performed at a wedding in 1502). His frottolas sometimes set verses by Petrarch, thus acquiring a seriousness of mood that looks ahead to the madrigal.

Frottolas in *IM* 1st ser., i, ed. G. Cesari and R. Monterosso; *SCMA* iv, ed. A. Einstein

Trope In medieval Roman liturgy, a textual addition to or gloss upon authentic texts, ranging from a few words interpolated into a Kyrie to lengthy explanatory sentences or entire poems. The shorter could be adapted to pre-existent chant melismas by singing one syllable to each note, otherwise tropes were set to new melodies. Tropes were abolished by the COUNCIL OF TRENT, but traces survive in the Kyrie names in plainsong Mass books (the *Kyriale*).

Troubadours, trobadors Aristocratic (and humbler) poet-musicians from the Provençal-speaking area of southern France. From *c*1100 they devoted themselves to the cultivation of chivalrous love through poetry and music. Some 2,600 poems in Provençal survive, together with 250 melodies, in their *chansonniers* or songbooks.

Trouluffe, John (d. 1473x74) English editor and composer. Canon of Probus, Cornwall, from 1448, but probably resided at Exeter; collaborated with Richard Smert in compiling the collection of hymns and carols which forms the oldest part of the Ritson MS (2 of the simple votive antiphons in the MS are by him and he may have composed a third jointly with Smert).

Trouvères Like the Provençal TROUBADOURS, trouvères were aristocratic poet-musicians; they were active in northern France from the mid-C12. Some 2,100 of their texts and 1,400 melodies are preserved; trouvère songs resemble those of the troubadours in being monophonic but place more emphasis on formal structure, being cast in forms of lasting importance such as the VIRELAI.

Trumpet Wind instrument with cup mouthpiece and no finger-holes. The medieval straight trumpet (the very long one was called buisine, and the shorter type clarion) could play only a few natural harmonics and was used largely for ceremonial purposes. In the C14 the buisine's overall length was reduced by bending it into a flat S-shape, and by the C16 the trumpet had acquired its familiar folded shape and was normally pitched in D. A century later the upper register was in use and elaborate polyphonic fanfares were being written. A mute could be used to raise the pitch by a tone.

The Slide trumpet developed from the S-shaped trumpet during the C14, the main body of the instrument being slid up and down a telescopic mouthpipe so as to give a chromatic compass of about 2 octaves. C15 pictures frequently show the slide trumpet playing with shawms for a basse dance, and some music apparently intended for it survives. It was an unwieldy instrument to play, however, and by c1500 had largely given place to the SACKBUT, which employed the slide principle more satisfactorily.

Turini, Francesco (b. Prague, c1589; d. Brescia, 1656) Italian composer. His father was in Imperial court service; he himself was sent by the Emperor to study in Venice and Rome before becoming court organist in Prague. In 1620 he became cathedral organist in Brescia. One of the pioneers of the baroque trio sonata, publishing many sonatas for 2 violins and continuo, he also published madrigals for 1 to 5 voices, solo motets, and Masses with continuo.

Turnhout, Gérard de (b. Turnhout, c1520; d. Madrid, 15 Sep 1580) Franco-Flemish composer. Worked in and around Antwerp from 1545 as singer and choirmaster, from 1562 at the confraternity of the Virgin and from 1563 at the cathedral; in 1571 became choirmaster to the Flemish chapel of Philip II of Spain. He published a volume of 3-part chansons and motets in 1569; a Mass and some 2- and 3-part chansons appeared in anthologies.

Sacred and secular songs in *RRMR* ix–x, ed. L. Wagner

Tye, Christopher (b. c1500; d. Doddington, 1572x3) English composer. May have been a choirboy at King's College, Cambridge, and was a lay clerk there in the late 1530s; he took Cambridge Bachelor and Doctor of Music degrees in 1536 and 1545. By 1543 he had become choirmaster at Ely cathedral, where he remained till 1561. He was thereafter rector of Doddington in Cambridgeshire. His Latin church music (Masses, antiphons, Magnificats, etc.) was probably written during Henry VIII's reign, though the fine 6-part Mass *Euge bone* may belong to the Marian period in the 1550s. Tye was an important composer of early Anglican anthems and service music, which show his thorough-going adoption of the Continental imitative style. He also wrote the *Acts of the Apostles* (1553), dedicated to King Edward VI (he was at that time a member of the Chapel Royal), and a quantity of consort and keyboard music.

Latin church music in *RRMR* xiii–xiv, ed. J. Satterfield; English church music in *EECM* xix, ed. J. Morehen; Instrumental music in *RRMR* iii, ed. R. Weidner

U

Ugolini, Vincenzo (b. Perugia, *c*1570; d. Rome, 6 May 1638) Italian composer. A pupil of G. B. Nanino and teacher of Benevoli; held posts as *maestro di cappella* at various Roman churches, including S. Maria Maggiore (1592–1603) and the Cappella Giulia (1620–6), and in 1609–15 worked at Benevento cathedral. A serious illness in 1604 left him in poor health for the rest of his life, but he published madrigals and many volumes of church music, some for 1 to 4 voices with continuo in the new manner, and some for 8 to 12 voices in a dignified and old-fashioned style.

Ugolino of Orvieto (b. ?Orvieto, *c*1380; d. Ferrara, *c*1457) Italian theorist. His *Declaratio musicae disciplinae* was the last of the great speculative treatises of the Middle Ages; later writers did not regard speculative justification as necessary to the practice of music.

Ulenberg, Kaspar (b. Lippstadt, nr. Paderborn, 1549; d. Köln, 16 Feb 1617) German ecclesiastic. Originally a Lutheran pastor, he became a Catholic in 1575 and rose rapidly from priest in Kaiserswerth (Düsseldorf) to Rector of Köln university (1592–1615). He made a German translation of the psalms with tunes, which was still being reprinted in 1710; 3-part settings of these melodies were made by Lassus. He also translated the Bible and wrote catechetical works.

Unversagte, Der C13 Minnesinger. His name means 'the Dauntless One', and his song *Der Kuninc Rodolp* praises a Hapsburg ruler known for his lack of generosity towards musicians.

Urreda (Wreede, Vrede), Johannes (b. ?Bruges; fl. 1476–81) Spanish composer of Franco-Flemish origin. In 1476 the Duke of Alba paid him to teach 3 Negro boys to sing, and from 1477 to 1481 he was *maestro de capilla* to Ferdinand V of Aragon. His 4-part arrangement of the Mozarabic *Pange lingua* and 3-part setting of the *villancico Nunca fué pena mayor* (from the *Cancionero de Palacio*) were very popular, and frequently used as the basis of works by other composers.

Use of Sarum (Salisbury) see **Sarum Use**

Usper (real name Spongia), Francesco (b. Parenzo [Poreč, Yugoslavia], end C16; d. Venice, beginning 1641) Italian composer and priest. A pupil of A. Gabrieli; worked as organist at S. Salvador in Venice from 1614, and in 1622–3 was deputy organist at St Mark's. In 1627 he became director of the Scuola di S. Giovanni Evangelista. He published madrigals, church music, and instrumental music in up to 8 parts, including a fine *sinfonia* for 2 violins, 4 viole, recorder and chitarrone which has brilliant concertino passages.

Utendal, Alexander (b. *c*1530; d. Innsbruck, 7 May 1581) Franco-Flemish composer. Served the widowed Spanish Queen Mary of Hungary in Brussels and Spain, and in 1564 entered the service of Archduke

Ferdinand in Prague and Innsbruck, where he became vice-*Kapellmeister* in 1580. His publications of church music, including Masses, motets and penitential psalms, and of German songs, are noteworthy for the very careful notation of accidentals; he was one of the first composers to use the natural sign (♮) to contradict an earlier sharp or flat.

V

Vacqueiras see **Raimbaud de Vacqueiras**

Vaet, Jacobus (b. Courtrai or Harelbeke, 1529; d. Vienna, 8 Jan 1567) Franco-Flemish composer. *Kapellmeister* to the Archduke Maximilian in Prague from 1554, and when Maximilian succeeded as Emperor in 1564 became court *Kapellmeister* in Vienna. His output consists almost entirely of church music, including many parody Masses on models by composers such as Josquin, Mouton and Crecquillon. His earlier work is solidly imitative in the manner of Gombert, but his later music shows the influence of Lassus in its freer textures and bold dissonances, and of the Venetians in his double-choir pieces.

Selected works in *DTO* xcviii, c, ciii–iv, cviii–ix, cxiii–iv, cxvi, cxviii

Vaillant, Jean Late C14 French composer. Ran a music school in Paris and had 5 pieces in the Chantilly MS; his style retains more of the clarity and simplicity of Machaut than does that of some of his contemporaries.

Secular works in *CMM* 53/i, ed. W. Apel.

Valderrábano, Enríquez de (b. Peñeranda de Duero, nr. Aranda de D., c1500; d. after 1557) Spanish vihuelist. Nothing is known of his life, but a motto at the end of his solitary publication suggests that he may have suffered great poverty. This *Libro de música* (1547) contains lute songs, many based on folk tunes or dances; arrangements of pieces by such composers as Josquin Desprez, Willaert and Morales for one

or 2 lutes; 33 imaginative and expressive fantasias; and *diferencias*, including a set of 120 variations on *Gúardame las vacas*.

Libro de música in *MME* xxii–iii, ed. E. Pujol

Valente, Antonio (fl. 1565–80) Italian (or possibly Spanish) organist and composer. He was blind, and from 1565 to 1580 was organist at S. Angelo a Nido in Naples. His *Intavolatura* of 1576, written in an unusual number notation, contains the earliest known written-out fantasia for keyboard, imitative ricercars, and variations which use stereotyped figurations. He also published a volume of canons for organ.

Intavolatura de cimbalo, ed. C. Jacobs (Oxford, 1973)

Vallet, Nicholas (b. Corbény, nr. Laon, c1583; d. Amsterdam, after 1626) French lutenist. He lived in Amsterdam from 1613 and published 2 volumes of lute music containing fantasias, preludes, dances (often based on themes also used by the English virginalists) and transcriptions of English, French and German songs. He also produced 2 volumes of psalms for voice and lute.

CE: in *CLF* x, ed. A. Souris and M. Rollin

Vaqueras, Bertrandus (b. Bresses, Ain, c1450; d. after 1507) French composer. A singer at St Peter's, Rome, in 1481–2, and Papal singer from 1483 until 1507; also at some time in Liège. Glareanus admired his compositions and quoted from his work; Petrucci's anthologies included one motet and one chanson by him, and 2 Masses and other works survive in MS.

Variation A form that developed with the rise of keyboard and lute music in the mid-C16. Spain was particularly important in the early stages, which culminated in the DIFERENCIAS of Cabezón and others. The English virginalists followed a novel trend towards the brilliant variation based on figuration patterns: technical and musical aspects were harmoniously balanced in examples by Byrd, as also in those by Sweelinck. Frescobaldi often used popular tunes or stock basses such as the ROMANESCA as the foundation for variations.

Vásquez, Juan (b. Badajoz, c1500; d. Seville, c1560) Spanish composer and priest. *Maestro de capilla* at Badajoz cathedral from 1545 and later served a succession of Spanish noblemen. Most of his output is secular, including 2 published volumes of ingeniously written *villancicos*; he also published a setting of the Office of the Dead in alternating plainsong and polyphony.
    Secular music in *MME* iv, ed. H. Anglés

Vautor, Thomas (b. ?Leicestershire, ?1580x90) English composer. In the service of the Duke of Buckingham, and published a volume of 5- and 6-part madrigals in 1619. These show some individuality of style; his best-known piece is *Sweet Suffolk Owl*.
    Madrigals in *EM* xxxiv (rev. edn.)

Vecchi, Orazio (bp. Modena, 6 Dec 1550; d. Modena, 19 Feb 1605) Italian composer. Took vows, and directed music at the cathedral of Salò in 1581–4, thence returning to Modena. In 1586 became choirmaster at the cathedral of Reggio Emilia and a canon of Correggio cathedral (nr. Modena), but long absences led to his dismissal from the former post. In 1596 he took over the choir of Modena cathedral, and 2 years later was put in charge of music at the Este court and the musical education of the Duke's children. A wicked intrigue on the part of his colleague Capilupi brought about his dismissal from the former post in 1604, and hastened his death.
    Vecchi published no less than 13 volumes of canzonets, madrigals, dialogues and madrigal comedies, and 4 of sacred music–motets, Masses and Lamentations. He was an inspired master of the light madrigal and canzonet, with its airy melodies and dance-like rhythms; but his fame rests on the MADRIGAL COMEDIES, especially *L'Amfiparnaso* (1597), in which a *commedia dell'arte* drama is acted out in madrigalian music of many sorts, including vulgar burlesque and dramatic dialogue (among groups of voices); there is no scenery, and the audience would have been the friends of the 5 singers, so this cannot be seen as a genuine forerunner of opera.
    Madrigal comedies in *CP* v, viii

Vecchi, Orfeo (b. Milan, c1550; d. Milan, before Apr 1604) Italian composer, not related to Orazio Vecchi. *Maestro di cappella* at S. Maria della Scala in Milan from at least 1590, and published many volumes of church music, including Masses with basso continuo, psalms and spiritual madrigals, some of which went into several editions. Among the spiritual madrigals are more than 20 adaptations to sacred texts of secular pieces by composers such as Merulo, Palestrina and Wert.

Velut, Gilet Early C15 Franco-Flemish composer, possibly from Liège. He was in Cyprus in 1411, and may have entered the Papal choir in 1421. Some chansons, Mass movements and motets (one is isorhythmic, on the subject of the Papal Schism) survive; he frequently employed a syllabic style.

CE: in *CMM* 11/ii, ed. G. Reaney

Venegas de Henestrosa, Luys (b. Henestrosa, nr. Burgos, 1500x10; d. ?Toledo, c1557) Spanish organist. In 1557 he prepared a volume of Spanish keyboard music (*Libro de Cifra Nueva*) containing 138 pieces–fantasias, *tientos* and arrangements of church music –by A. de Cabezón and others.

Ventadour see **Bernart de Ventadour**

Vento, Ivo de (b. c1544; d. Munich, 1575) Composer, probably of Netherlands descent and a pupil of Merulo in Venice; an organist in Munich in 1564, became ducal *Kapellmeister* at Landshut in 1568, and was appointed court organist at Munich, under Lassus, in 1570. He published many German songs; those in 4 to 6 parts are on the whole conservative (one of his prefaces takes exception to the idea of madrigalian word painting) but those in 3 parts owe something to the villanella style. He also published motets.

Verbonnet see **Ghiselin**

Verdelot, Philippe (b. ?Caderousse, Orange; d. ?Florence, before 1552) ?French composer; seems to have lived in Italy from 1505, possibly studying with Obrecht at Ferrara. Directed music at the Baptistery of S. Giovanni in Florence in 1523–7, was in Rome from 1529 for up to 4 years, and held a secular appointment in Venice in 1533–5. His career is hard to follow after 1539.

Verdelot was one of several non-Italian composers who settled in Italy and dominated the early development of the madrigal. He published 9 volumes of madrigals, and his church music (Masses and motets) was published in anthologies all over Europe. Though many of his 4-part madrigals are chordal and song-like, as are Arcadelt's, he sometimes wrote in a more flowing, imitative style, as in the fine *Madonna il tuo bel viso*. He also developed 5-part writing, varying the music with delicate contrasts of texture and careful attention to individual words or phrases, or enjoying the rich sonority of multiple low voices.

CE: *Opera omnia* (*CMM* 28), ed. A.-M. Bragard (Rome, 1966–   )

Verdonck, Cornelius (b. Turnhout, c1563; d. Antwerp, 4 July 1625) Franco-Flemish composer. A pupil of Cornet and Waelrant, he was from 1579 in the private service of various wealthy citizens in the Low Countries. He published chansons (whose preface deplores the poor state of music in the Netherlands) and madrigals; he is represented in *Musica Transalpina*, and a motet he composed for an archducal visit to Antwerp is said to have been performed by 6 boys on the back of an elephant.

Verse anthem see **Anthem**

Verso, Antonio il (b. Piazza Armerina, Sicily, before 19 Jan 1569; d. Palermo, ?Aug 1621) Italian composer. An infant prodigy–he is said to have composed a 2-part ricercare at the age of 10–he was a pupil of Pietro Vinci and spent most of his working life in Palermo, though he may have visited Venice c1600–3. Only Monte was a more prolific madrigalist than il Verso, whose 39 publications included 23 madrigal books, the remainder comprising church and instrumental music. His style shows many characteristics of MANNERISM; his early work however owes more to Wert than to Gesualdo.

Concerti and madrigals in *MRS* vi–vii, ed. A. Watanabe and P. Carapezza

Vespers see **Office**

Viadana, Lodovico Grossi da (b. Viadana, nr. Mantua, c1560; d. Gualtieri, 1627) Italian composer, possibly a pupil of C. Porta. Became a Franciscan monk in 1596; in 1593–7 directed music at Mantua cathedral, and was probably still working in that city in 1600. His next recorded post was as choirmaster in Fano (1610–12); he later visited Venice and finally returned to Mantua.

Viadana was a prolific church composer, publishing no less than 22 volumes of motets, psalm collections, etc.; he also wrote 4 books of madrigals and canzonets and one of instrumental *sinfonie*. His historical importance lies in the fact that he established the small-scale CONCERTATO style and the use of the continuo in church music with his epoch-making *Cento concerti ecclesiastici* of 1602 (2 further volumes appeared later). In writing for between 1 and 4 voices with indispensable organ accompaniment, he proved that the new medium was feasible for church music, and though the musical results were often modest or even backward-looking, the influence of the collection was immense. The preface contains important information on the new art of continuo playing. Some of the motets do show the chromatic or true monodic or duet writing of the *stile moderno*, and illustrate neatly-conceived formal structures.

Vicentino, Nicola (b. Vicenza, 1511; d. Milan, 1576) Italian composer and theorist. A pupil of Willaert in Venice, he was court music director and teacher at Ferrara before 1539, and then joined the retinue of Cardinal Ippolito d'Este in Rome. He was cathedral *maestro* at Vicenza in 1563–5 and a priest in Milan in 1570. He is chiefly known for the advanced theories in his *L'antica musica ridotta alla*

moderna prattica (1555) on supposedly Greek enharmonic music; he divided the whole tone into 5 parts, devising an instrument called the archicembalo with a 31-note octave capable of distinguishing F sharp from G flat, for example. His madrigals exploit these microtones. The musical establishment opposed his ideas, though he was asked by the progressive fathers of the Council of Trent to write a 'chromatic' Mass as a sample of liturgically acceptable polyphony.

CE: *Opera omnia* (*CMM* 26), ed. H. Kaufmann (Rome, 1963)

Victoria, Tomás Luis de (b. Ávila, 1548; d. Madrid, 27 Aug 1611) Spanish composer. Possibly a pupil of Escobedo, he was sent to Rome to study at the Jesuit German College and may also have studied with Palestrina at the nearby Roman Seminary. He succeeded him there as choirmaster in 1571, and held the same post at the German College in 1573–8, becoming a priest in 1575; he resigned in 1578 and went on to work as a priest at S. Girolamo della Carità. In 1585 he returned to Spain, though continuing to visit Rome frequently; from 1586 until his death he was in Madrid, serving the Empress Maria and later her daughter, as teacher, organist and choirmaster in the convent of the Descalzas Reales.

Victoria was one of the most widely respected of the late Renaissance polyphonists. His works include 20 Masses, 44 motets, and a number of important liturgical collections – hymns, Magnificats, 2 Requiem Masses, and music for the Holy Week Offices. It is the latter which contains the famous Tenebrae RESPONSORIES, in which he clothes plangent texts with music of great intensity without departing from the strict textual repetition scheme; much the same could be said of the lesser-known Lamentations. Though he wrote no secular music, Victoria was as capable as any late Renaissance composer of infusing church music with a spiritual fervour in keeping with the spirit of the Counter-Reformation – this is often misleadingly referred to as 'Spanish mysticism'. The hymns, Magnificats and Masses, however, breathe a suave and less emotional spirit; the hymns often use soaring contrapuntal lines against a plainsong cantus firmus, while the Masses are mostly of the parody type, making imaginative use of models by Victoria himself (the *O quam gloriosum* Mass, for instance) or by others. His control of vocal sonority is evident in the various pieces for double choir, for one of which he provides an organ part. In general he was less reticent than Palestrina in details of style such as tonal colouring, and vocal line and rhythm; though he worked for so long in Rome, his music often has a distinctive Spanish quality that is obvious to the ear but less easy to describe in words.

CE: *Opera omnia*, ed. F. Pedrell (Leipzig, 1902–13); rev. edn., ed. H. Anglés (Rome, 1965–   ) in *MME*, various vols.

Vidal see **Peire Vidal**

Vide, Jacques (fl. 1410–33) Franco-Flemish composer. An ecclesiastic in Bruges in 1410, he served the Burgundian court as *valet de chambre* and secretary to Philip the Good 1423–33. He seems neither to have sung in a church choir nor to have left any sacred music, but he composed some fine chansons, several of which make bold use of dissonance. *Las j'ay perdu*, complete in 2 parts but with a blank extra stave, may be an attempt at visual illustration of a text, while in *Amans double*, *à 4*, both top parts are of equal importance.

Vihuela Plucked string instrument

peculiar to C16 Spain and southern Italy, and properly called *vihuela da mano*. Similar in size to the modern guitar, it had tied-on gut frets and 6 double courses of gut strings, giving a lute-like sound; it was played with the fingers. During its brief career its prestige was equal in Spain to that of the lute elsewhere, and it was used for virtuoso solo playing as well as for accompaniment; music was provided for it by the principal Spanish composers. In the C17 its history merges with that of its more popular relative, the guitar.

Vila, Pedro Alberch (b. Vich, nr. Barcelona, 1517; d. Barcelona, 16 Nov 1582) Spanish composer. *Maestro de capilla* at Barcelona cathedral from at least 1538, and was also adviser on matters concerning organs to all the Catalan cathedrals, and a noted organ teacher. He was regarded as one of the leading Spanish composers of the day; his surviving works include a volume of madrigals to Spanish, French and Italian texts, pieces in the Flecha *ensalada* collection, a dramatic 3-part Lamentations setting and some dignified organ *tientos*.

Villancico C15–16 Spanish poetry of an idyllic or devotional type, frequently set to music for 3 or 4 voices, as in the CANCIONERO DE PALACIO (c1500) in a mainly chordal style. Later *villancicos* were set for voice and lute to Spanish or Portuguese words. In form they resembled the French VIRELAI.

Villanella A type of light C16 Italian secular music originating in Naples (as 'canzon villanescha') as a less polished and more folk-like counterpart to the serious madrigal. It was usually strophic, sometimes laid out in the form *AABCC*, and often contained a burlesque element in 'rustic' consecutive 5ths. The earliest collections were published by NOLA, CIMELLO and WILLAERT in the 1540s.

Villotta A north Italian type of light secular music of the C16, having the character of a popular dance or street song, sometimes with nonsense syllables; its idiom was even more folk-like than that of the VILLANELLA, with which it however became synonymous after about 1540.

Vincenti Venetian music publishing family active from 1583 until 1665. Giacomo Vincenti (d. 1619) founded the business in 1583, at first in partnership with the firm of Amadino; he worked alone after 1586, and his son Alessandro took the firm over after his death. It published many collections of madrigals, villanellas and canzonas, and much sacred music.

Vincentius, Caspar (b. S. Omer, ?1580; d. Würzburg, before June 1624) Franco-Flemish composer. After a period at the Imperial court, where he was a pupil of Monte, he worked as organist in Speyer and Worms, becoming cathedral organist in Würzburg (where he quarrelled with the builder of the new organ) in 1618. His continuo parts for Lassus' *Magnum Opus Musicum* were published posthumously in 1625; his own music appeared in anthologies.

Vincenzo da Rimini C14 Italian composer. An abbot at either Rimini or Imola, and is portrayed in the Squarcialupi Codex. His output consists of 4 madrigals and 2 *cacce* (this is unusual, as most composers produced only one *caccia*).
CE: in *CMM* 8/iv, ed. W. Apel; in *PMFC* vii, ed. W. T. Marrocco

Vinci, Pietro (b. Nicosia, Sicily, c1540; d. Nicosia, JulyxDec 1584) Italian composer. *Maestro di cappella* at S.

Maria Maggiore, Bergamo, 1568–80, and from 1581 held various similar posts in Nicosia and other Sicilian cities. His many volumes of madrigals received frequent reprintings, and he also published church music; his style is simple and restrained for its period, yet effective. As the teacher of Antonio il Verso and others he may be seen as the founder of a school of Sicilian composers.
Vocal works in *MRS* ii–iii, ed. P. Carapezza

Vinier, le see **Gilles** or **Guillaume le Vinier**

Viol Bowed string instrument. Not a medieval instrument, or related to the violin; it emerged in the later C15, possibly in Spain. The viol had 6 strings (occasionally 5, or, on some C17 bass

Tenor viol, 96 cm

instruments, 7) tuned similarly to the lute. It was lightly constructed with flat back, deep sides, sloping shoulders, fretted fingerboard and C-shaped sound-holes, and was less tightly strung than the violin. Ganassi (1542) describes 3 sizes–treble, tenor and bass. All were bowed underhand and were usually held downwards, resting on the player's knee. An instrument for the cultivated amateur as well as the professional, it was suitable for many kinds of music; consorts for up to 6 viols were especially popular in England.

Viola bastarda Continental equivalent of the DIVISION VIOL; a small bass viol played with virtuoso technique. Praetorius however describes it as an accompanying instrument.

Violin Bowed string instrument; a fusion of FIDDLE, REBEC and LIRA DA BRACCIO which emerged in the early C16. Originally with 3 strings, by the 1550s it had 4, and had acquired its familiar shape; it was bowed overhand. Initially used mainly for dance music, it had in little more than a century from its arrival become the principal bowed string instrument, with a large and technically difficult solo repertory and an important part in ensemble playing. There were important schools of violin-making in the C16 at Brescia and Cremona.

Violone Bowed string instrument with 6 strings, fretted and tuned like a viol, which acted as a double bass to the viol family from the mid-C16 to mid-C17. Though larger than the bass viol, its precise pitch is not certain; it was more probably an intermediate instrument, used alone on bass lines, than a 16-foot instrument used for octave doubling. The name is somewhat ambiguous, being applied also to the standard bass viol.

Virdung, Sebastian (b. Amberg, ?19x20 Jan 1465; d. c1511) German singer and composer. His treatise *Musica getuscht* (1511) is the earliest known work to describe musical instruments and instrumental practice in any detail.

Virelai An important type of French poetry and music, c1150–1500. Those of the trouvères were monophonic; Machaut wrote both monophonic and polyphonic *virelais*, and the form was cultivated also in Italy (the early LAUDA and BALLATA) and in Spain (CANTIGA, VILLANCICO). Its musical structure is *A b b a A* (capitals indicate textual refrain, lower case fresh sections of text). C14 French and Italian examples had three stanzas in this form.

Virginal Plucked string keyboard instrument, differing from the harpsichord in its oblong shape, with strings parallel to the keyboard. In use by the late C15, it had one set of strings with a 4-octave compass. In England the name was used for all plucked string keyboard instruments.

Vitali, Filippo (b. Florence, c1590; d. Florence, after Apr 1653) Italian composer. Except for a period in Rome as Papal singer (from 1631) spent his life in Florence, becoming *maestro di cappella* at S. Lorenzo there in 1642. He published both 5-part madrigals and pieces for 1, 2 and 3 voices in the modern style, as well as a little church music in a more archaic idiom. His opera *L'Aretusa* (1620), though musically undistinguished, is important as one of the first productions of the kind in Rome; he also wrote music for *intermedi*.

Vitry see **Philippe de Vitry**

Vivanco, Sebastián de (b. Ávila, c1550;

d. Salamanca, 26 Oct 1622) Spanish composer. He worked in Lérida, Segovia, Ávila, Seville and Salamanca, where he was *maestro de capilla* at the cathedral from 1602 and professor of music at the university from 1603. He published several volumes of church music, and more survives in MS.

Masses in *RRMR* xxxi, ed. E. Arias

Vrede see **Urreda**

Voces musicales see **Hexachord**

Vogelweide see **Walther von der Vogelweide**

Volta A late C16 dance in triple time, regarded as somewhat lascivious.

Voluntary A free form of English organ music to be played at a church service. The early examples, those from the Mulliner Book and others by Byrd and Gibbons, are somewhat similar to the fantasia in their contrapuntal element.

Vulpius, Melchior (b. Wasungen, nr. Meiningen, *c*1570; bd. Weimar, 7 Aug 1615) German composer. Schoolmaster and cantor at Schleusingen (near Meiningen) from 1589, and town cantor at Weimar from 1596. He published many volumes of motets in up to 8 parts and German sacred songs (which introduced new tunes to the congregational repertory), some of which went into several editions.

W

Waelrant, Hubert (b. Tongeloo, Brabant, c1517; d. Antwerp, 19 Nov 1595) Franco-Flemish composer and publisher. Possibly a pupil of Willaert in Venice, he can be traced as singer, teacher and publisher in Antwerp 1544–58. In 1554 he and Jean Laet founded a publishing business which issued anthologies of motets and chansons, including some of his own works; 2 of these were confiscated by the Inquisition on the grounds of suspected heresy, and certainly there is nothing specifically Catholic about the texts of Waelrant's motets. More of his music was published in 1588, and 36 villanella-like 3-part pieces survive in an English MS; his style is notable for its use of bold dissonances in word painting.

Waissel, Matthäus (b. c1540; d. Königsberg [Kaliningrad], 1602) German lutenist and composer. From 1573 headmaster of a school at Schippenbeil near Königsberg, he published in that year a volume of lute arrangements of vocal pieces; in 1592 he issued a collection of German dances for lute, which was the last lute tablature to be published in Germany for many years.

Walter, Johannes (b. Kahler, Thuringia, 1496; d. Torgau, 25 Mar 1570) German cantor and composer. In 1517 he belonged to the chapel of Friedrich the Wise of Saxony, and became a friend of the reformers Luther and Melancthon, and a collaborator with Luther in the organization of music for the Reformed services, including the provision of chorale melodies. He was cantor at the Latin school at Torgau in 1526 – one of the first to occupy a type of post held by many leading Protestant musicians in Germany – and from 1548 directed music at the Saxon court chapel there and later at Dresden (where the court transferred). He retired to Torgau in 1554.

Walter's *Geistliches Gesangbüchlein* of 1524 marked a historical beginning for Lutheran music as the earliest collection of chorale settings; it also included motets. He published several more similar volumes and a book of Magnificats, while his Passion settings and instrumental canons survive in MS. Walter did not create a new form in his approach to the chorale; rather he adapted the best techniques of existing secular polyphonic song by Senfl and others, slightly modernizing their contrapuntal idiom or writing in a fairly homophonic manner, so that the text was clear. The chorale itself usually lay in the tenor part.

CE: *Sämtliche Werke*, ed. O. Schröder and others (Kassel, 1943–73)

Walther von der Vogelweide (b. ?Tyrol, c1170; d. Würzburg, c1230) Poet and Minnesinger. A member of the lower aristocracy; lived for some time at the Vienna court and also attended such great occasions as the coronation of the King of Swabia at Worms in 1198 and the Reichstag at Frankfurt in 1212. Some time after 1220 he abandoned his wandering life and settled down on an estate in Würzburg. His famous and very beautiful *Palästinalied* probably dates from the Crusade of 1228, and was only rediscovered in 1910; it is the earliest surviving Minnesinger melody (in

fact a variant on a Provençal troubadour song) and his style in general
combines courtly and more popular
elements.

Ward, John (bp. Canterbury, 8 Sep
1571; d. 31 Aug 1638) English composer. In the service of Sir Henry Fan-
shawe of Ware, he published a volume
of madrigals in 3 to 6 parts in 1613,
contributed to Ravenscroft's psalter,
and composed anthems, viol fantasias,
and keyboard pieces. One of the best
and most serious of the English madrigalists, at times approaching the standard of Weelkes. There are traces of
Italian influence in his music; his
anthems contain some extravagant
word painting, and his viol music is
distinctively instrumental in style.

Madrigals in *EM* xix (rev. edn.)

Weelkes, Thomas (b. *c*1575; d. London, 30 Nov 1623) English composer.
Became organist of Winchester cathedral in 1598, and in 1602 took the
Oxford degree of Mus. Bac. and moved
to Chichester cathedral as organist.
During his time there he was several
times in trouble with the authorities for
being slack and erratic at his job, and
even for drunkenness.

Weelkes was one of the leading
English madrigalists, publishing 4
collections for 3–6 voices; he also wrote
some 10 services and 40 anthems. As a
madrigalist he preferred larger combinations of voices and more pano-
ramic musical designs than Morley.
His balletts are sometimes quite intricate, moving far from the original Italian model. In the madrigals of 1600 he
shows a brilliance and impulsive boldness in his writing for large sonorities
and graphic illustration of words, as in
the remarkable geographical madrigal
Thule, the period of cosmography. His
occasional chromatic writing, though
uncharacteristic of English madrigals,
is restrained by comparison with that

of contemporary Italians. As a church
composer, Weelkes is rather more traditional, though his anthems breathe a
worldly spirit and the best of them
have a monumental quality. He also
wrote a few keyboard and consort
pieces.

CE: Madrigals in *EM*, ix–xiii, rev.
edn.; Anthems in *MB* xxiii, ed.
D. Brown and others

Weerbeke, Gaspar van (b. ?Oude-
narde, Flanders, *c*1440; d. after 1518)
Franco-Flemish composer. From 1472
he was in the service of the Sforza
family in Milan, with Josquin and
Compère, and he sang in the Papal choir
in 1481–9 and between 1499 and 1515; in
the 1490s he made a triumphal return
to his native Flanders. He wrote some 8
Masses, 2 Credos, 28 motets, 2 motet
cycles and 5 chansons; the motet cycles
were early examples of pieces intended
to be substituted for the Proper of the
Mass. A highly esteemed member of
the Josquin generation, he wrote in an
Italianate manner for an airy 4-part
texture; his style shows great euphony
and harmonic clarity, though he was
also skilled in canon and the notational
intricacies of northern music. Five of
his Masses were issued by Petrucci.

Masses and motets in *AMMM* xi, ed.
G. Tintori

Wert, Giaches de (b. Wert, nr. Antwerp, 1535; d. Mantua, 6 May 1596)
Franco-Flemish composer. From an
early stage he lived in Italy, at first as
a choirboy in Naples and Novellara
(near Modena), and then as a pupil
of Rore at Ferrara (*c*1550–5). He directed music at the court of Novellara
before 1558, and then served the Duke
of Mantua and (in 1561) the Duke of
Parma. In 1563 he was in Milan, directing music for the Spanish governor,
but he returned to Mantua in 1565 to be
choirmaster at the ducal chapel of S.
Barbara where he stayed till 1583. His

personal relationships were stormy; his wife deserted him, and he had an ill-fated love affair with a singer at the Ferrara court.

Wert was one of the leading 'virtuoso' madrigalists of the late C16, and the last of the great Flemings who settled in Italy. He published 13 volumes of madrigals (mostly à 5), one of *canzonette*, 2 of motets and one of hymns, and much more appeared in anthologies. He stands as the link between Rore and Monteverdi, whose early madrigals show his influence very strongly. Wert developed a fastidious attention to declaiming the texts he set, using a kind of choral recitation; he often favoured brilliant virtuoso scoring with the 3 upper voices emphasised – in recognition of the talented court singers for whom he was writing; and his vocal lines are highly individual and dramatically angular in certain 'mannerist' works. He was a friend of the poet Tasso, whose verses he liked to set.

CE: *Opera omnia* (*CMM* 24), ed. C. MacClintock and M. Bernstein (Rome, 1961–)

Whole consort see **Broken consort**

Whyte, Robert (b. 1535x40; bd. London, 11 Nov 1574) English composer. Chorister at Trinity College, Cambridge, in 1554–5, and took the Cambridge Mus.B in 1560; the following year became choirmaster at Ely cathedral, in succession to his father-in-law Tye, holding the same post at Chester (c1567) and later (1570) at Westminster Abbey. His works fall into 2 groups; those for Catholic use at the time of Queen Mary, and those written during Elizabeth's reign. The former include antiphons, hymns, a respond, and a fine large-scale Magnificat à 6 in which the plainsong psalm tone is clearly audible in the polyphonic verses. The latter include some impressive psalm-

motets, a few of which use solo/full textural contrasts, and 2 sets of Lamentations which rival Tallis in their sombre intensity. Whyte also wrote some Anglican services and anthems, and instrumental music.

Vocal works in *TCM* v; Instrumental music in *MB* xliv, ed. P. Doe

Whythorne, Thomas (b. ?Somerset, 1528; d. Aug 1595) English composer and writer. Travelled widely in Europe around 1553, and taught music in Cambridge and London. His volume of songs in 3 to 5 parts (1571) is the only secular publication to appear in England between 1530 and 1588; its preface contains some useful information about the state of secular music in England, and its contents show traces of foreign influence. Some of the pieces are in the old-fashioned part-song style; *Buy new broom*, the earliest printed English solo song with accompaniment, belongs to the consort song type. His 1590 volume of 2-part pieces contains the earliest printed English instrumental music; he also wrote an interesting autobiography.

Widmann, Erasmus (bp. Schwäbisch Hall, 15 Sep 1572; d. Rothenburg ob der Tauber, 31 Oct 1634) German composer. Worked as organist, teacher and cantor in Graz and Hall before becoming court *Kapellmeister* at Weikersheim (near Bad Mergentheim) in 1602, and then teacher and cantor in Rothenburg in 1613. He was one of the first German composers to publish instrumental canzonas; he also published ensemble dances (many have girls' names as their titles), motets in old and new styles, and German songs, which were several times reprinted. His volume of student songs (1622) sets many of his own topical texts, dealing with current political events, and contains the earliest known student drinking song.

Selected works in *EDM* Sonderreihe iii

Wilbye, John (bp. Diss, Norfolk, 7 Mar 1574; d. Colchester, Sep 1638) English composer. At the age of 20 he became a household musician to Lord Kytson at Hengrave Hall, spending most of his time there or at the family's London house. One of the most distinguished of the English madrigalists, he published 2 books of madrigals, and contributed 2 sacred pieces to Leighton's *Teares*. He is a subtle contrapuntist with a feel for formal balance and restraint, shunning the splashy colour of Weelkes' larger pieces and the frivolity of Morley's ballett style; in the fine *Draw on sweet night* he delicately contrasts major and minor mode.

Madrigals in *EM* vi–vii (vii in rev., edn.)

Wilder, Philippe van (fl. 1525–50) Franco-Flemish composer and lutenist. Entered Henry VIII's service in 1525, became lute teacher to the future Queen Mary in 1529 and the King's lutenist in 1538, and was Keeper of the Instruments at Westminster when Henry died in 1547. Two of his sacred pieces are in the Gyffard partbooks; he is represented in several Continental anthologies, and church music, lute pieces and In nomines survive in MS.

Willaert, Adrian (b. ?Bruges, 1480x90; d. Venice, 7 Dec 1562) Franco-Flemish composer. Nothing is known of his early life and training; he studied law in Paris before turning to music, which he may have studied with Mouton. In 1522–5 he served at the Este court in Ferrara, and then sang for his patron's son, the Archbishop of Milan. In 1527 he became *maestro di cappella* at St Mark's, Venice, remaining there until his death (though occasionally returning to the Netherlands) and building the choir's reputation up to considerable heights and gathering round him a distinguished circle of pupils.

Willaert's output consists of 7 volumes of church music (Masses, motets, psalms and hymns), one each of chansons, villanellas and instrumental music, many madrigals published largely in anthologies, and the *Musica Nova* of 1559 which contains both madrigals and motets. His appointment to St Mark's can be seen as a turning-point in European music; he 'Italianized' the Franco-Flemish style by his cultivation of harmony and sonority, and was a most influential teacher of northerners and Italians alike. His *Salmi spezzati* (1550)–psalms for separated choirs–firmly associated the polychoral idea with St Mark's. In madrigals he conveyed the inner rhetoric of the words by close attention to harmony and scoring as well as to vocal line, while his sacred music shows the contrapuntal (and canonic) fluency of Josquin Desprez.

CE: *Opera omnia (CMM* 3), ed. H. Zenck and W. Gerstenberg (Rome, 1950–)

William IX (b. 1071; d. 1127) Duke of Aquitaine, the first of the noble troubadours; his are the earliest troubadour songs to survive. His art had great influence on medieval literature and the concept of courtly love; His daughter Eleanor, who became Queen of England, was a patron of troubadours, especially Bernart de Ventadour, and her son Richard I was a trouvère. Eleven of William's poems survive, but the only extant melody is incomplete.

Wizlaw III von Rügen (b. *c*1265; d. Barth, nr. Stralsund, 8 Nov 1325) Prince of Rügen, the last ruler of this Slav dynasty; Minnesinger who associated with poets, scholars and musicians such as Heinrich von Meissen.

His 17 surviving songs are in a popular rather than courtly style; *Ich warne dich* is unusual in its elaborate ornamentation, and lacks the simplicity characteristic of the Minnesingers.

Wolfram von Eschenbach (fl. 1207) Poet and Minnesinger. Took part in the *Sängerkrieg* at the Wartburg in 1207 which appears in Wagner's *Tannhäuser* (the real TANNHÄUSER was also present), and is further connected with Wagner in that *Parsifal* is based on his epic poem *Parzival*.

Wolkenstein see **Oswald von Wolkenstein**

Wreede see **Urreda**

Wylkynson, Robert (fl. 1496–1515) English composer. Parish clerk at Eton from 1496, and master of the choristers there from 1500. Only 3 of his 8 pieces survive complete in the Eton Choirbook, but they show him to have been extremely skilled at handling rich sonorities and complex rhythms. His *Salve Regina* is the only known 9-part work of the period and his Credo is a unique 13-part round, in which each voice covers the range of a 13th. It is also unique as the only Eton piece to exist in a much later source; it was copied into a commonplace book of *c*1600 as a 'curiosity'.

X

Xylophone Melodic percussion instrument, with tuned wooden bars— M. Agricola (1528) illustrates one with 28 of these, though others were smaller. The earliest references belong to the early C16; it has always had a particular association with the macabre.

Y

Yonge, Nicholas (b. Lewes, Sussex; bd. London, 23 Oct 1619) English musician. A singer at St Paul's cathedral, and a convenor of amateur music-making at his London home, where the English taste for singing Italian madrigals developed. To satisfy a growing demand he edited 2 volumes of MUSICA TRANSALPINA (1588 and 1597) containing Italian madrigals with English singing translations.

Z

Zacharia, Zacharias, Zacharie Recent researches suggest that a number of late C14/early C15 pieces in various styles but under some form of this name should be attributed to 3 separate identifiable composers:

Antonio Zacharia da Teramo, from Teramo in S. Italy, who may be the 'Zacharias' of the Old Hall MS. All but one of his 10 surviving secular pieces are *ballate*; he had a liking for unusual texts with a mixture of languages and bizarre, even Satanic, overtones. His *Rosetta* was extremely popular both as the basis for parody Mass movements by himself and others and in highly ornamented keyboard arrangements.

CE: in *CMM* 11/vi, ed. G. Reaney; in *PMFC* x, ed. W. T. Marrocco

Magister Zacharias, an Italian who was a Papal singer around 1400 and wrote motets, including *Sumite carissimi*, whose rhythmic complexities are somewhat in the French style, and secular pieces. His lively *Cacciando per gustar* is set in a market-place and incorporates the traders' cries; it is the last known *caccia*.

CE: in *CMM* 11/vi, ed. G. Reaney; Secular works in *PMFC* x, ed. W. T. Marrocco

Nicolas Zacharie (Niccolo Zaccaria), who may have come from Brindisi and was a Papal singer in 1420 and 1434. His music is found in MSS in Bologna, Oxford and Aosta.

CE: in *CMM* 11/vi, ed. G. Reaney; in *PMFC* x, ed. W. T. Marrocco

Zarlino, Gioseffo (b. Chioggia, before 22 Apr 1517; d. Venice, 14 Feb 1590) Italian theorist and composer. Became a Franciscan monk, and went to Venice in 1541 to study with Willaert. From 1565 onwards he was *maestro di cappella* at St Mark's. Though he wrote church music and madrigals (2 books of motets survive), he is chiefly important as an outstanding theorist of international influence. His main work, *Istitutioni harmoniche* (1558), describes the position of excellence reached by music in the high Renaissance (he calls it the *ars perfecta*) though aware of improvements that could come about through a study of the ancients; he also discusses intervals, modes, word underlay and the art of counterpoint.

Zielenski, Mikołaj (b. *c*1550; d. 1615) Polish composer. One of Poland's leading early baroque composers; from 1608 to 1615 in the service of the Archbishop of Gniezno, who at the King's instigation sent him to study with Gabrieli. Venetian influence is present in his volume of Offertory settings, all for two 4-part choirs (except for a Magnificat for 3 choirs with 8 trombones, which was performed at the Chopin centenary celebrations at Lwów in 1910). His Communion settings are more varied, including polyphonic pieces in 3 to 7 parts, and solos and duets, with and without instruments; the volume also contains the earliest known Polish instrumental fantasias.

Zoilo, Annibale (b. Rome, *c*1537; d. Loreto, 30 June 1592) Italian composer. Worked as *maestro di cappella* at S. Luigi dei Francesi, at the German College in Rome, and at Todi cathedral, before becoming *maestro* at the Santa

Casa in Loreto in 1584; he was also for a time a Papal singer, and it was during this period, in 1577, that he and Palestrina began work on a revised edition of the *Graduale*, which was never finished. He published a volume of madrigals, and more of his music survives in anthologies and MSS.